NICK CLEGG

Nick Clegg was Leader of the Liberal Democrats for eight years from 2007 and Deputy Prime Minister from 2010 to 2015. He has been the Liberal Democrat MP for Sheffield Hallam since 2005, and was previously MEP for the East Midlands.

Nick and his wife Miriam were married in her home town in Spain in 2000 and have three young sons – Antonio, Alberto and Miguel. He speaks five European languages.

Nick Clegg

Politics

Between the Extremes

VINTAGE

1 3 5 7 9 10 8 6 4 2

Vintage
20 Vauxhall Bridge Road,
London SW1V 2SA

Vintage is part of the Penguin Random House group of companies
whose addresses can be found at global.penguinrandomhouse.com

Penguin
Random House
UK

First published in Vintage in 2017
First published in hardback by The Bodley Head in 2016

penguin.co.uk/vintage

A CIP catalogue record for this book is available from the British Library

ISBN 9781784704162

Printed and bound by Clays Ltd, St Ives Plc

Penguin Random House is committed to a sustainable future
for our business, our readers and our planet. This book is made
from Forest Stewardship Council® certified paper.

Politics

Contents

FOREWORD

With hindsight, it makes perfect sense; at the time, it really didn't.

It was the spring of 2014, and Nigel Farage and I were debating whether Britain should be in or out of the European Union on live television. I was already struggling to understand his arguments – let alone their strong public appeal – when Farage expressed his admiration for Vladimir Putin. At the time, Russia's aggressive role in the bloody violence in Syria was becoming evident, and Putin's cynical annexation of Crimea and assault on Ukraine threatened to destabilise Europe. Farage argued in our first TV debate that, in the face of the EU's proposal for a strengthened relationship with the Ukraine, Putin's actions were understandable, and went so far as to declare that the EU had 'blood on its hands'. I was aghast.

I had long advocated inside the coalition government a tough line against Moscow, viewing Putin then, as I do now, as a dangerously unscrupulous leader determined to weaken Western multilateral resolve at all costs. (Little wonder that I was put on a visa 'blacklist' by the Russians shortly after I left office.) Three months after that TV debate with Nigel Farage, Malaysia Airlines Flight MH17 was shot down over Ukraine by a Russian surface-to-air missile, killing all 283 innocent passengers and fifteen crew on board. I assumed, then, that any

British politician whose loathing of the EU should lead him to sympathise with Vladimir Putin would put himself firmly on the wrong side of public opinion.

The result? An overwhelming triumph for Nigel Farage. However questionable the science of instant opinion polls, the message after both debates was unequivocal: Farage was deemed to be the winner by a significant majority of viewers.

As is often the case in political commentary, much of the immediate analysis dwelt on superficial minutiae, such as Farage's sweaty brow in the first debate, and my excessive waving of arms in the second. What was missed – though it seems crystal-clear now – was the significance of Farage's emotional, anti-establishment appeal, which resonated powerfully with many angry and bewildered voters. I was the establishment figure, tarnished by several bruising years in office, defending a flawed status quo. Nigel Farage was the man who shared people's frustrations, who could be relied upon to rattle the cage of an unresponsive political elite. Whether he loved or loathed Putin made little difference to those many voters who were keen to give the establishment a good kicking.

All the ingredients for what has happened subsequently – Brexit, Trump, the eruption of populism, growing Russian influence – were foreshadowed in that spring of 2014. Emotion over fact. Fury at the establishment. And an unlikely partnership between populism in the West and strongman politics in the Kremlin. If someone had told me then that Russia would mount a huge covert operation to influence the US presidential elections, including the hacking of emails belonging to Hillary Clinton's team, and that Nigel Farage would be the first British visitor – photographed grinning with schoolboy excitement – to meet the new US President, I would have scoffed in disbelief. Yet, in many ways, all the clues were there in those TV debates, along with the pent-up public appetite for something different that they exposed. It was only a matter of time before the politics of rage espoused by Farage, Trump and others would triumph in the ballot box.

I began writing the main text of this book at the end of 2015 and completed it in the summer of 2016, within a few weeks of Britain's EU referendum. It took some effort to keep up with events. Since then, the pace of change seems only to have got faster. As a result, whilst much of what is described in these pages happened very recently, the coalition government of 2010–15 with which the book begins already feels like a throwback to a more staid, conventional past – just as President Obama's cerebral moderation already seems out of step with the temper of American politics today. As well as this foreword, then, a new afterword now accompanies the text, reflecting on what has happened in the months since it was first published and what might happen in the months and years ahead.

Yet it has become equally obvious that the bigger forces that shaped my time in government – the effects of the financial crash of 2008, the rise of violent extremism, conflict in North Africa and the Middle East, economic turmoil in the eurozone, public disenchantment with politics – also explain much of the force of populism today. Indeed, it will be impossible for the politics of moderation and reason to make a comeback in the years ahead without a full understanding of what has led to the state of politics we now face today.

To that extent, if no other, I like to think the relevance of this book is as great, if not greater, now as it was when I first set about writing it.

INTRODUCTION

From Rose Garden to Cenotaph

It was as brutal as it was unexpected.

Miriam and I had just returned to our flat in south-west Sheffield after a day of knocking on doors across my constituency. I was wolfing down a bowl of pasta, and we'd switched on the TV to catch the news headlines at ten o'clock.

The BBC's exit poll predicted that the Lib Dems would be hammered – down to ten seats from fifty-seven. Miriam held her hand to her mouth in shock, turned to me and said, 'Can't be?'

'Of course not,' I muttered in reply. 'They've got it wrong.'

In the event, they *were* wrong: we got eight seats.

Over the next twenty-four hours I endured braying crowds of Labour activists in a sports centre in the Don Valley at 4 a.m. as Sheffield's election results were announced; explained to our children on the phone before they went to school what had happened, so that they wouldn't be taken by surprise by any unkind comments in the playground; drafted my resignation speech in a sleepless state of despair; delivered the speech on arrival in London; and then, at a VE Day commemoration event in which everyone painstakingly pretended nothing had happened, mustered what little dignity I had left, to stand next to David Cameron and Ed Miliband in front of the Cenotaph – and the nation's media.

To say this was a far cry from the sun and unbridled optimism of the press conference that David Cameron and I had held together, five years earlier in the Downing Street Rose Garden – after an election that saw more people voting for the Liberal Democrats than at any time since the party was formed – is a considerable understatement.

This book is not a blow-by-blow account of what happened between Rose Garden and Cenotaph, between the formation by the Conservative and Liberal Democrat parties in 2010 of the first coalition government in Britain since the Second World War and the Liberal Democrats' spectacular loss of power in May 2015. Nor is it a kiss-and-tell revelation of my time as Deputy Prime Minister, designed to settle scores with my erstwhile coalition partners, tempting though that undoubtedly is. And it is most definitely not a self-congratulatory rewriting of history – I've made too many mistakes to make that possible.

Instead, it is a candid reflection on my experiences, and an attempt to understand why politics has become so volatile and unpredictable in recent years. It is also an attempt to suggest how the politics of reason and reform – the politics of the centre ground – can compete with the politics of anger and grievance, which is on the rise across the developed world.

I have experienced the full rollercoaster that politics has to offer: from 'Cleggmania' to tuition-fee protests. The sharp fall from fresh outsider to unpopular insider is a pattern seen a lot more in politics these days – I was an early pioneer. I occupied a ringside seat as the Conservatives lurched rightwards under the pressure of an insurgent UK Independence Party (UKIP) and reopened their festering disagreement over Europe, culminating in Cameron's spectacularly misjudged referendum on the UK's membership of the EU. I spent five years at the top of a government charged with an unenviable fiscal clean-up job after the calamitous financial crash of 2008, a task that led us to offend many of our traditional supporters. I watched as the politics of give-and-take, of compromise, in which I believe, was branded an act of treacherous betrayal. And I spent half a decade working with governments and leaders across Europe and America who were just as bewildered as I was by the rising tide of popular rage that was to sweep many of them out of power, too. This book is born of a turbulent time and is my attempt to make some sense of it all.

It includes some personal reflections on life in the public and political spotlight – stories from the top and bottom of British politics. It dwells on the numerous frustrations I encountered as a newcomer to Whitehall, when trying to introduce reform into a political system engineered to resist change; and on some of the unexpected victories, too. It reflects on the difficulties facing multi-party, coalition government in an age of polarised politics – especially for smaller parties, which have tended to fare badly in coalitions throughout Europe. It is a reflection on the perilous predicament of British liberalism: a rational, reasoned political creed that is out of step with the populist mood of our times.

Learning from defeat is crucial in life – most especially in politics. As Colm O'Connell, an Irish missionary and retired teacher who went on to coach world-beating Kenyan distance runners, so pithily put it: 'The winner is the loser who evaluates defeat properly.' At no point do I seek to absolve myself of responsibility for the mistakes and miscalculations that contributed to the political difficulties of the Liberal Democrats in the last parliament.

But whilst I will not duck the things I got wrong, this book will be a disappointment to those who believe I should disavow all that the Liberal Democrats did during the coalition – or, conversely, those who believe we should never have had the temerity to be in government in the first place. As I will explain, it is my view that the Liberal Democrats were right, in the absence of any practical alternatives, to forge a coalition with the Conservative Party. Indeed, I remain immensely proud of the way the Liberal Democrats stepped up to the plate at a time of national need, and equally proud of the many things we achieved in power.

The ferocity with which both the left and the right in British politics condemned the role of the Lib Dems in the coalition was matched only by the satisfaction they shared at the drubbing meted out to us at the 2015 election. The political and media establishment was quick to resume business as usual, and the oddities of a government composed of more than one party were quickly airbrushed from public discourse with equal relief by commentators on both sides. Disraeli was right, you almost heard people mutter: 'England does not love coalitions.' Let the familiar ding-dong pendulum of left–right politics resume its legitimate place at the heart of the nation's political debate, they seemed to say. But I believe they're wrong, much as conventional wisdom in Westminster is often wrong.

The parliamentary majority of Theresa May's Conservative Government cannot hide its threadbare legitimacy: three-quarters of eligible voters voted for other parties, or did not vote at all, in 2015. As I will seek to explain, even though that election delivered a conventional, one-party government, it disguised a deeper, unconventional shift in politics, which the old duopoly at Westminster will ignore at its peril and which was so starkly highlighted by the EU referendum result.

Identity politics – where you live, what country you come from, what community you inhabit, what religion you practise – is displacing conventional left–right arguments about state, market, tax and spend. Many people are giving up on conventional politics altogether. Four million people voted for a party, UKIP, whose principal appeal rests on a return to past certainties – secure borders, the impregnable nation state – in the face of the churning uncertainties of globalisation. And a party of undisguised national chauvinism, the Scottish National Party (SNP), has turned one part of the UK into a one-party state. The referendum vote to quit the EU has exploded the settled order of things. The traditional moorings of British politics are being dragged from their fixed anchors. At the next general election, these profound shifts may, as I will argue, lead to a far-reaching realignment of British politics.

Meanwhile, as the Conservative Government's fixation on Europe continues and as it struggles to absorb the Brexit vote, meaningful government has been reduced to a standstill; the Labour Party is experiencing a slow-motion split between left and centre-left; the ludicrous nineteenth-century mannerisms of the House of Commons and the even more preposterous House of Lords continue unabated; Whitehall remains over-centralised; big money still distorts our politics; politicians and the media are locked in an unhealthy love–hate embrace; and the hyperbolic fury of online political debate is deeply unappealing to any normal person.

Across Europe and America a similar phenomenon is unfolding, as a succession of anti-establishment populists, from both left and right, march from the political margins to the heart of power. From Donald Trump in the USA to the radical anti-austerity party Podemos in Spain, from Viktor Orbán in Hungary to Marine Le Pen in France, the telltale signs are the same everywhere: furious popular disgust at the status quo is overwhelming mainstream politicians and is releasing a heady mix of nationalism, protectionism and populism into the arteries of democratic debate.

New divisions are hardening in our society between those who feel comfortable with the pace of change in a modern, globalised economy and those who feel disoriented by it; between those who feel at ease with the growing diversity of society and those who feel alienated by it; between those who relish the opportunities offered by information technology and those for whom it remains a mystery; between those who celebrate the openness of Britain to the outside world and those who wish to seal her off from the outside world.

These profound differences of outlook – optimist or pessimist; keen on change or alarmed by it; open or closed – take many forms. Self-evidently, those with the good fortune to have benefited from a sound education with transferable skills will feel more confident about the opportunities available to them than those without. Older workers with basic skills feel particularly – and understandably – overlooked and left behind, as their place in a fast-changing labour market is taken by others or abolished altogether by technology. At the same time, many young people feel that their life chances are still determined by the income of their parents rather than by their own talents. Sharp generational differences are opening up in society that must be healed, if we are to maintain social cohesion between young and old.

These new fault lines trump the old left–right terms of trade of British politics. That is why immigration, community relations, ethnicity, religion, identity politics and nationalism – all readily exploited by the politics of fear – now loom as large as the furious debates about taxation, public-service reform and privatisation used to. It is why parties like UKIP and the SNP – and numerous other nationalists and chauvinists across Europe, from the Finns Party to Alternative für Deutschland, from Geert Wilders in the Netherlands to Norbert Hofer in Austria – are doing so well, just as liberal parties that eschew identity politics are doing so badly.

But this is also why rational liberalism is more needed than ever before.

The reasons for this profound shift, for the rapid fracturing of conventional politics, are complex: the end of the Cold War era in which the world was neatly bifurcated between East and West, communist and capitalist, left and right; the extraordinary velocity of change brought about by economic globalisation, where decisions taken in boardrooms and trading floors halfway round the globe affect the fortunes of every working family; the crushing effects of the 2008 banking crash, ushering in the longest squeeze on people's living standards in the post-war period; the mass movement of people across Europe on an unprecedented scale; the threat of Islamist violence and terrorism in our cities; the effect of the digital revolution, giving people access to information and choices previously hoarded by the rich and powerful.

In the face of this widespread rejection of mainstream politics – and in the wake of the shattering defeat that the Lib Dems suffered at the 2015 election – it may be tempting to give up on the politics of the centre ground altogether. Perhaps the future is now firmly in the hands of those who shout loudest – or those, like the Conservatives and the SNP, who have the deepest pockets and a monopoly on the grievances of a nation. I refuse to accept, however, that this is an irreversible political fate. There are millions of British citizens who are searching for moderation against the extremes, who want evidence and not prejudice to govern decisions, who understand that in a complex world the politics of give-and-take has its place. The messy compromises of mainstream politics may not be pretty, but they still offer the surest route towards real answers to people's everyday concerns. Populism, by contrast, offers anger without solutions. Liberalism may not be the loudest voice in politics, but, as I will argue, it is a voice of calm reason, which – once lost – would be much missed.

Liberalism, of course, does not just reside in the Liberal Democrats. In fact this book is not really about the Liberal Democrats, though my experiences in recent years as party leader and Deputy PM provide the backcloth to many of the views I have reached. It is about the politics of reason, compromise and moderation in society at large. Nor is my defence of the centre ground an argument for insipid, pastel-coloured politics. One of the many impressions I failed to correct during my time in government was that ours was little more than a split-the-difference approach – highlighting the dangers of a lurch to either the left or the right – rather than an appeal based on a distinct set of values and ambitions. As I hope to convey in the following pages, there was nothing insipid about the huge reforms we pushed through and the way we fought tenaciously to keep the government anchored in the centre ground, as the Conservatives kept veering off to the right. Nonetheless, our efforts at promoting what we did were always swamped by accusations from both left and right of passivity and weakness. As I will explain, successful politicians tell compelling stories that encourage people to follow them on a journey. Unfortunately, I soon lost any real control over the story I was seeking to tell.

By the time of the 2015 election, whether I liked it or not, the primary appeal of the Lib Dems had been reduced to a kind of insurance policy against the excesses of other parties, rather than as protagonists of our own beliefs and values. Given the palpable public fear of further economic volatility under a Labour Government, or excessive and unfeeling austerity under a Conservative Government, it made sense to explain our role as a guarantee against both threats. But, in the event, that appeal simply couldn't compete with the visceral fear, which dominated the latter stages of the campaign, of a hapless Labour Government in Number 10 dancing to the tune of the SNP – a fear that was so effectively exploited by the Conservatives. One of the things I want to achieve in this book is to dispel the notion that the role of liberals is merely to act as a kind of political prophylactic, blocking the ambitions of other parties. Liberalism is, and always has been, a movement of far-reaching reform.

The irony is that – far from subsiding into a colourless centrist mush – my own views became steadily more anti-establishment, the longer I was in government. As I will describe, forcing through change in Whitehall and Westminster is one of the toughest challenges any politician will face. There are powerful vested interests that resist change at every turn, especially when power, money and patronage are at stake. My liberalism is driven by an abiding impatience with the status quo. Far from viewing the centre ground as the location for insipid compromises, I view it as the terrain where real, lasting reform of our broken political and economic system can be forged.

The referendum on Britain's membership of the EU was, in many ways, a lightning conductor for the clash between the politics of anger and grievance and the politics of compromise and moderation. It exposed gaping divisions in society between young and old, metropolitan and provincial; between those in secure employment and those not; between those with university and college degrees and those without; between diverse ethnic communities and a disenfranchised white working class. The instant judgement after the shock referendum result – which occurred just as I was putting the finishing touches to this book – was that it was all about immigration. As I will seek to demonstrate, whilst immigration was undoubtedly the motive many voters cited for backing Brexit, I believe it served more as a symptom rather than a cause for a deeper malaise: a woefully lopsided economy in which opportunity, security and essential public goods, notably housing, are out of reach for too many people.

I regard the referendum outcome as one of the greatest acts of national self-immolation in modern times, which over the long term will probably lead to the break-up of the UK, the possible disintegration of the EU itself, significant economic and social damage to the fabric of our society and, to all intents and purposes, the end of Britain's role as a major world power.

I do not agree with the assertion that it could all have been fixed in Brussels – that if only David Cameron had got a marginally better deal on the freedom of movement of EU workers, all would have been well. No, the source of the Brexit decision and the focus of any longer-term solution lies in our own hands. Until we address the profound economic and political disenchantment that led millions of voters to put their faith in the mendacious claims of a ragbag group of political malcontents, populists and opportunists, it will be difficult for our country to dream of a common future again.

This requires, as I describe in the final chapter, a radical rewiring of our politics and our economy, and a willingness on the part of liberals everywhere to demonstrate a new, authentic patriotism of their own. The reassertion of centre-ground politics will not happen by default; it requires big changes in the way mainstream politicians think and behave.

*

Tony Blair once famously said that the problem in politics is that you start at your most popular and least capable, and you end at your most capable and least popular. I now know what he means.

The 2010 general-election campaign was dominated by public disgust at the rash of scandals surrounding the misuse of MPs' expenses. The Labour Party was tired after thirteen years in government, led by a brooding and resentful leader in Gordon Brown, who was unable to answer the public's appetite for change. David Cameron was held aloft by hagiographic flattery in the Conservative supporting press, but came across as inauthentic in his appeals for a new politics. Perhaps, with the benefit of hindsight, the sudden surge in popularity of the Liberal Democrats, after the first of the televised live leaders' debates, is not as surprising as it seemed then: the Liberal Democrats are nothing if not a movement of political reform, and my repetition of the long-standing liberal belief that British politics needed to be overhauled fell on very fertile ground at the time. The stratospheric (if fleeting) rise of the Liberal Democrats to more than 30 per cent support in the opinion polls, revealed a huge public appetite for something different from the stale duopoly of British politics. No wonder, then, that our subsequent entry into government with the most establishment of all British political parties, the Conservatives, led to a sense of betrayal among those who had invested in us their hopes for a New Jerusalem.

The point at which the Liberal Democrats would move from being a party of protest and opposition to one of government and responsibility was always going to be a perilous transition. Ironically enough, it was made all the more fraught by the very success that made it possible in the first place: we wouldn't have been in a position to enter into government if we hadn't been able to galvanise public opinion in 2010, yet the public expectations of what we could deliver ran well ahead of what was possible in a coalition at a time of economic turmoil.

Could I have foreseen this rollercoaster, from expectation to disappointment? Clearly the debacle over tuition fees sharpened the accusation of betrayal – although, as I will explain, I suspect it would have been levelled at us even if we hadn't altered student funding at all. Nor could I entirely control the way I was put on a pedestal one moment and then demonised the next: within a week, I went from being 'the most popular party leader since Winston Churchill', according to the *Sunday Times*, to peddling a 'Nazi slur on Britain', according to a characteristically splenetic headline in the *Daily Mail*. I knew that the very act of entering a coalition would lead to disappointment from some supporters, even anger from others.

Nonetheless, I remained firm in my view – a view I still hold today – that a political party that is not prepared to take risks to put its ideas and policies into practice isn't much of a political party at all. Political parties are not like think tanks or pressure groups; they are not like academic departments or commentators. Political parties are the means by which high ideals and values can be translated into policies, which can then be put into practice to change society for the better. And that can only be done through the exercise of power. There is nothing grubby about getting one's hands dirty in order to get things done.

This is especially true when a country is in serious economic turmoil and is crying out for political stability, as the UK was in 2010. I remember being telephoned by senior denizens of Whitehall and the City of London at home in Putney the weekend after the 2010 election – on one occasion, when I was furiously trying to blow up balloons for my middle son's sixth birthday – pleading with me to accelerate the negotiations to form a new government, for fear that a failure to do so would lead to a rout in the bond markets the following week. There was an overwhelming sense at the time that UK plc was living on borrowed time and that market instability, even chaos, beckoned if we didn't get our act together. Very few things concentrate the mind more sharply than a sense of impending economic catastrophe – and it was a feeling that loomed over the many meetings and debates the party held at that time. So the tension between public expectations of a new beginning and the economic and political realities in which we had to operate was something of which I was acutely conscious.

Looking back on subsequent events, it is obvious that such a balancing act was nigh-impossible to pull off. But while it may have eluded me, it is nonetheless a balancing act we will have to learn to master as a country. Coalition government will, I am sure, return to Westminster at some point in the not-too-distant future – indeed, a Government of National Unity may soon be required to pull the country back from the brink, where it has found itself after the referendum vote. The Labour Party cannot, in my view, win power again in its own right, under the present electoral arrangements, unless they make a spectacular comeback against nationalism in Scotland or against the Conservatives in England. Neither seems remotely likely. And the Conservatives cannot for ever rely on older English voters – and a cynical demonisation of the SNP – to sustain their grip on the levers of power, with barely a quarter of the popular vote. Something will have to give. Party political realignments, as I will explain, may happen. And the sharing of power as the political landscape fractures is inevitable.

So I hope the lessons to be drawn from my own experiences will also help future coalition governments, and especially the smaller parties within them, navigate the difficulties that await them. Because I believe, when set against all the available alternatives, that the coalition was a good, sane government at a time of unprecedented economic and political turbulence. Over time, I believe it will serve not as a one-off departure from business as usual, but as a useful model for how reasoned politics can serve a country well, against a rising tide of populism and unreason.

On the morning after I resigned as party leader, rather than moping at home, I decided to go out and buy a new mobile phone, as I assumed that an efficient Home Office official would soon demand the immediate return of my security-vetted BlackBerry. So I went to the nearest high street with my oldest son, determined to cheer myself up by going on a shopping spree for new gadgets. I was braced for some awkward sideways glances from fellow shoppers, given the very public drubbing the country had just dished out to the Liberal Democrats. Instead, person after person came up to me to express their sorrow at what they considered to be an unfair outcome. One lady even embraced me tearfully and declared what a loss it was that the Lib Dems were no longer in government. I thanked her warmly for supporting the Lib Dems and agreed that it was a crying shame – to which she burst out, 'But I didn't even vote Lib Dem, I voted Green!'

So maybe, just maybe, the seeds of recovery are sown at the moment of harshest defeat. There is certainly a gaping, liberal-shaped hole in British politics right now, which cannot be filled by the Conservatives or Labour or by the populism of nationalists north or south of the border.

I have been told countless times that the history books will judge my record more favourably than the voters did in 2015. This is no history book. But it may help shed some light on an unusual chapter in Britain's political history. And it may, most importantly of all, contain some clues as to its future, too.

CHAPTER 1

The Political Zoetrope

In his book *The Political Brain*, written shortly before Barack Obama's rise to the presidency, the American clinical psychologist and Democrat adviser Drew Westen identified what he considered to be the source of their Republican opponents' greater success at communicating to voters:

> Republicans have a keen eye for markets, and they have a near monopoly in the marketplace of emotions. They have kept government off our back, torn down that wall, saved the flag, left no child behind, protected life, kept our marriages sacred, restored integrity to the Oval Office, spread democracy to the Middle East, and fought an unrelenting war on terror. The Democrats, in contrast, have continued to place their stock in the marketplace of ideas. And in doing so, they have been trading in the wrong futures.

I know how they feel.

Socialism, Conservatism and nationalism all emit powerful emotional depth-charges: socialism fights inequality; Conservatism protects tradition; nationalism defends identity. When articulated skilfully, each can trigger something deep in our psyche. So where does that leave liberals? After all, liberalism is a philosophy of rational enlightenment, of head not heart. Liberals believe in evidence, reason and logic – hardly the best tools to pack an emotional punch.

Like all great political movements, there are different, sometimes conflicting, cross-currents in the Liberal tradition. The very creation of the Liberal Party in 1859, founded on a belief in parliamentary politics, religious tolerance, free trade and social reform, brought together Whigs (non-conformist parliamentarians who opposed the Tories), Peelites (a breakaway faction of the Conservatives who favoured free trade) and Radicals (middle- and working-class supporters of universal suffrage). Ever since, the Liberal and Liberal Democrat Parties have contained divergent attitudes, most especially towards the role of the state and the primacy of the market. Nor is liberal thinking confined to the Liberal Democrats – countless politicians from other parties, from Winston Churchill to Tony Blair, have at different times sought to define themselves as liberals. Indeed, most of the liberal shibboleths of the nineteenth and early twentieth centuries – human rights, the extension of the democratic franchise, universal pensions and benefits, free schooling, free and fair trade – have long been hard-wired into all mainstream political parties. Nowadays, liberalism infuses much of our culture.

Yet there is still something that sets liberals apart today, which can be traced back to its deepest origins in the convulsions of the English Civil War and the Glorious Revolution, and in its founding assertion of parliamentary power against the absolutism of monarchy: a simple belief that power should be dispersed and held to account; and that the individual flourishes when she or he is empowered to make the most of their own lives. As Conrad Russell so memorably explained in *An Intelligent Person's Guide to Liberalism*, liberalism abhors the 'arrogance of power', wherever it is found. That is why liberals seek to defend privacy and civil liberties, to reform our lopsided electoral system, to spread competition and break up monopolies, to mock snobbery, to devolve power to localities, to challenge class-based politics and to spread educational opportunity to disadvantaged children. All of them, in different ways, help to disperse power.

But 'dispersing power' can seem like a remote preoccupation to many people, especially at a time of heightened fear and insecurity. Populists, by contrast, offer instant, simple solutions to the frustrations and injustices of life. Some versions of populism are pretty benign. No one, for instance, would disagree with populism if it simply referred to the expression of popular, public opinion against unresponsive elites. Mahatma Gandhi was a populist of sorts. But much of the populism now on the rise across Europe and America has a far darker side. Today populism, on both left and right, relies in different ways on three pernicious assertions: first, it seeks to apportion blame for people's frustrations to another group, nation or community. For Donald Trump, it's the Mexicans. For Nigel Farage and the Brexiteers, it's Brussels. For Alex Salmond, it's England. For Marine Le Pen, it's the Parisian elite. For Viktor Orbán, it's Islam. Second, populists all claim that we must return to a mythical past of simpler truths and happier times. For populists and separatists in Catalonia, Scotland, Flanders, the Basque country, the Balkans and countless other regions and nations, there is a ready cast of myths, traits and characters, from Braveheart to the peculiar blood type of the Basque people, which sets their histories apart. Populism thrives on this appeal to the past. Third, populists claim that complex problems can be solved by simple, invariably divisive, solutions. Build a wall to keep out the Mexicans. Pull out of the EU. Pull apart the UK. Reduce immigration. Blame Islam. Arrest bankers. Stop free trade. Populism offers silver-bullet solutions to our problems. Liberalism, by contrast, does not rely on simple solutions, embracing instead the complexity of the world.

Building walls, dividing nations and stopping commerce do not help anyone in the long run, especially the poor and vulnerable. But, as policies, they excel in the marketplace of emotions: it feels good to know who to blame. It feels good to return to a simpler past. It feels good to wish all our difficulties away with one simple solution. Liberalism excels instead in the marketplace of ideas. And one thing I've learned the hard way in politics, confirmed most recently in the EU referendum, is that the heart invariably trumps the head.

This is not to say that Liberalism is incapable of engaging the emotions. At its best, it is a creed that preaches optimism, tolerance and generosity. When contrasted clearly with a tired and tawdry status quo, it can appeal to a longing for change. The spectacular Liberal victory in 2015 of the Canadian Prime Minister, Justin Trudeau, may have had a lot to do with the unpopularity of his Conservative predecessor, Stephen Harper, but it was also built on an avowedly liberal and reformist message. So too the (albeit short-lived) enthusiasm for the Liberal Democrats in the 2010 general-election campaign may have had a lot to do with the weariness of the outgoing Labour Government and with distrust of the Conservative Party, but it was also built on a Liberal message of fairness and reform. But an emotional appeal is not enough in and of itself. Simply appealing to hope, optimism or a better life is nothing more than an emotional spasm unless it is wedded to a compelling story about who you are, what you're trying to do and why you're trying to do it. Stories enable you to understand something instinctively, to feel and see it for yourself, in a way that is much more compelling than simply following a logical argument to a rational conclusion. It's the difference between showing and telling.

In the end, people follow stories, not policies, in politics. Governments and leaders who have a clear story that has a beginning, middle and end will generally be rewarded. Margaret Thatcher was successful because she told a story of past failure – trade-union domination, Labour recklessness, national decline – to which she was the only compelling answer. Tony Blair was successful because he told a story of past wrongs – a heartless Conservative Party interested only in itself – and presented himself as the herald of a new dawn. The Brexit campaign told a story – Britain can be great again if it 'takes back control' – which was far more compelling than a barrage of statistical predictions about household finances from George Osborne.

Perhaps the master of political storytelling was Ronald Reagan. He told the American people a story about freedom and American exceptionalism. He said that America was a 'shining city on a hill' – a phrase he used repeatedly in his speeches – in which every citizen was born free, but that their unique way of life was under threat from the tyranny of communism, a threat they had to take on and defeat. What was remarkable about Reagan was not the strength of his story, but the consistency with which he told it over time, in simple terms, and the way he managed to embody it. As an actor during the Second World War, he made propaganda films for the US Army. As President of the Screen Actors Guild, he fought against communism in Hollywood. And as President of the United States he fought against the Soviet Union until Mikhail Gorbachev tore down that wall. At every stage, it was the same message: America is a great country full of free people, and that freedom must be defended from tyranny. It was a message that appealed directly to the hearts of millions of Americans, and Reagan delivered it time and time again with effortless showmanship. Poor old Jimmy Carter and Walter Mondale – his opponents in his two presidential elections – never stood a chance. Their rival stories were sincere, rational, yet lifeless when compared to Reagan's Story of America.

Most normal people, of course, don't follow politics at all most of the time, certainly not the day-to-day assembly line of policies and announcements, headlines and soundbites. For most normal people, politics is something that burbles along in the background, catching their attention only from time to time at the point when they are asked to make a choice. So how does the public build up a sense of the story a politician is telling, if they're only listening to it fitfully? In other words, if good politics is all about good storytelling, how is a story told well to millions of people who'd rather be listening to something else? The clue, in my view, lies in the zoetrope.

Zoetropes, the direct predecessors to motion pictures, were hugely popular in the Victorian era. They are cylinders with slits cut vertically in the sides, with a series of sequenced images painted on the inside. When spun around in front of the human eye, the images seen through the slits turn into a moving picture. A successful politician will tell her or his story in the same manner as a zoetrope – through a series of separate snapshot images, which, when seen together, amount to a clear moving sequence.

So much of the everyday stuff of politics has no bearing on the perception – the zoetrope – of political parties and leaders, because so much of politics is taken up with frenetic activity that is either uninteresting or simply invisible to the public eye. This is especially true of the House of Commons. Most of what passes as significant within the Chamber is in truth wholly insignificant, because no one outside is listening or watching. William Hague trounced Tony Blair at the Despatch Box – but Tony Blair's story was immeasurably stronger, so Hague's snapshots of parliamentary brilliance didn't stick in the public mind. Conversely, there are crucial moments, instants, when people *will* look up from what they are doing and register what a politician is saying or doing. The art of political storytelling is to recognise that fleeting moment when people might actually care to listen to what you have to say. Times of crisis, change and heightened controversy are the most common moments when a snapshot image of a politician may lodge itself in the public imagination.

If you're a lucky or skilled politician, that series of snapshots will cohere into a broadly positive sequence that depicts a clear narrative of who you are and what you are trying to do. Once that happens, a positive reputation starts to settle and the spinning political zoetrope reinforces that reputation over and over again. Equally – as I found to my considerable cost – one's political zoetrope can be made up of snapshots that tell a negative story, leaving the positive images invisible to the public eye.

I suspect, for many people, my zoetrope is made up of the following snapshot moments: the first leaders' debate in April 2010, which sparked 'Cleggmania'; the Rose Garden press conference with David Cameron the following month, which marked the start of the new coalition government; the tuition-fees protest in November 2010, which saw tens of thousands of people demonstrate on Whitehall, burn me in effigy and trash the Conservative HQ at Millbank Tower; the video in which I apologised for tuition fees, or rather the spoof version of it that was set to music, in September 2012; and my resignation speech on the morning after the general election in May 2015. In other words, the zoetrope of images that forms the story of my journey in and out of government is one of fresh promise at the outset, followed by controversy in the middle and electoral defeat at the end. I worked night and day for five years to insert positive images that would have told a different story – of policies delivered, liberties defended, taxes cut, children helped, resilience rewarded – but, in truth, my political zoetrope had taken on a life of its own over which I had precious little control.

It went a little something like this . . .

It was April 2010, three weeks before election day. I had been leader of the Liberal Democrats for two years and had languished during that time in relative anonymity. With no partisan newspapers to champion our cause and no expectation that a party of perennial opposition would get anywhere close to power, it was difficult to get a public hearing for the Lib Dems. As a result, the early days of the election campaign involved a series of uninspiring clashes between a clearly exhausted Labour Party led by Gordon Brown, on its way out after thirteen years in office, and a Conservative Party led by David Cameron that had as yet failed to generate much real enthusiasm from the British public. Very few people knew who I was or what the Lib Dems stood for.

Looming large over the election were two great recent crises: the financial crash of 2008 and the MPs' expenses scandals of 2009. Many voters were angry, anxious or apathetic. It was commonplace to hear MPs described as crooks and liars. Goodwill was running low. Optimism was out. And it was in that volatile atmosphere that the three of us – Cameron, Brown and I – took to the brightly lit stage at ITV's Granada Studios in Manchester for an event that would change my political career utterly.

Our entire campaign had been based around making the case for a 'new politics', ending the old red–blue duopoly and reforming a disgraced and broken political system. With the unstintingly loyal help of John Sharkey, Jonny Oates, Lena Pietsch, Polly Mackenzie, Sean Kemp, Danny Alexander, David Laws and others in my team, I sought to deploy simple, accessible language to tell our story. The most memorable thing I said that evening – which was repeated in news coverage for the rest of the campaign – was 'The more they attack each other, the more they sound exactly the same.' It was a form of words that John Sharkey, chair of the campaign team, and I had been playing around with. Clearly, it tapped into a pent-up appetite for someone, and something, different. Over the next few days the Lib Dems surged in the opinion polls, wildly hyperbolic claims about our prospects were made, and the two other parties went into blind panic. Mission accomplished.

I carried an optimistic message – that things could be better, if only we tried something different – but it was one that played on a profound sense of grievance. In a way, I was tapping into a very similar mood to that which the populists are tapping into now. The SNP and UKIP may offer very different solutions, but they are all fishing in the same pool of discontent. All, in different ways, are appealing to that volatile and abstract desire for change.

While I had deliberately set out to tap into that mood, two things nonetheless took me by surprise. First of all, while it was intentional, it was hardly new. I had been communicating exactly the same kind of message for the past two years, but to no avail. I didn't say anything in that debate that I hadn't said dozens of times before. The difference, of course, was that most people simply hadn't tuned into it yet. I knew that the TV debate would have the largest audience of any event I had taken part in since becoming leader and, as such, was the biggest opportunity I would have to get my message across, but I hadn't anticipated quite how transformative it might be. It was like taking a sailing boat out on the water and, out of nowhere, catching a huge gust of wind.

The second, and related, surprise was seeing for myself quite how volatile that pent-up mood was. Most election campaign events these days are carefully choreographed, tame and poorly attended. In the 2010 election campaign, by contrast, we held a succession of rallies with thousands of people who weren't even members of the Liberal Democrats clamouring to join in. They were raw, uncontrolled, spontaneous and heartfelt. This posed some difficulties for my close-protection team. Like all party leaders, I had a team of specially trained close-protection officers from the Metropolitan Police assigned to me during the campaign, and then throughout my five years as Deputy Prime Minister. At times, especially when out on the campaign trail, I would spend more time with them than I would with my own family. Many of them became, and remain, good friends. I was always hugely impressed and grateful for all they did to keep me and my family safe. But I hardly expected that one of the earliest occasions when they would have to take action to get me out of harm's way would be not in the face of a hostile menace, but at a rally at the height of so called 'Cleggmania'.

I was on a campaign visit to a beautiful rural pub in Worcestershire, where I was supporting our parliamentary candidate, Richard Burt. It was a warm evening, and it was instantly clear when we arrived that many people had been drinking outside in the sun while waiting for our banana-coloured campaign bus to heave into sight. When I stepped out of the bus, there was a sea of people surging forward, chanting, jostling. I remember a hapless Spanish TV journalist shouting out to me to say a few words to her in Spanish, before she was virtually trampled underfoot. At first the mood was happily upbeat as I slowly made my way through the hot, roaring, swaying crowd. But then it started to turn a little too manic; small scuffles broke out, the mood of exhilaration turned in an instant into something more uncontrolled and menacing, as people tried to force their way to the front. My protection team moved swiftly and bundled me into the bus, and we backed out of an increasingly agitated scene.

In the end, we didn't even win the constituency.

Being unknown to so many people, prior to the 2010 election, gave me the advantage of surprise in the TV debates. Another reason why our message resonated was that we sought to convey it in a way that was unthreatening, and not angry. I offered people a new choice – but it was still a safe one. I suspect if I had been some red-faced, banner-waving hothead angrily yelling the same words onstage next to Cameron and Brown, it wouldn't have had the same effect. As Alex Salmond's grandfather is reported to have told him at the start of his political career thirty years ago, 'If you're going to say something radical, make sure you wear a suit.'

I was keen that my message shouldn't appeal just to those of an anti-establishment bent who demanded immediate and wholesale change, important though that was. I also sought to reach out to moderate, middle-of-the-road voters, many of whom might have voted for Labour under Tony Blair and were at risk of being tempted to vote for Cameron's Conservatives. That's why, when the Tories realised this, they stopped treating me as a curiosity and turned their guns on me instead. It was no surprise that on the morning of the second TV debate, every right-leaning newspaper carried banner headline stories attacking me. As well as being accused of a 'Nazi slur on Britain' in the *Daily Mail*, I was alleged to have received dodgy payments into my bank account in the *Daily Telegraph* – all complete nonsense of course. It was a coordinated attempt to derail the momentum we'd generated from the first debate, orchestrated (I was later told) by George Osborne and the press team at Conservative Party HQ. No wonder David Cameron came up to me backstage before the second debate and mischievously observed, 'Well, you've had quite a day of it.'

I think – I hope – I responded to all this by keeping my feet firmly on the ground. Perhaps others will tell me otherwise. But I have Dutch blood: a blood type that isn't prone to great rushes to the head. I felt at the time that I was becoming a screen onto which people were projecting their hopes and aspirations, some of which were not realistic. A gap opened up between who I was and what my supporters imagined me to be. I knew it couldn't be sustained, although I did hope – when I saw the polls – that it might lead to an electoral breakthrough for the Lib Dems. So I just tried to keep a level head and to focus on the election outcome. I also spent precious little time thinking about how I might manage the party's descent back to earth. Perhaps a soft landing might have proved impossible anyway, but I did little to prepare for or mitigate the crash that was to follow.

The next snapshot moment was the Rose Garden press conference a few weeks later. On the face of it, it was an event that epitomised the new politics I had campaigned for. What could better illustrate that we were doing things differently than presenting the two heads of the new government to the country, side by side on equal terms, after decades of single-party rule? The sun was shining and there was a palpable sense that we were doing something new and exciting.

But, buried in the bonhomie of the occasion, there were also the first seeds of its undoing. For me, to begin with at least, demonstrating that we could arrive at agreements across party lines was the essence of the new style of coalition politics. The birth of the coalition was greeted by a near-universal prediction

among commentators that it would not last more than a few
months – a couple of years at best. At the same time, given the
economic crisis, the country desperately needed a government
that could function, and function well. So, for me, showing that
coalition could work and that difficult decisions could be
taken collaboratively was an early priority – and setting a
cooperative, positive tone in the Rose Garden seemed like the
right thing to do.

But what seemed logical to me appeared deeply unsettling
to many people who had voted for the Liberal Democrats,
especially those who had done so out of an implacable dislike
of the Conservatives. However much I may have felt – and still
feel – that governing together with an opponent is an inevitable
consequence of the pluralist politics that Liberals have long
espoused, tribal dislike of the Conservatives prevented many
Lib Dem voters from seeing it that way. To them, the Rose
Garden press conference may have looked like new politics,
but it wasn't the sort of new politics many had imagined they
were voting for. To them, the Rose Garden became emblem-
atic of a loss of political identity, an excessive willingness to
compromise, the abandonment of reformist zeal in a cloying
stitch-up with the most establishment of all parties: the Tories.

Some people have argued that I was mistaken in appearing
too enthusiastic about the coalition at the outset. Far from
appearing relaxed or positive in the Rose Garden, I should
have made clear that the coalition was a cold, transactional
arrangement, which I was only prepared to endure through
gritted teeth. While I accept that to many people the event
came across as excessively chummy – and symbolic of the
loss of autonomy, for the smaller party in the coalition – I
remain of the view that a grim, joyless announcement of its
formation would have squandered the early momentum that
is so important to any new government. Despite appearances,
the Rose Garden press conference certainly wasn't intended as
some sepia-tinted bromance in which flighty sentiment trumped
hard-headed political calculation. Indeed, David Cameron and

I found ourselves grappling with serious disagreements within a matter of days. Instead, it was a sincere attempt to underline that a government composed of two parties could have big ambitions and expectations.

Either way, it is clear that in the spinning zoetrope that depicted the story of the formation of the coalition, the Rose Garden press conference took on a much greater significance than I realised at the time. For many people whose hopes had been raised – possibly excessively – by the prospect of a new politics at the time of the 2010 general election, the relaxed atmosphere of the Rose Garden press conference looked anything but new.

By the time of the third snapshot moment, I had completely lost control of the story that was being told about me.

As thousands of protesters descended on Whitehall on 10 November 2010, I was due to go to an event at the National Liberal Club at the top end of Whitehall near Trafalgar Square. I was told by my protection team to duck down and lie flat on the back seat of my car as we travelled there, in case I was spotted by the protesters who were milling around in the Whitehall traffic. As my effigy was later being burned on Whitehall, to the chants of 'Clegg, Clegg, shame on you, shame on you for turning blue', I was smuggled back to the Cabinet Office like a guilty secret via an underground tunnel from the Ministry of Defence. In just seven months, rapturous crowds outside a pub in the West Midlands had morphed into an angry mob in the heart of Whitehall. How on earth had this happened?

On one level, the tuition-fees furore is the clearest example of the dangers of taking policy decisions based solely on their merits, rather than their emotional impact. It was precisely because I and others felt that the scrapping of tuition fees – which would be funded in large part by taxpayers who hadn't had the good fortune to go to university themselves – was not realistic, at a time of unprecedented fiscal restraint, that we had attempted to change our party's policy prior to the 2010 election. Our higher-education spokesman, Stephen Williams, spent a huge amount of time and effort valiantly trying to devise new funding systems for students and universities, but was ultimately unsuccessful at getting agreement from the party's Federal Policy Committee. Vince Cable, who was responsible for the party's economic policy at the time, was particularly opposed to a no-fees policy, which he felt was fiscally incredible – a case he made in vain to the committee. With the decision then made according to the party's internal democratic process, the most Stephen could achieve was to shift our position to a gradual phasing out of the fees system over six years. Vince made it clear all along that he considered even that commitment to be financially unsustainable.

As the election approached, the National Union of Students ran a campaign to get MPs to sign up to a pledge to vote against any future rise in tuition fees, a prospect made all the more likely by an impending review of university funding commissioned by Labour and carried out by Lord Browne. Given that it was in line with our collectively agreed party policy, Lib Dem MPs were encouraged to sign up to the pledge, which we duly did – a terrible misjudgement, for which I would later apologise very publicly.

Conscious of the fraught internal tensions surrounding this policy, I was adamant that it should not feature as a do-or-die commitment in our 2010 manifesto. The policy was not even a campaigning priority – most of my efforts during the election campaign were devoted to highlighting the policies on the front cover of our manifesto: 'fair taxes', which meant a rise in the tax-free personal allowance to £10,000; a 'fair start', which meant a 'pupil premium' of £2.5bn of additional funding for the poorest children in schools; a 'fair future', which meant tackling the deficit and investing in low-carbon technology and green jobs; and a 'fair politics', which meant voting reform, a right of recall over corrupt MPs and a 'Freedom Bill' to scrap ID cards, twenty-eight-day detention without charge and to repeal some of Labour's more authoritarian legislation. We made very clear in public, over and over again, that these were our top priorities.

Except, of course, that I did have a fateful photo taken with a pledge-card on tuition fees, on a campaign visit to Cambridge, and recorded online videos advocating our agreed policy. While it would have been impossible for me as party leader to disavow a decision that had been properly and collectively taken, given my own private doubts about our party's policy, I shouldn't have done either.

Our dilemma only got worse when we entered into coalition talks with both the Conservatives and Labour immediately after the election – because they agreed with each other more than they agreed with us: both were determined to raise fees. The Labour Party had introduced fees in 1998, and then raised them in 2004 (ironically, given the piety with which Labour condemned our U-turn, despite their own manifesto commitment not to do so). The Browne Review was a clear sign of their intention to do so again. Meanwhile the Conservatives had long been clear that they wanted a full-scale market reform of higher education, including new private universities and variable fees. So it was instantly clear – irrespective of my own doubts about our party policy – that whichever party we ultimately entered into coalition with, we would be faced with an agonising dilemma.

During the coalition negotiations we chose to postpone a final decision on university funding until the Browne Review had reported, and instead agreed a set of criteria against which we would test its findings, notably its impact on students from disadvantaged backgrounds. These criteria at least had the virtue of placing the emphasis where it belonged: on providing stable finances to our world-class universities; and on ensuring that access to university remained open to all. We also agreed that if the government could not reach an agreement on the issue that was acceptable to the Liberal Democrats, we would reserve the right to abstain in any vote in Parliament.

At my insistence, David Cameron and I decided who to appoint to lead each Whitehall department only after the policies had been thrashed out in the coalition Agreement, including on tuition fees. I insisted on this sequence because I believed that a government without a coherent policy platform would have been a disaster, and because I didn't want to lose leverage over those policy decisions by getting drawn into early horse-trading about ministerial posts. My subsequent decision to put Vince Cable in charge of the Department for Business, Innovation and Skills (BIS) – the department that, among many other things, was responsible for higher education – was simply based on wanting to give him a big economic portfolio. Vince was, and remained, sensitive to the perception that he would be playing second fiddle in economic policy-making to people – George Osborne and Danny Alexander – who he felt did not have his pedigree in economics. In the event, he put his leadership of BIS to great effect by pioneering policies on industrial strategy, apprenticeships, science and further education. Indeed, one of the reasons why Vince devised and advocated the new tuition-fees policy was his understandable fear that, in the absence of reform, the higher-education budget would increasingly encroach on his other departmental priorities. Equally understandably, he did not want to vote against or abstain on an issue for which he was the responsible Secretary of State. I backed him on both counts.

The approach of the universities themselves did not exactly help. I remember vividly, as we agonised over the decision, Vince Cable and the Universities Minister David Willetts coming to see me in my office. 'Why can't we delay it for a year?' I asked, looking for some way to postpone the day of reckoning.

'The universities will go nuts – they have to issue their prospectuses to new students now,' came the answer.

If only I had dug my heels in and let them go nuts: maybe then they might have said publicly what they were insisting on in private, that university funding was in a state of crisis. We had failed to spell out how unsustainable the existing financial regime was for universities. If the universities themselves had been forced to sound the alarm about their own financial predicament over the course of a year, perhaps it would have been easier for people to understand why the government was taking such a controversial decision. This was another lesson I learned the hard way: if you don't spend enough time spelling out in lurid terms what the problem is, don't expect people to accept a controversial solution on faith.

Over the course of the summer and autumn of 2010, a communications disaster of epic proportions unfolded. Draft documents from Lord Browne's review leaked. Stories appeared about a plan to raise tuition fees with no cap at all. Any chances we might have had of presenting the new policy on our own terms were sunk from the start. While this was happening, Vince let it be known that he favoured a straight graduate tax – that is, an additional tax on the income of graduates, rather than a loan system – which I was keen on, too. Indeed, a considerable amount of work went into trying to make a graduate tax work. I asked Jeremy Heywood, the Cabinet Secretary, to lead a group of senior officials to look into the feasibility of a graduate tax. His conclusion, however, was that it wasn't workable for a number of reasons, not least that there would be no way of recouping it from overseas students, or British students who left the country after graduating; and because public accounting rules meant it would have added to the government's fiscal liabilities.

In response, Vince spoke out shortly before the final tuition-fees policy was announced, to explain why a graduate tax would not work after all, and attacked the Labour Party for pushing the idea. This last-minute change of heart only deepened the impression that a radical policy was being developed on the hoof.

The great irony is that the policy adopted in the end was effectively a form of time-limited graduate tax and was a significant improvement on the old system: no students would pay a penny up front, ending the discrimination against part-time students; the earning threshold was raised significantly, so that graduates would pay back less each month, and nothing at all if they were low-paid; a progressive repayment system was put in place so that the highest-paid graduates would pay back the most and the lowest-paid would pay the least; and a much more generous system of grants, bursaries and incentives to support students from the poorest backgrounds was created (some of which, sadly, have been scrapped by the new Conservative Government). Together, those measures have led to more young people going to university than ever before, including, crucially, more students from disadvantaged backgrounds. But as far as our political fortunes were concerned, none of that mattered a jot.

Any way you look at it, the Liberal Democrats were clearly between a rock and a hard place. Our own implausible policy, a fiscal crisis, the personalities in government and the pressure of compromise within a coalition put us in an invidious position. We had overstated what we could in practice deliver, and we compounded our woes by advocating a policy that many people at the top of the party did not believe in. To that extent, we were rightly found out and punished.

But the Liberal Democrats are not the first or last party to be in that position. My political competitors at the time, Ed Miliband and David Cameron, were hardly paragons of consistency: one was part of a government that had pledged to end 'boom and bust', before crashing the economy; the other had solemnly pledged to reduce net immigration to the tens of thousands, before consistently breaking his word. In my view, the reason why the tuition-fees controversy became the politically self-harming Exocet missile it did was that it grievously offended the most basic, emotional instincts parents have: the dream that their children will do better than they themselves did; the pride in seeing the framed picture of their son or daughter on the mantelpiece in their graduation robe; the deep aversion to the idea that debt is placed on the shoulders of the young. These fears provoked an intense emotional backlash – far stronger than that caused by Labour's or the Conservatives' broken promises on the economy or immigration. Still, today, it is the aspirant parents of working-class kids who are most resentful about the decision, even though their own children have long got used to the new system.

Even so, I didn't think tuition fees would be an albatross around my neck for ever. Just as I had not got carried away at the heights of Cleggmania, neither did I get fatalistic at the depths of the tuition-fees trauma. I continued to try to explain the merits of the change in policy. As protesters were demonstrating on Whitehall in November 2010, I even went live on Jeremy Vine's BBC radio show and spoke to one of them, attempting to persuade the protesters of the logic of the policy. How wrong I was. I might as well have sought to persuade them that the moon is made of cheese. My rational explanation was no match for visceral emotion.

The tuition-fees decision crystallised the sense of unease, or even betrayal, that many voters felt about our entry into government with the Conservatives in the first place. It became a lightning conductor. If tuition fees had never been increased, I imagine another policy decision might have taken its totemic place, perhaps the NHS reforms or the 'bedroom tax'. But whether or not that would have been the case is moot. It was the tuition-fees decision that came to symbolise the growing narrative about us: that our behaviour in the coalition was one of weakness and loss of principle.

That story – that I had betrayed my principles for power – was remorselessly repeated by critics from both left and right. I was grilled about the tuition-fees decision and its consequences in every interview I gave, at every public meeting and at every constituency visit from then on. In the summer of 2012, one opinion poll found that I was less popular than Genghis Khan: quite a distance to fall, from Winston Churchill. I knew that, in one form or another, I would have to try to deal with it publicly and draw a line under the matter.

Which led me to the next snapshot moment in my zoetrope: the apology video.

I had been mulling the idea of making a very public apology for most of the summer of 2012. This was arguably the shakiest point of the coalition: the economy showed few signs of life; the 'omnishambles budget' had been a disaster; we were at loggerheads over House of Lords reform and a host of other issues; the Conservatives were increasingly pandering to their right wing; Lib Dem poll ratings were in the gutter, and so was my reputation. George Osborne had been loudly booed at the Olympics – a fate I narrowly avoided when I was invited to address the crowd at the Netherlands–GB men's hockey match (by saying a few words in Dutch halfway through my appearance, I managed to elicit a roar of appreciation from the orange army in the stands, which drowned out the hecklers). Privately, I gave myself a year. If I didn't see signs of recovery by then, I would fall on my sword.

But, first, I would do something politicians rarely do. I would say sorry.

I tested with a number of close friends and advisers the idea of publicly apologising for making a promise on fees that I could not keep; some of them supported it and some of them hated it. I tried it out on audiences of Lib Dem activists at private meetings around the country that summer, who overwhelmingly supported the idea. I knew in my gut I had to do it. I felt like I had been holding my breath, and I needed to exhale.

I hoped that by apologising, people might come to see that we'd tried our best in extremely difficult circumstances. Above all, I hoped that by doing so I might clear the air and get a fresh hearing for the bigger story – the positive snapshots I hoped would be included in the Lib Dem zoetrope – of the many successful changes we were making in government.

I worked on some words while on holiday in August at a hotel Miriam and I often go to with our boys, on the stunning, wild Atlantic coast of northern Spain. It had to be short, plain, authentic. I scribbled several versions. I then recorded the apology at home back in Putney that September, and it was released as our party political broadcast on the eve of our autumn conference in Brighton.

I woke the morning after it was broadcast to find that some bright spark from the satirical website The Poke had re-edited it and set it to music, with my voice auto-tuned so that I sang the words in an instantly catchy melody. It had already gone viral on social media, when The Poke asked if they could release it as a charity single, which I agreed to on the condition that the proceeds went to the Sheffield Children's Hospital, where Miriam was a patron. The single was a hit of sorts – one of my sons even started singing it loudly when we were in a supermarket together, despite my frantic attempts to divert him with some sweets.

To some extent, notwithstanding the inevitable mockery, it also had the desired effect: in the months that followed, public hostility waned a little and the cloud lifted a little. At the height of the tuition-fees controversy I noticed that some people avoided catching my eye as they passed me in the street. At least people began looking me in the eye again. Most importantly, I regained the ability to talk about other things – the economy, tax, mental health, civil liberties, school education – rather than facing a wall of questions about fees every time I appeared in public.

Ultimately, of course, it wasn't enough. Or at least the lingering feeling that we had sold ourselves short, and compromised on principle, remained right through till the election in 2015. By the time of that election there was a tangible sense that we had earned back some respect for sticking with the coalition through thick and thin, and a widespread recognition that we had brought welcome restraint to Conservative instincts, as well as putting in place some priorities of our own. But there's no doubt that tuition fees – fair or not – became one of the defining points in the story, the zoetrope, of my time in government.

It wasn't until we had received our punishment in the ballot box that it felt as if things had finally moved on.

The last snapshot moment was the morning after election day, when I stood, bleary-eyed and crestfallen, in front of a packed room of party staff, supporters and journalists and delivered my resignation speech. I had been up all night and had written the speech with the help of my superb speechwriter, Phil Reilly, travelling in a sleepless state between Sheffield and

London. I offered what I hoped was a defence not only of my party's role in government but also of liberalism more generally, an optimistic creed that was being swept aside across Europe by a tide of rising populism and grievance.

The response was warm and immediate. Within weeks, nearly 20,000 new members had joined the party, many citing the speech as the motivating factor. I received thousands of messages of support and gratitude. One of my caseworkers in Sheffield captured this generous, if sudden change in public mood very well. 'I think people wanted to give you a bloody nose,' she observed, 'but they didn't want to throw you to the bottom of the stairs.'

In many ways, my rise and fall were symptomatic of the feverish, unsettled and volatile political time in which we live. I was swept into public awareness on a wave of breathless expectations, an unknown figure with an optimistic message that spoke to a widespread yearning for a clean start. But, as with all waves, it quickly broke. Many populists, from the SNP to UKIP, have caught that same wave. And each has done so with an emotionally compelling story to tell. Alex Salmond and Nicola Sturgeon tell a story of a proud people ruled from afar by English elites who do not have their best interests at heart; they promise that, with just one more push, they can be free from the shackles of Westminster and make Scotland the master of its own destiny once more. Nigel Farage told a strikingly similar story, of a once-great nation that has ceded control of its laws and its borders to a foreign elite that does not care about its citizens and does not respect its culture; he promised to take back control and return the country to a halcyon age when it ruled the waves and played on no one's terms but its own. Jeremy Corbyn, too, successfully appealed to a simpler, purer past: he took the Labour leadership contest by storm, by promising to free his party from the compromises of Blairite modernism and return it to a golden age when it was true to its socialist roots. Each is a powerful story for its intended audience.

As I learned the hard way, riding a wave of discontent can take you far, but it is nigh-impossible to sustain, if you actually take power. The SNP may have sustained their power in Holyrood, but they have done so by blaming the English in Westminster for every difficulty they face. In national government, I had no convenient scapegoat I could blame – in fact, I soon became everyone else's favourite scapegoat. The left shouted betrayal at the sight of Lib Dems in power. The right spluttered outrage at the sight of anyone but the Conservatives in power. I became Deputy Prime Minister at a time of economic instability in which there was no hiding place from the brutal realities of a fiscal crisis. My optimistic story could not be sustained. I had promised a fresh start, but it ceased to feel so fresh once the cuts and compromises set in.

One of the great ironies of all this is that I felt the coalition did have a pretty compelling story at its heart: the country had suffered a near-death experience in 2008 and a political crisis in 2009; an indecisive election result risked untold further damage to people's livelihoods if politicians failed to get their act together; the coalition was an exceptional government formed in exceptional circumstances to fix our broken economy and restore faith in our political system. Over time, however, three things happened: the political reform narrative was eclipsed by the economic one; the economic narrative became synonymous with deficit reduction alone, a task overwhelmingly associated with the Conservatives; and any progress in fixing the economy was, as a result, viewed as a triumph of Conservative fiscal orthodoxy rather than as an example of balanced coalition policies.

For a while I retained an old-fashioned belief that in the end the truth would triumph. Surely people would see that the person who was doing much of the heavy lifting in the Treasury to reduce the deficit was a Liberal Democrat, Danny Alexander? Surely people would see that deficit reduction alone is not the only thing a government needs to do to stimulate growth, and that many of the long-term ideas – apprenticeships, the

Green Investment Bank, infrastructure investment, Industrial Strategies – were being put into place by Lib Dems like Vince Cable and Ed Davey? People, surely, would see that a strong economy is not much use unless it is put to the purpose of creating a fair society? Why else would Steve Webb devote so much of his time, and unparalleled expertise, to designing a new, fairer pension settlement, providing greater dignity and choice in retirement? Why else would David Laws spill so much sweat and blood in government giving free pre-school support for the first time to two-year-old toddlers? Why else would I wage – and win – a lengthy battle to provide free school meals to children at primary school? Why else would Danny Alexander and I bang the Cabinet table before every budget and every Autumn Statement for five years, insisting that our tax priority must remain taking more and more people on lower pay out of income tax? Alas, none of what I thought would become obvious to the country could penetrate the fog of derision and misrepresentation that had enveloped us within months of the coalition being formed.

But if we didn't manage to interest the country at large in our ideas and achievements, the Conservatives were no slouches in appropriating them for themselves. Pensions reform. Apprenticeships. Decentralisation. A northern economic hub. The pupil premium. Equal marriage. Raising the tax allowance. Mental health. Regional growth funds. Increasing the minimum wage. Tackling female genital mutilation. The list goes on. Policy after policy that had initially met resistance from the Conservatives within government were adopted by them with aplomb as their own, the moment they saw it helped them politically. The Conservatives are the intellectual magpies of British politics – brilliant at picking up anything that shimmers and shines, shamelessly pinching other people's prized possessions for their own purposes. We may have produced the best ideas, but the story we were trying to tell about ourselves was weaker than the stories being told about us by our opponents. As the zoetrope spun, the Conservatives and their supporters wrote us out of the story of the government, while Labour, reinforced by the left-wing commentariat and the online echo-chamber, told everyone we were weaklings and traitors.

All good stories involve simple choices. It is no different in elections: a choice between one lot saying it's time for a change and another lot saying it's no time to rock the boat. Just as we failed to 'own' the story of the coalition govern-ment, so we were also condemned to miss out on the story of that choice, too. We ended up saying a bit of both: don't risk the economy; but we need a change, too.

When people said they didn't know what the Lib Dems stood for, I think this is what they meant: they didn't know what our story was. By the end of five years, the only positive aspect of our story – repeated to us over and over again by members of the public – was a grudging acknowledgement that we had moderated the Conservatives. So we played on that (accurate) perception. But restraining the unattractive instincts of another party was never going to be a story that could compete with the visceral choice which confronted the electorate in the end. Ours was a rational, moderate pitch rather than an emotional one.

Just as we appealed too much to the head rather than the heart, and dwelt on policy rather than story, so we also failed to look after our own vested interests. Owing to the crippling financial circumstances in which we came into power, we were condemned to offend teachers, nurses, doctors, social workers, students – the educated middle classes and the public sector – who were the closest thing the Liberal Democrats had to a 'core vote' in 2010. We had won their support in large part because of our opposition to Blair's public-sector reforms and the appeal of our policies on issues like public-sector pay and pensions. Any government coming into power in 2010 would have had to make controversial savings in the public sector. Indeed, progressive or left-wing parties elected by public-sector support at times of economic hardship will always find themselves vulnerable when they have to confront reality. From François Mitterrand in the early 1980s to Syriza's government in Greece in 2015, politics is littered with such examples. So perhaps it was unavoidable.

But there was something else at play, too: a dignified, if naive, focus in the Liberal Democrats on elevating good policy over good politics; of attaching greater significance to the coherence of our ideas than to the needs of our supporters. The Conservatives, on the other hand, always knew which side their bread was buttered. That's why Cameron vetoed the introduction of higher taxes on very expensive properties, telling me quite openly that his donors wouldn't wear it. It's why they chose to plough more money into childcare for middle-income families instead of the poorest, despite all the evidence saying the latter would make a much bigger difference to the life chances of the poorest kids.

As it happens, I always thought that being the voice of the public sector was not a viable long-term vocation for a liberal party anyway. While I was braced for a loss of support from that quarter once we'd entered into coalition and started the gory job of repairing the public finances, I harboured the ambition that we would emerge over time as a mouthpiece for a wider constituency across the country: that great swathe of British society which believes in fairness, which is open to innovation, liberal in its instincts about lifestyle choices, internationalist in outlook, concerned about long-term challenges like climate change, and modern and hard-headed in its attitude towards the economy. In short, liberal Britain. As the gamble of forming the coalition was vindicated by a strengthening economy, I hoped that a growing centre-ground, liberal constituency would build behind the party. I wasn't alone in that view. Veteran politicians from other parties – from Ken Clarke to Jack Straw – all assumed in private conversation with me that we would rebound over time. But from the moment we lost control of our own story, the prospect of that rebound became more and more remote. Liberal Britain didn't hear our story, because the stories they heard about us from our opponents were more potent.

Anyone who wants politics to remain sane and rational must learn to speak to the heart, and not just the head. But above all, if they want to compete with the populists and fear-mongers, liberals have to offer people the most emotionally compelling weapon at their disposal: a story of optimism about the future and faith in the ability of politics to bring about positive change. Unreason and fear thrive in the seedbed of cynicism that has gripped mainstream politics. So confidence in the process of politics itself is vital in safeguarding the country against the appeal of populism.

Unfortunately, that task is made considerably harder by the dysfunctional way in which Westminster and Whitehall currently work. As we shall now see, even the briefest peek behind the curtains of power reveals a system marooned in the past.

CHAPTER 2

Welcome to Westminster

Being – I like to think, most of the time – a courteous individual, when I turned up in the House of Commons for my first day at work as a Member of Parliament I greeted my new colleagues with a smile and an outstretched hand. Instead of the gesture being reciprocated, however, it was met with the sort of pained expression usually reserved for a guest who breaks wind loudly at a party. MPs must not shake hands in Parliament. This, I soon realised, was one of the many bizarre unwritten rules that govern the birthplace of modern parliamentary democracy.

MPs are not allowed to clap in the Commons Chamber, either, so instead they slap their thighs, wave their 'order papers' (the official printed agenda for the day) and guffaw wildly, like caged monkeys. They are not allowed to refer to each other by name, instead using euphemistic titles such as 'my right honourable friend' or 'the gallant and learned Member for . . . ' Each sitting of the House begins with 'prayers', during which members must stand facing the wall. Apparently they stand because standing is preferable to kneeling if one is wearing a sword. Not that it should be a problem: the cloakrooms include sashes for members to hang their swords on, anyway.

During the seven years I led the Liberal Democrats, all the leaders of the three main parties – David Cameron, Gordon Brown, Ed Miliband and I – had young children. Yet, until 2010, the Palace of Westminster did not house a crèche. It did, however, house a rifle range. I never found it, but the *Guardian* writer Simon Hoggart did, in the basement of the House of Lords. 'You could borrow a .22-calibre single-shot rifle and ear defenders,' he wrote in 2013, 'and blaze away while an instructor, who was always present, told you to "squeeze the trigger, don't tug at the bloody thing!"' All, naturally, at the taxpayers' expense. The parliamentary estate has no fewer than eight subsidised bars in which parliamentarians, their staff and guests can drink away the long Westminster nights, but there is a shortage of ladies' loos and a distinct lack of convenient disabled access.

In Michael Cockerell's 2015 BBC documentary *Inside the Commons*, David Cameron described the Palace of Westminster as 'half like a museum, half like a church, half like a school'. Ignoring the mathematical error in that statement, the last comparison is particularly telling. Parliament is like school – if you went to an oak-panelled public school. It is full of private codes, unspoken rules and bizarre rituals. The architecture is grand and Gothic. Many of the staff wear oddly old-fashioned uniforms. The dining areas feel like public-school canteens. It all reinforces an elitist atmosphere – if you are raised in a certain way, it is a world that you implicitly understand. If not, it can seem as if you've landed on another planet. I went to an outstanding – and exclusive – private school myself, just a stone's throw from Parliament, yet even I have spent the last decade feeling that other people know the secret to how Parliament really works.

Perhaps Parliament's most unattractive quality is that it deliberately orchestrates and amplifies confrontation. Winston Churchill, accidentally or otherwise, had a significant hand in ensuring this was so. After the wartime bombing of the House of Commons Chamber by the Luftwaffe, Churchill argued that it should be rebuilt in such a way that there would not be enough space to fit all the MPs at once. He argued:

> The essence of good House of Commons speaking is the conversational style, the facility for quick, informal interruptions and interchanges. Harangues from a rostrum would be a bad substitute for the conversational style in which so much of our business is done. But the conversational style requires a fairly small space, and there should be on great occasions a sense of crowd and urgency.

He certainly created a sense of crowd and urgency – when the Chamber is packed with MPs standing, squatting and hunched in every available spare space, there are few experiences that compare to the wall of white noise generated by hundreds of puce-faced middle-aged men shouting at each other from benches just a few feet apart.

Trying to make yourself heard in the face of the antics of some MPs is not always easy. At least Winston Churchill did not have to speak, as I did once, with Jack Straw, the respected elder statesman of the Labour Party, gurning hysterically at me, his eyes wide and his face bright red as he counted out the (incorrect!) number of my supposed sexual conquests on his fingers. Some MPs crouch in the gangway out of the Speaker's line of sight and out of earshot from the hanging microphones, shouting expletives at each other. The Labour MP Sarah Champion described an insidious sexist culture in which some MPs can often be found 'gesticulating about female assets'. Indeed, in 2004 researchers from Birkbeck College reported what they described as shocking levels of sexist abuse, with male MPs pretending to juggle imaginary breasts and shouting, 'Melons' as female MPs spoke in the Commons.

Parliament is famously unrepresentative of the population at large. We may have a female Prime Minister, but women make up little more than a quarter of all MPs (with none in the much-depleted Lib Dem parliamentary party). Just forty-one

of 650 are from ethnic minorities. Almost one-third of current
MPs went to a private school, of whom one in ten went to
Eton. More than a quarter of MPs went to university in Oxford
or Cambridge. Westminster is not a 'normal' place, and most
politicians I know are not especially 'normal' people, either.

But then politics is not a 'normal' job. It is a competition
for power pursued by people who are often powerless; a
race for voters' affections by people who are invariably held
in contempt by them; a clash of high ideals steeped in petty
rivalries; a vocation devoted to shaping the future, conducted
in an out-of-date setting; a game of teamwork populated by
fragile egos and loners; a profession that requires calm, considered judgement, composed of individuals who are strung
out and exhausted; a trade that relies on the semblance of
normality, conducted according to the most peculiar traditions in the land. All this is, perhaps, unsurprising. After all,
to put oneself before the judgement of thousands of one's
fellow citizens in a particular community at election time
is a peculiarly brazen thing to do. The belief of politicians
that – unique among men and women   they have something
special to contribute, which gives them the right to shape the
rules by which everyone else has to live, is, well, not quite
normal, either.

And yet: my own appetite for politics remains undimmed;
my respect for the ideals of politics remains as strong as ever;
and my belief in the value of democratic argument greater still.
More than that, I think politicians have become ludicrously
stereotyped as craven, scheming beings who pollute public life.
On the whole, I have found the majority of politicians I have
got to know – from all parties – to be flawed, driven and intelligent, but not venal or corrupt. Of course I have come across
the time-servers, careerists and opportunists who simply join
a political party (usually the Conservatives, because of their
unsentimental interest in power) because they want a go in a
ministerial Jag. But the vast majority I have known start out
with a genuine, occasionally naive, belief that the world can

be changed through political will and that their beliefs will help to make it a better place. The innocence of those beliefs may become a little tarnished over time, but scratch even the most world-weary MP and below the surface there still lurks someone with worthy dreams and ideals.

Indeed, one pattern I have noticed is that the public stereotype of individual politicians is often an inversion of the truth: Charles Kennedy, Ken Clarke and Boris Johnson all have a particular place in the public's affections because of their sociable bonhomie. They're the kind of MPs most people would 'like to have a pint with'. Yet each of them was, or is, by turns more complex, shy or lonesome than the public might expect. George Osborne, in private, is mischievous, gossipy and thoughtful – quite different from the pallid bean-counter of public perception. I never quite knew how to react when people who had met me for the first time during my time in government used to exclaim, 'Oh, wow, I never expected you to have a sense of humour.' I took it as a compliment, of sorts.

The reason I keep my faith with politics is precisely that it is not for the faint-hearted, it isn't a nine-to-five existence, it is wildly unpredictable. It is populated by interesting, intriguing and downright odd characters. Despite its numerous sins, shortcomings and sacrifices, it remains the best way for society to thrash out our differences without violence and give people a voice in how our governments are run.

On 3 June 2013, the then Lib Dem chief whip, Alistair Carmichael, and I found ourselves standing in a crowd of pink-clad, smiling, singing campaigners on the road outside the House of Lords. Inside the Lords, last-ditch arguments against gay marriage were being made by a series of peers who claimed that it would be an aberration of faith, country and tradition to allow gay couples to celebrate their love through marriage. But we knew the vote would succeed in favour of reform in the end. Outside, Alistair and I were being serenaded by the London Gay Men's Chorus. We stood a little awkwardly – side by side – as if we were part of a spontaneous marriage ceremony ourselves. As the chorus of Abba's 'Dancing Queen' reached its stirring fever pitch, I couldn't help but choke up a bit. Because this was politics at its best. I had been the first leader of a major political party in the UK to advocate equal marriage, three years earlier. It was a Liberal Democrat, Lynne Featherstone, who decided to take on the cause of equal marriage as a one-person crusade, when she became a minister in the Home Office. And thousands of campaigners – hundreds of whom were lined up outside Westminster that afternoon, singing Abba songs at the top of their voices – had lobbied, harried and cajoled MPs into doing the right thing. The pace of change took everyone by surprise. It confirmed that things – important things, like how people celebrate their love for each other – can be changed with the right mix of passion, guile and political grit. It was an uplifting moment that made all the cuts and bruises of politics bearable.

This is the kind of politics I believe we should celebrate and preserve: full of conviction and controversy; driven by ideals and strength of personality; drawing people in from outside Westminster; showing that change is, at least sometimes, possible.

There are many things that threaten the authenticity of that kind of politics: the elitist and confrontational nature of Westminster; the cynicism with which politics is portrayed in the press every day; the cynicism with which politics is conducted every day; the rise of angry populism; the impatience of direct online democracy; the collapse of old ideological certainties; the fact that most politics, most of the time, is more humdrum and dreary than the drama of a vote on gay marriage. But there is something else, too: we are drifting towards a time when only people who behave like robots, monks or nuns will be able to succeed in politics. The combination of arcane decision-making in Westminster and Whitehall, on the one hand, and the frenzied twenty-four-hour media examination of every aspect of a politician's life, on the other, is making our already unrepresentative politics increasingly unattractive to – or simply impossible for – individuals with an independent mind or a colourful life beyond politics.

So much of the mechanics of politics in Westminster and Whitehall is slow, unresponsive and cut off from modern Britain; yet so much of the scrutiny of politicians is manic, censorious and turbocharged by social media. This means that only those who really enjoy the peculiar traits of Westminster politics feel comfortable entering into politics in the first place – hence the conveyor belt of parliamentary assistants, special advisers and party researchers who become MPs – and only those who have nothing embarrassing or dodgy about their pasts are brave enough to expose themselves to the ferociously intrusive judgement of the press and social media. This will spell the end of authentic, heartfelt politics. Instead, an insipid, callow politics made up of party apparatchiks – the robots – and people with blemish-free pasts – the monks and nuns – will be all that remains. The political class will appear even more cut off from everyday life and ever more like a decision-making caste talking to itself. Judgement, instinct and conviction will give way to the politics of calculation, one-upmanship and public relations. At a time when politics across the developed world is fragmenting and anti-establishment populism is on the rise, the last thing mainstream politics needs is a loss of colour, character and conviction. The rise of an ever more pasteurised, professional political class has fuelled, and will continue to fuel, those who want to pull politics to the extremes.

Meanwhile, politicians will only have time for . . . politics. The space for modern politicians to be rounded human beings is narrowing all the time. This wasn't always so. William Gladstone, when Prime Minister, used to enjoy long, solitary walks across the British countryside. Famously, he had a passion for chopping logs, which he would do hour after hour. When he died, his library – much of it annotated by hand – amounted to more than 32,000 books. Winston Churchill once went on a cruise across the Mediterranean that lasted several weeks. US President Dwight Eisenhower had a putting green installed in the White House and played more than 800 rounds while in office. And more than a century earlier, his predecessor John Quincy Adams could often be found skinny-dipping in the Potomac River in the early mornings. These men are among the great figures of modern political history. They navigated their countries through wars, social unrest and great economic change. And they did it all without iPhones and BlackBerries. Without a news channel permanently on at low volume, on a television in the corner of the office. Without the instant judgements and gossip of social media. Without emails, without faxes, without Skype. So how come the present generation of politicians – all political pygmies compared to the giants of the past – is run ragged in a way that would have been regarded as unnecessary and unhealthy in earlier times?

All MPs, from the most high-profile minister to the most anonymous backbencher, live by definition a double life. They dwell in two places – London and their constituency – with their families inevitably ensconced in one or the other. Even for London MPs, life is split between Parliament and their constituencies. Votes in Parliament often keep them there until past 10 p.m. on Monday to Thursdays. Most then dash back to their constituency, to spend their Fridays holding surgeries and handling casework in their constituency offices, and find their weekends absorbed in a mix of doorstep campaigning, church fetes and, if they're lucky, a little time with their families. Then it's back to Westminster to start it all again. When Parliament is in recess, far from being holiday time, most MPs can be found back in their constituencies hard at work. Those who accept ministerial jobs or other party responsibilities in Westminster pile these on top of the dual role they already carry out as MPs.

I am only one of many MPs who has tried to juggle this life with the responsibilities of raising a young family – I was already party leader when our youngest son Miguel was born. Danny Alexander's wife Rebecca gave birth to their second daughter, Isla, in May 2010, less than two weeks after we entered government. Liberal Democrat MPs Jo Swinson and Duncan Hames married during the last parliament, splitting their lives between each other's faraway constituencies – East Dunbartonshire in Scotland, and Chippenham in south-west England – and Westminster. Jo became pregnant with their son Andrew while serving as a BIS Minister. Shortly after he was born, Andrew would be a regular attendee at our parliamentary party meetings, gurgling from the back row as we discussed weighty matters of state. While Jo was on maternity leave I appointed Jenny Willott in her place, who was already balancing the dual life of being an MP, as well as a government whip, with raising her two young sons, Toby and Joshua, who, like Andrew, were a regular presence in the corridors of power.

Physical and emotional resilience is probably the most important, and most overlooked, requirement for a contemporary politician on the front line. An MP can be the clearest thinker, the most inspiring speaker and the most authoritative statesman or stateswoman, but if they cannot put in the physically and emotionally draining shifts required for leadership in the age of twenty-four-hour news, they will falter at the first hurdle. For any MP, keeping oneself healthy and sane, and protecting loved ones from the side-effects of politics, is a high-wire act that few can truly claim to have mastered. Frontline politicians have it harder still: they are always on display, always on the move, always subject to forensic scrutiny – and always bereft of a good night's sleep. Party leaders, especially those in government, are subject to a relentless and all-consuming level of exposure. This takes its toll on their well-being, their family, their colleagues and – crucially – their performance in their job.

The circumstances of my own journey in government were fairly unusual, but I suspect many of my experiences are pretty typical of the tensions of all life in power and the public eye, and while I like to think I navigated the stormy seas with some success, at least when it came to shielding my family from the worst of it, I'd be lying if I claimed I was operating at 100 per cent throughout, especially in the early days of government.

From the outside, the first day of the coalition government looked just about as smooth a transition of power as you could wish for, but behind the doors of 10 Downing Street and 70 Whitehall, home of the Cabinet Office, it was anything but. With the coalition negotiations wrapped up in just five days – no time at all, by continental standards – the Prime Minister and I spent the morning of Wednesday, 12 May 2010 in Downing Street appointing ministers to our first Cabinet, before sharing the stage in the sun-drenched Rose Garden for that good-humoured and now infamous press conference. When Cameron turned to me shortly afterwards and told me that 'We may have overdone it a bit', he was probably right. It was easy to get a little carried away with the 'new dawn' feel of the occasion, especially after the intense and uncertain experience of the election campaign and the negotiations that followed. But the bonhomie masked not only physical exhaustion but institutional disorganisation, too. I soon found out that not only was I physically unprepared for government; government was physically unprepared for me.

On that first day in Downing Street, there was no office waiting for me. The in-house team at Number 10 quickly switched into gear for the incoming Prime Minister, but had little idea how to handle a Deputy Prime Minister sharing power at the top. I was ushered upstairs to the 'White Room', one of the first-floor state rooms given their names according to the colour of their walls (next door is the 'Terracotta Room'). There I spent several hours, accompanied by Danny Alexander, my chief of staff in opposition and a close friend whom I would soon appoint to the Scotland Office and then the Treasury, and a small number of my closest advisers, while the Civil Service buzzed around the building supporting the new PM and largely ignoring us. There wasn't even a phone.

Eventually the Cabinet Secretary, Gus O'Donnell, the government's highest-ranking civil servant, took me to the neighbouring Cabinet Office to look at a number of rooms. I plumped for one that had until that week belonged to Peter

Mandelson. In it was a desk, a sofa, some eerie modern art and a long oak table that I sat at with my senior advisers Jonny Oates, Lena Pietsch and Polly Mackenzie, all of whom had fought the election at my side every step of the way and would loyally see the coalition right through till the very end, five years later. As the door closed behind us, we sat there wondering what on earth we were supposed to do next.

While the 200 or so staff in Downing Street leapt into action to support the new Prime Minister, I was given just a single civil servant: the good-humoured and inexhaustibly hard-working Calum Miller, who became my first Private Secretary. In those early days I relied an extraordinary amount on Calum, without whose wise counsel and Herculean efforts the coalition simply wouldn't have got off the ground. The problem was, however, that Calum was but a single person, was relatively junior in the Civil Service pecking order and so lacked the clout to match the administrative firepower in Number 10.

Not only did I lack Civil Service support, but I immediately had my technological wings clipped, too. Having worked from my laptop every day for years, I was told that for security reasons I could no longer do so. Likewise, newly appointed ministers were told not to use iPhones. Instead, we had to conduct all our business via secure BlackBerries. There was a desktop computer in the office, but it sat there forlorn and unused for the next five years, because Whitehall still did most of its work, extraordinarily, on paper.

What all this made embarrassingly clear was that the Civil Service had no real idea how to serve a coalition government. The entire Civil Service is designed as a pyramid, with a single point at its apex: the Prime Minister. It is not structured for power-sharing and there was no evidence that any substantive thinking had been done as to how it might effectively become so. My mistake, at least at first, was to accept the model presented to me. Having negotiated the Coalition Agreement without the help of civil servants, and with no experience in government myself, I simply didn't see the need to surround myself with teams of officials. In any event, having witnessed the infantile Whitehall turf war waged by Gordon Brown's courtiers against Tony Blair in Number 10, I thought it best to avoid rival power centres immediately springing up in our new coalition government. The idea of maintaining a minimal office was also endorsed by the senior Civil Service – though the error, such as it was, was evidently mine. Whatever the reasons, I was left trying to do my job at one end of the coalition see-saw with a tiny fraction of the support provided at the other. It would be the best part of two years before I was able to build up a Deputy Prime Minister's Office with the sort of administrative oomph I needed in order to do my job effectively.

The most unforgiving consequence of the lack of Civil Service support was the tsunami of unprocessed paperwork that fell directly to me to contend with. Every night I left the office with hundreds of pages of dense official advice crammed into my lead-lined ministerial box to be signed, commented on and approved in time to be fed back into the Civil Service machine in the morning. It spanned every conceivable aspect of government policy and procedure, often in painstaking detail. I was asked my opinion on things I didn't have the remotest clue about – dense, technical issues to do with the mechanics of everything from local-government finance to energy subsidies. Every evening I would plonk myself on the sofa at home with my box and sit there dutifully wading through it, as family life happened around me. Such was the volume of it that I would stay there virtually every night until the early hours of the morning. Then I would go to bed to grab a few hours' sleep, which were disturbed most nights by our then one-year-old son Miguel, only to get up early to help get our two older boys fed, changed and packed off to school.

The effect was not only physically draining, it was politically debilitating, too. Very quickly it became obvious that the central nervous system of Whitehall lay in the daily negotiations between me and David Cameron. In departments where there was a solitary Lib Dem minister working to a Conservative

Secretary of State, the only way we could enforce our views in areas of contested policy was by bringing it to my desk so that I could argue the case with the Prime Minister. At the same time, the two most senior Liberal Democrats in the Cabinet – Vince Cable and Chris Huhne – were, notwithstanding their obvious intellectual strengths, not known as nature's keenest team players. From the outset, their focus was devoted to their own departmental bailiwicks – the Department of Energy and Climate Change and the Department for Business, Innovation and Skills – and their own political reputations. While they did this to great effect (and I encouraged them to do so), it also meant, in the early stages of the government at least, that I was unable to rely on others to defend in the media what we were doing. While the party had strong public performers in Norman Lamb, Jo Swinson, Ed Davey, Lynne Featherstone and others, the broadcast media did not always accept them as surrogates for me as leader. What's more, I soon became such a focal point for anger that I felt the impulse to defend myself publicly. No wonder George Osborne said somewhat smugly in an interview in the *Financial Times* early in 2011 that, having expected to become British politics' public enemy number one, he 'hadn't reckoned on Nick Clegg'.

It was only later that Danny Alexander assumed the stature necessary to take up the cudgels on my behalf, and that former party leader Paddy Ashdown and Malcolm Bruce, the party's deputy leader later in the parliament, volunteered to take on some of the squalls of bad news, rather than leaving me to do so on my own. In the last year or so of the parliament it was a wonderful relief to be able to turn on the radio in the morning and hear the sombre tones of one of these two wise old heads taking on the difficult questions, instead of me. But by then, of course, so much damage had already been sustained.

The combination of inadequate official support, huge volumes of unfiltered advice, the tendency for every problem to float upwards to me and the PM, and the lack of a coherent senior team meant I had neither the time nor the energy to step back and properly consider the wider politics of what we were doing. I have only myself to blame. I took the old-fashioned view that I had to do my homework, master as much policy detail as possible and make sure I stayed on top of every decision. But, determined to keep abreast of every minor twist and turn, I became too immersed, wading through the weeds rather than surveying the landscape. The upshot, of course, was that I risked missing the wood for the trees.

Take, for example, the coalition's controversial NHS reforms. These were presented to David Cameron and me in great detail and with great enthusiasm by both Andrew Lansley, the Conservative Health Secretary, and Paul Burstow, the Liberal Democrat minister in the department. They were even presented to a rare gathering of the Coalition Committee, a meeting composed of senior members of both parties, whose purpose was to agree any departure from the terms of the Coalition Agreement. I was joined by Vince Cable, Chris Huhne, Danny Alexander, Mike Moore and a number of our Conservative counterparts – everyone expressed scepticism about the plans at that point. Later, as the final reworked proposals were presented to the Cabinet, most ministers had persuaded themselves that the reforms might prove to be a useful synthesis of Conservative and Lib Dem thinking – ensuring greater responsiveness within the NHS by radically localising decision-making. But with my political antennae and perhaps those of everyone else around the table dulled by exhaustion, I simply didn't spend enough time asking myself how this would be received by the public – or by an NHS workforce fed up to the back teeth with constant organisational upheaval. I realise now, with hindsight, that however inaccurate it was for opponents of the reforms to characterise them as creeping privatisation of the NHS (in fact we ended up legislating to stop some of the botched privatisations of the New Labour era), the distrust of Conservative motives when it comes to the NHS is so entrenched that a caricature of the reforms was bound to trump reality.

If these self-inflicted errors were not bad enough, they were compounded by unexpected events. The first was losing my close friend and colleague David Laws from government after just seventeen days. David resigned from his position as Chief Secretary to the Treasury after being exposed by the *Daily Telegraph* for claiming expenses for rent paid to his partner, James Lundie, who owned the London property they lived in together, something that owing to a recent Commons rule change was no longer allowed. It didn't matter that David's motivation was not financial gain – he could have legitimately claimed more, if he had arranged his affairs differently – but the protection of his privacy. David feared that if he changed his arrangements, it would be exposed that he was in a gay relationship, something that he had kept hidden for many years. Instead, it was exposed by the *Telegraph* and David immediately resigned.

I received the news while in Paris, on what was supposed to be my first weekend away with my family after months of gruelling campaigning. Having been informed of what had happened, I went back to the Gare du Nord and was shown into a little room where Eurostar staff hang up their coats and bags. I spoke to Cameron and Osborne from the cloak-room and told them I intended to replace David with Danny Alexander. David and Danny were my most trusted colleagues, always willing to put their own necks on the line for the party and for the Lib Dem governing team. Yet within three weeks of entering government I had effectively lost both from my office, as David resigned and Danny moved to the Treasury to replace him, a position that demanded a huge amount of his time and energy. All of a sudden I was left not only with modest administrative support in my office, but also without the presence of my two closest allies.

Most cruelly of all, I also lost the help of a significant number of advisers in Parliament and Lib Dem Headquarters, who abruptly lost their jobs straight after we entered into government. As a result of our ascent to power, the party was no longer eligible to receive 'Short money', the state funding allocated to opposition parties in order to allow them to fund policy development and other basic political functions. This is designed to compensate opposition parties for the fact that the governing parties have access to the Civil Service. The withdrawal of Short money led to dozens of talented and dedicated staff being pointed to the exit door, through no fault of their own. Given that these staff had just helped deliver a campaign that saw us win more votes than at any time since the party was founded, being rewarded for their efforts with a P45 was a very bitter pill to swallow.

Finally, to complete this somewhat beleaguered picture, I was also under political siege in my own constituency in Sheffield. Within months of the coalition being formed, the people of Sheffield were being warned by no less a figure than David Blunkett that they would soon be 'fending for themselves' in a 'post-Soviet' meltdown, as a result of coalition cuts that were, inevitably, held to be the sole responsibility of the perfidious Lib Dems. The trade union Unison even unveiled a huge poster of me – branded 'Cleggzilla' – stomping like a demented giant on the city, and it remained plastered prominently on a wall by one of the city's roundabouts.

It was against this backdrop that we hosted the party's 2011 spring conference in Sheffield. On the advice of Med Hughes, the former Chief Constable of South Yorkshire Police, a 'ring of steel' was erected around the conference centre to protect the delegates from those who wished them ill. As a result, we spent our biannual gathering in what felt like a parody of a medieval fort, with a steel fence separating us from hundreds of angry trade unionists and Labour activists yelling at the somewhat bewildered Lib Dem conference delegates within.

While much of what I have described here was atypical – ours was the first-ever fully fledged coalition government to include a party that had never been in government before – I don't for a moment presume that I had it any harder than others who have found themselves thrown onto the front line of contemporary politics. Life at the top has always been a madhouse of sorts.

That's why it is odd that people seem so surprised when leaders get health scares. Politicians are human and get sick just like anyone else. Tony Blair caused a ripple of uncertainty by falling ill during his premiership. Given the relentless physical strain he was under, it is no surprise at all. When I became Deputy PM, I struggled at first to keep my head above water. During those long months from the comprehensive spending review in autumn 2010 to the local elections and the Alternative Vote referendum in spring 2011, I was both drained and physically unfit. I smoked several cigarettes a night. I got virtually no exercise. During the campaign that spring I developed a bad bronchial condition and was popping strong antibiotics. Since becoming leader of the Liberal Democrats, I had dealt with pneumonia, chest pains, a broken toe, chronic coughs and bronchitis – while trying to look perky in public at all times. And throughout all of this, I would regularly criss-cross London in the early evening to help put our three young boys to bed at home in Putney, especially if Miriam had to work late, before returning to Westminster later. No wonder there was a 'Nick Clegg Looking Sad' website. They could have added Nick Clegg looking fat, pale and unhealthy, too.

It all took its toll on the way I came across in public. I was no longer the fresh-faced newcomer of the 2010 leaders' debates. My body language was weary. And body language is remarkably important. I have lost count of the number of times people have said, 'I thought you were very good in that interview', but when asked what they thought it was that hit the mark, they replied, 'I can't remember what you said, but you looked calm/healthy/happy', et cetera. Conversely, after I'd given what I considered to be a strong speech or interview, I would receive polite criticism or comment based entirely on my physical demeanour instead of what I said. 'You looked tired,' they'd say, or 'You didn't seem quite yourself.' I used to think that those who said they judge a politician by turning the volume down on the television and looking at them, rather than listening to them, were talking nonsense. Now, I think they may be right.

Part of the reason for the relentless pressure of modern politics is, of course, the transformation of media scrutiny, aided by new technologies. The unforgiving glare of close-up television means the public can peer at the demeanour of a politician in a way cartoons, lithographs and photographs never allowed. A gaffe by a politician visiting a primary school in rural Lincolnshire can be retweeted in Australia within seconds.

Social media has also transformed the way in which politicians, commentators, advisers, spinners, journalists, activists and other members of the political and media elite speak to each other. Instant judgements are now cast within seconds, arguments rage and subside within minutes, announcements flare and bomb within hours. It's as if a whole new Petri dish of communication has been created for the few thousand people who follow the daily ins and outs of politics.

Much of this is healthy. Anything that forces the powerful to stay on their toes is a good thing. The democratisation of opinion, in which anyone can pitch in their ideas through social media, has to be a good thing, too. But there are also downsides: the fact that anyone can join in doesn't actually mean that everyone does, and so a false impression of openness is created. Far from opening politics up to outsiders, the shrill and angry language in which insiders debate politics alienates most normal people. I remained pretty immune to the kind of abuse that is hurled around by the Twitter zealots – but it's the kind of language that seems utterly bizarre to the casual observer. This, in turn, can lead politicians to confuse the political noise on social media with wider public opinion. I remember Labour politicians in 2015 claiming that the fact that a couple of thousand of young activists clamoured to hear Jeremy Corbyn speak in town halls, and the enthusiasm with which they lauded him on social media, represented some kind of people's revolution. This was always a delusion – a few thousand enthusiasts don't speak for forty-seven million voters, most of whom prefer to be left alone by politicians from one election to the next.

The instant rage and indignation of social media also have their echoes in the print media. In my time in frontline politics, I have witnessed a distinct shift in press coverage from reporting to opinion, from acting as the public's witness to acting as participants in politics. Partisan coverage of politics is now the norm. There may be many reasons for this: the personal preferences of individual proprietors and editors; the need to match the opinionated vibrancy of social media; the increasingly cut-throat competition in an industry that is losing customers; the prominence of issues that aggravate the press itself, such as the phone-hacking scandal and the subsequent Leveson Inquiry into the conduct of the press. Whatever the reasons, the upshot is that the press and politicians are increasingly locked in an unhealthy, twenty-four-hour embrace disfigured by mutual need and loathing. This, in turn, contributes to a non-stop atmosphere of harassed insecurity among politicians. At any instant, a minister's day can be upended by an article, blog post, tweet, diary column or anonymous quote that – whether true or not – requires instant response and rebuttal.

In late 2010, after a number of stories were published on a prominent political blog site insinuating that William Hague had once had a gay affair with a young adviser, the then Foreign Secretary felt the need to make a highly personal statement. He not only denied that he had behaved improperly with the staff member in question, or had ever had a homosexual relationship, but also revealed that he and his wife Ffion had tried to have children, but that Ffion had suffered a number of miscarriages. The blog stories – and the Westminster village gossip and newspaper attention they had generated – were clearly deeply distressing for the Hagues. William, I imagine, had hoped that by making such a deeply personal statement he would be able to draw a line under them. And in a way he did, but at the cost of giving national newspaper editors licence to print his statement – and recount the accusations it was addressing – on their front pages. It was a nasty, intrusive media frenzy that engulfed two decent individuals and forced them into exposing the most intimate and painful details of their own lives, details that should be no business of anyone else's.

Inevitably, far too much government time is devoted to taking the minute-by-minute pulse of the media, worrying about the fickle ebb and flow of opinion-makers in the Westminster village. In those first few months of government, I tried to follow the currents and cross-currents of media opinion about the coalition and the Liberal Democrats. I tried to read newspapers, listen to the morning radio news, catch the evening television news, and so on. But I soon realised it was a hopeless task – hugely time-consuming, enervating and detrimental to the basic job of taking decisions in government.

I bumped into John Major shortly after the coalition had been formed, and the one recommendation he gave me was not to read the newspapers every day. With characteristic grace, he explained to me how he had become too fixated about what the newspapers said about him when he was in office, and that he wished he'd taken a greater distance from the daily press. When I arrived in government, Whitehall was awash with stories of Gordon Brown scouring the early editions and firing off angry emails in the dead of night from his lair in Whitehall, in response to unflattering articles. So I decided to avoid the same fate and soon I simply stopped reading any newspaper properly. Instead I would take a quick look at the headlines online and ask someone from my press team to alert me to any stories I needed to be aware of.

As the portrayal of both the government and my role in it deteriorated in significant parts of the press, this was not always an easy task. As diplomatically as they could, my press team would have to explain the zany things that were said about me – from the *Daily Mail*'s claim that I had knowledge of child-abuse offences that occurred before I was even born, to the unflattering photograph of me on holiday in Spain under the headline 'Who Ate All the Paella?', or the suggestion that because I was unable to make a meeting or two of the Privy Council, I was somehow 'snubbing the Queen'. That suggestion was something that evidently frustrated James McGrory, my outstanding and inexhaustibly loyal press spokesperson, even more than it did me, leading to this snippet making it into the *Daily Telegraph* in 2013:

> 'I can't believe we are having this f-----g conversation again,' an aide to the DPM emoted in a tirade worthy of Malcolm Tucker in the television series *The Thick of It*. 'The f-----g fact is he can't f-----g be everywhere, but I know you are going to go off and write that the DPM has f-----g snubbed the Queen once a f-----g gain.'

I never contacted newspaper editors in response to negative coverage about myself – I felt there was zero chance of persuading them to change their views, so I didn't bother. But perhaps I should have done; with hindsight, the daily media flogging I received, especially in the early months of the government, had a lasting and damaging effect. My only exception to this rule was when my family was affected. The tendency in some parts of the press to attack a politician by attacking their family, with claims that are either false or irrelevant to the role of the politician, is a fact of political life. But it doesn't make it any less gruesome, or the duty to protect one's own family any less pressing. The attack on Ed Miliband's father – described by the *Daily Mail* as 'The Man Who Hated Britain', because of his Marxist beliefs – was not only malicious and false, but also of no relevance to Ed Miliband's fitness for office.

Every few weeks, Miriam and I had to devote a fair amount of time – and a considerable amount of emotional energy – to rebutting ludicrous claims made about her or the education of our children: that Miriam was somehow responsible for human-rights abuses in Western Sahara; that she was guilty of tax irregularities in her law firm several years before she was even employed by it; that the channelling of government money to a literacy charity was decided at her behest; that our decision to send our Catholic children, who had attended a Catholic primary school, to a Catholic secondary school was a sign of hypocrisy. And so on.

Responding to false and silly claims in the press just goes with the territory for any modern politician. I'd rather live in a country where politicians are harassed by the press than a country where the press can be harassed by politicians. But I am nonetheless struck by how all-consuming an activity it has become in contemporary politics. So much of the semi-neurotic pace of political life today can be explained by the evolution in technology and the relationship between the media and political classes. Gladstone and Churchill would, I suspect, have been nonplussed at the huge amount of time and energy their political successors now spend on monitoring, shaping and reacting to daily news.

My early experience of the physical and emotional pressures of high office was shaped by an unusual election outcome, and by inexperience. Over time I worked out a better balance for myself. After the disastrous local elections and the loss of the referendum on electoral reform in May 2011, I realised I had to change my ways. I beefed up my office by employing a larger team of civil servants and special advisers; I took up kick-boxing classes at 6 a.m. every Monday at a local gym and had a rowing machine installed in a cubbyhole near my office; I cut down on the cigarettes and started to eat better. I even managed to handle the vast amount of paperwork more effectively, by tackling the majority of it early in the morning instead of late at night, a switch of technique that I later discovered David Cameron had adopted, too. Of course, the person whose advice I should have taken was Ken Clarke, who cheerily told me that the way he avoided having to wade through vast reams of paperwork at home was to instruct the civil servants in his office that no one was to leave for the day until his box work was complete. He soon found that his ministerial box became a lot lighter and he barely needed to take home any paperwork at all.

But while some of my experiences may have been atypical, what I witnessed nonetheless reveals a wider truth: we are governed by a political class that exists not only in a bizarre Westminster world, but also under permanent physical and emotional strain. Politicians in government endure a decision-making process that is antiquated and laborious; MPs out of government have to spend their time in an increasingly dilapidated House of Commons, away from home, with only cheap alcohol and an unlimited supply of political intrigue to keep them company. There are many jobs that place a great strain on individuals, from head teachers to hill farmers. Politicians should not seek or receive special sympathy for their predicament – to serve as a Member of Parliament is a great honour that, rightly, comes with significant duties. But the country should worry about the quality of decision-making that occurs within such a hothouse atmosphere. I am sometimes told that chief executives of major companies endure a similar degree of pressure as senior government ministers. Yet, in my experience, senior business people are not subject to remotely the same level of public scrutiny, do not need to balance conflicting public interests in the same way, are often treated with kid gloves by underlings in their organisations, and rarely need to take multiple decisions with the velocity required in government. This is not to denigrate the excellent work of highly professional private-sector executives – it is merely to highlight the atypical, and peculiarly unhealthy, way in which politicians are expected to take decisions.

Over time, I discovered that one of the best ways to master the dysfunctional worlds of Westminster and Whitehall was simply to work outside them as much as possible. Having spent much – too much – of the first year of the coalition holed up in Whitehall thrashing out policy compromises across government, I increasingly spent as much of every working week as I could visiting other parts of the country.

I restarted my pre-election habit of holding public question-and-answer sessions. I hugely enjoyed seeing for myself how policies that the Lib Dems had championed in Whitehall – most especially the Pupil Premium, which channels additional money to schools for the most disadvantaged pupils – were starting to have a transformative effect. I even started my own call-in show on LBC Radio with the veteran radio presenter Nick Ferrari, following a chance conversation I had with the then Mayor of New York, Michael Bloomberg. He said his own radio phone-in show in Manhattan had helped him regain some political momentum, so I thought I'd give it a try. Needless to say, it was immediately condemned as a foolish risk by many in the Westminster village – yet quickly proved to be sufficiently popular that a number of other politicians followed suit.

If Churchill or Gladstone would have struggled to comprehend the breathless way in which politics functions under the modern media glare, I suspect they would have been even more dismayed by the Americanisation of our attitude to politicians' families. One way or another, the pressure on frontline politicians to display their children and to confect an impression of 'normality' in their family life has increased dramatically in recent years. It is a trend that, like so many trends, appears to have started in the USA, where families are now part of the stock-in-trade of a politician's public wares. I imagine this has happened because it works: there's nothing that humanises a politician better than letting the cameras capture a warm family hug. In my time as party leader, I watched how David Cameron built his early reputation on unprecedented access to his home life, and how Ed Miliband sought to salvage his later reputation with similar access to his family during the 2015 election campaign. I have no doubt they were both effective – the repeated insights by way of 'WebCameron' into life in the Cameron household provided a powerful contrast to the stuffiness of previous Tory Leaders, and the sight of Ed Miliband walking with his children in a North London park during the election campaign helped to show a warmer side to him.

When my own political fortunes started to plummet, it was gently suggested on a number of occasions that I might want to consider exposing my devotion to my own children, in order to offset the bloodless caricature that was being made of me by my critics. But Miriam and I never countenanced doing so. We wanted to protect the innocence of our children. It was not their fault that their dad had decided to go into politics, and I always felt they were as entitled to a carefree childhood as any other child. I do not in any way seek to judge the decisions of other politicians – all parents should be left to take their own decisions – but Miriam and I asked ourselves what it would feel like for Antonio, Alberto or Miguel to turn up at school and find that their classmates were talking about their appearance on TV or in a magazine. It would, we feared, make our children feel very different – separate even – from their peers at school. To be known as the son of the Deputy Prime Minister was a sufficient burden, we reckoned, and we didn't want to add to it by bringing their faces, and their innocence, into the public gaze.

One of the best decisions I ever took – or, rather, that Miriam rightly insisted on – was to stay in our own home instead of moving into a government flat in Whitehall. In the first few days of the coalition, I was advised by officials to consider moving my family to an apartment in Admiralty House that had previously been occupied by John Prescott. They didn't exactly say that I had to be there for my own safety, but it was certainly presented to me as a much better option than staying in our corner house in Putney. So I went to check out the flat: it was vast, quiet, with beautiful views over Horse Guards Parade and utterly soulless, like a stale, beige-carpeted National Trust interior. When I got home that evening I tried to present it to Miriam in as neutral a way as possible, but her response was immediate. No chance. Absolutely not. No way.

Her instinct was absolutely right. We would have hated it there. It would have been hugely disruptive for the boys who, at that time, were eight, six and one. If we had moved there, they would have had to change school and lose the friendliness of the neighbourhood they were used to. It would have been like living in a goldfish bowl. In fact, remaining in our own home in Putney became a real tonic for us, over time. Our children lived largely normal lives, shielded from the spotlight, with a lot of people always looking out for them. Their schools were particularly helpful, always shutting up shop the moment the press tried to intrude.

Of course, as much as adults in the public eye try to give their children the normality they deserve, it is invariably small children who are better at enforcing normality on adults. I remember the evening in 2007 when Ming Campbell announced suddenly – and to my complete surprise – that he was resigning as leader of the Liberal Democrats. My phone immediately went berserk with people calling to find out whether or not I intended to stand in the leadership contest. Jonny Oates, at that time Ming Campbell's chief of staff, suggested to me that I should escape Westminster, so I immediately left Parliament for Putney. I got home to discover a crisis unfolding: Alberto, only three at the time, was distraught because his black-and-white spotted leopard toy had gone missing. I had to search the house inside out – looking under every sofa and bed and in every box and cupboard – while the phone rang off the hook. There I was, worrying about whether I would become the leader of a political party and the impact it would have on my career and my family, and all of that was put on hold to search for a missing cuddly toy.

My children also kept my feet firmly on the ground when I later entered government. In the midst of all the excitement that followed the 2010 election and the formation of the coalition, my eldest, Antonio, asked me earnestly why I had gone from being the *Leader* of the Liberal Democrats to being *Deputy* Prime Minister. He clearly viewed it as a steep demotion.

There is so much in modern politics that is artificial and unnatural, and so much that is expected of modern politicians that is odd and intrusive, and while it is naive to imagine it might be otherwise, there is already a very real risk that future generations of politicians will have to be blamelessly dull or political obsessives, to survive the scrutiny of their youthful indiscretions recorded for ever on social media. I shudder to think what the censorious headline-writers of today would make of my bad behaviour in my wild twenties. I am immensely grateful that Facebook, Instagram and Twitter were not around to record the misdemeanours of my youth. If all that were not discouragement enough for most people, the prospect of also having to subject loved ones to the contorting artifice of family photo opportunities will surely discourage the rest. British democracy will suffer in the future, if Westminster is populated by people who have never committed a sin or by those whose political ambitions trump the right to privacy of their own children. We don't need to be like America. Politicians stand for election; their kids don't. They have as much right to an innocent childhood as anyone.

But if it is difficult to keep children away from the cameras, it is impossible to keep spouses hidden from public view. Understandably, the media want a glimpse of politicians with their husbands or wives. Miriam readily accepted the fact that, especially at party conferences and state events, she would publicly accompany me from time to time. Yet there is something faintly absurd about the modern expectation that spouses should, most of the time, be seen but not heard. They will be admired if they speak their mind, but mustn't speak too much; they must appear normal, without being plain; glamorous, without being showy; they must have their own career, but must stand loyal and mute next to their spouse.

This wasn't always easy for Miriam. My wife is successful in her own right. Her intelligence and independence are part of what makes her the exceptional person she is. Yet she was as surprised as anyone when she caused a stir during the 2010 general-election campaign by making the flamingly obvious point that she wouldn't put her own life on hold for the election, telling ITV's Mary Nightingale: 'I don't have the luxury of a job I can simply abandon for five weeks, and I imagine that is the situation for most people in the country.' Since then, she has been scrutinised like a catwalk model and judged, as a woman and as a mother. One newspaper even insinuated, after she and I were photographed visiting a school, that since Miriam was a working woman, she couldn't possibly know what life at a school was really like. Regardless, Miriam pulled it all off brilliantly. She never changed who she was; never acted differently for the cameras. She coped with the intrusion and the rigmarole with as much good grace as could reasonably have been expected. And she managed to win legions of fans in the meantime.

The days of mute spouses are over. Women, in particular, should not be expected to mimic some false pastiche of a dutiful 1950s wife staring adoringly at her swashbuckling husband as he makes his way through the political jungle. Things are, thankfully, changing. During the time I was a party leader, all three (male) party leaders were married to working women. Sarah Vine successfully combined life as an outspoken columnist with being the wife of Michael Gove when he was in the Cabinet. Jeremy Corbyn admirably dispensed altogether with the traditional kiss-and-hug routine with his wife, Laura Alvarez, at party conferences. Somehow we need to find a new balance: one where politicians are politicians, and their spouses can live as they like.

Much of what I have described here might seem like the footling ephemera of political life – the effect of politics on body, family and spouse. But I believe it lifts the lid on something more serious: politics is already populated by a surfeit of political professionals and apparatchiks; if we want people with an independent turn of mind who have led normal, sometimes blemished, lives to represent our country in Parliament in the future, there will need to be a shift in what is expected of them and their families.

There is a human cost to life in the public eye. No one should go into politics expecting an easy ride. The public and the media have every right to challenge, probe and provoke those who seek power. Yet if every youthful misdemeanour is recycled on social media for ever, if the media and political classes continue to slug it out in such a venomous manner, if the dysfunctional operation of Whitehall continues to expect too much of people at the top, and if politicians cannot protect their loved ones from unfair abuse and scrutiny, then we should not be surprised if in future Parliament is populated by robots, monks and nuns. I have nothing against them, but they are in short supply and do not represent contemporary Britain in all its flawed glory.

British politics – indeed, politics across much of the developed world – is in the throes of a major change, as old certainties collapse and the rise of a more fragmented, volatile and angry politics takes root. Conventional politics will not be able to fight back if it is hobbled by its own deficiencies, and filled with people who increasingly resemble a caste apart.

But public trust in politics relies not just on the character and quality of politicians, but also on an accurate and realistic account of the powers they possess and what they actually do in office. Politics may be the art of the possible, but too often politicians choose to promise the impossible. The private reality and public perception of power diverge. To understand why, we need to expose the unhealthy gap between the imperfect way decisions are taken and the grandiloquent behaviour of politicians.

CHAPTER 3

The Plumage of Power

David Cameron seemed a little on edge. We were alone in his study in Number 10, very shortly after the formation of the coalition, and he wanted to ask me something that had clearly been preying on his mind.

'This is terribly awkward,' he admitted. 'The thing is . . . George has for so long had his eye on Dorneywood . . . He's very close to me . . . Would you mind if he used Dorneywood instead of you?' He then proposed that I share the Foreign Secretary's traditional grace-and-favour countryside retreat, Chevening, rather than Dorneywood, which was ordinarily used by the number two in government.

I was a bit taken aback. I had thought he wanted to ask me something important. I had never even heard of these places. I knew of Chequers, the Prime Minister's country pad, but that was about it. It hadn't really occurred to me that I might get a grace-and-favour retreat in the countryside to use at weekends, still less that there was any great distinction between one or the other. David Cameron's plea on behalf of the Chancellor suggested that George Osborne had been measuring up the curtains for years.

So, with that, I accepted the new arrangement and found myself sharing Chevening – a grand mansion in the Kent countryside near Sevenoaks – for the next five years with the Foreign Secretary, first William Hague and later Philip Hammond. Not at the same time, I hasten to add; that would have been taking coalition cooperation a little too far. We simply stayed there on different weekends. By the end of the parliament, not least because Miriam didn't take to the somewhat overbearing atmosphere of such a palatial building, we limited our stay to one or two nights every month or so.

Whether or not occupying Dorneywood made any difference to anything, I couldn't say. But, like Westminster itself, many of the so-called trappings of power – grace-and-favour mansions, grand offices, ministerial Jaguars, the pomp and ceremony of state events – can seem completely alien to people who have not spent their lives preparing for power. As such, it is easy to underestimate their importance. As I came to realise later, the plumage that surrounds high office can matter a huge amount. The symbolism and imagery of power shape people's perceptions of who is wielding it. And perception is nine-tenths of the reality of power.

At the start of the coalition, I didn't think too much about the fixtures and fittings of my role as Deputy Prime Minister – there was just so much else going on. As I explained in the previous chapter, when I first arrived in Whitehall I was of the view that the last thing the coalition needed was a rival power centre to Number 10 in my office, so I consciously made do with fewer officials, less space and more limited resources. When it was suggested that I take an office with no publicly recognisable entrance of its own, I didn't mind, as I thought I wouldn't need an equivalent of the Number 10 door at which to receive guests. When it was decided where I would sit in the House of Commons at Prime Minister's Questions, I thought it made sense to sit supportively next to the PM, to show that the coalition could work smoothly.

Big mistakes. All of them.

The way power is organised and communicated is an essential ingredient for the legitimacy with which authority is wielded.

If people cannot readily visualise who occupies positions of power, what they do in those roles and why they do it, then the fragile acceptance of authority in an age of widespread public cynicism soon evaporates. The days when people would give governments the benefit of the doubt, when diffidence prevailed, are thankfully long gone. Of course, power has always been questioned – at least since the days of Magna Carta. But with the collapse of class-based politics and the rise of individual choice, people are more empowered today (at least as consumers) than ever before, so they rightly don't want to be taken for granted by their politicians. What I learned during five years of government is that, in a climate such as this, every time a politician boastfully exaggerates their authority or modestly fails to explain what they have achieved, every time a government overstates its ambitions or refuses to come clean about its ambitions, the result is the same: the public feel that they're being patronised or excluded by those in power, and naturally they don't like it.

Most people most of the time don't follow the ins and outs of politics, still less internal Whitehall politics. Life is too short, and people rightly care more about their own lives, their own families, their own communities. But the sense – which is stronger now than ever before, because of the greater scrutiny placed on governments – that the powerful occasionally try to pull the wool over their eyes understandably enrages people. This is why it is so easy for populists from the extreme right and left to appeal to a lurking resentment towards all forms of authority. If power seems opaque, if the powerful appear to be tricksy, if decisions are made in a way that people find difficult to follow, then resentment and cynicism only grow – and the politics of rage with them.

I mistakenly assumed that if I worked hard within government, did my homework and took decisions on their merits, then, one way or another, the truth – that the coalition was acting out of reasonable motives – would become plain to see, and political dividends for the Liberal Democrats would follow. What I did not anticipate was what actually happened: I worked hard, did my homework and took decisions on their merits as far as I could – and no one knew about it. This enabled critics from the left to lampoon the Liberal Democrats as spineless, and critics from the right to lambast Liberal Democrats as illegitimate irritants who shouldn't have been in government in the first place. Finding it hard to work out exactly what the Liberal Democrats were doing within government, the public readily turned away from us and towards other parties. In short, I failed to realise an interesting paradox of modern politics: in an age of unprecedented transparency, the reality of power can still remain obscure to the public.

During my time in office it was striking to observe how two of our political cousins – the French and the Americans – managed this balance between the plumage and the plumbing of power, for the political figures whose roles were also one notch down from the top: the French Prime Minister and the US Vice-President. In France, they don't shirk from furnishing the office of the Prime Minister, subservient though he is to the President, with some illustrious trappings. I was greeted by two French PMs while I was in government, François Fillon and, later, Manuel Valls, on the grand steps of the magnificent Hôtel Matignon in Paris, which served as their official residence and office. It seemed a world away from the comparative invisibility of my offices in Whitehall. The institutional accoutrements of the American vice-presidents are equally imposing. They work from the White House and rarely appear without a backdrop of US flags and a lectern displaying their somewhat regal-looking seal. I met and spoke to Vice-President Joe Biden regularly during my time in office and grew to like him immensely. But while the French Prime Minister is afforded both plumage and authority, the US Vice-President is famously granted some of the former, but much less of the latter. Joe Biden's role was significant because he was a widely respected figure in Congress and clearly enjoyed the trust of President Obama on matters of foreign policy – but that said more about his own gifts than it did about the formal powers of the Vice-Presidency. The 'Veep' may be 'a heartbeat away from the Presidency', yet the role was described as 'not worth a bucket of warm spit' by one of its previous occupants, John Nance Garner.

If the French provide their number two with both pomp and power, and the Americans provide theirs with pomp but less power, I was a third type: no pomp, but real power. The Conservatives may have had far more seats in Parliament than the Liberal Democrats – 307 to 57 – but they did not have a majority, and therefore if I didn't agree to something, they could not force it through. I was able to wield a veto over much of government policy. The role of the Deputy Prime Minister was, in this sense, quite different from that of John Prescott or Michael Heseltine: every significant decision over the five years required agreement from both me and the Prime Minister. The difference in votes received by the two parties was also much slimmer – 10.7 million for the Conservatives compared to 6.8 million for the Lib Dems, a ratio of roughly three to two – so the government relied on us not only for a parliamentary majority, but also, in a less tangible way, for its democratic authority.

Behind the scenes, then, I was a co-author in government. Not only did I wield a veto, but I also oversaw some of the key decision-making bodies. One of these was my role as chair of the Home Affairs Cabinet Committee, which administered collective responsibility for most areas of domestic policy beyond budget decisions, ranging from education and transport to health and justice. The committee was important not just because it met regularly, at least at the outset, but also because for all significant domestic-policy decisions that were made, Cabinet Ministers had to 'write round' – circulating memos that detailed their proposals, and responding to those put forward by others – a process for which I was the adjudicating chair. The meetings themselves, particularly in the early days of the coalition, were some of the most enjoyable and productive in government. They took place in a grand eighteenth-century meeting room in the Cabinet Office, innocuously named Conference Room A. In the centre was the old Treasury Board table, which was once used by Chancellors to lay out the Exchequer Rolls in the days when everything was recorded by hand. Oddly, I was placed at the far end of the table in front of an old throne that was apparently last used by George III, the last monarch to attend Cabinet meetings, who famously went mad. At their best, the Home Affairs Committee meetings became a useful forum for discussion of some of the big, and often intractable, issues of the day. There were challenging, collegiate debates between ministers on both sides of the coalition on everything from the future of social care to early-years provision – debates that were not possible in the more perfunctory format of the weekly meetings of the Cabinet. Cameron would sometimes joke, rather archly, 'I hear you're having all the interesting discussions in the Home Affairs Committee.'

While the committee was initially one of the most productive in government, its purple patch soon faded. As the coalition went on, Conservative ministers became less engaged and would complain privately that it was just a means by which pesky Lib Dems sought to keep a check on the decisions they were taking. A low point was reached in February 2014, when I had to stop a meeting of the committee altogether following a crass attempt by Chris Grayling, then Secretary of State for Justice, and a very overexcited Michael Gove, then Secretary of State for Education, to bounce the meeting into agreeing proposals for new offences for knife crime about which there was no consensus, not least because senior Conservatives such as Ken Clarke disagreed with them just as much as I did.

Other government committees fared considerably better with the passage of time – most notably the National Security Committee, of which David Cameron was chair and I was vice-chair. While there were occasional points of tension on issues of disagreement such as Trident, surveillance powers, the Middle East and Europe – I tried in vain on a number of occasions to hold a strategic discussion in the NSC about Britain's place in Europe – it remained a largely consensual and cooperative forum. This was partly due to my own view that, whatever other differences we had in the coalition, on core issues of national security it was important that the government should present a common position; and partly because David Cameron often chose to focus on operational defence matters, such as troop movements in Afghanistan, on which he appeared to have a clear grasp of the detail and there was no cause for party political argument.

The real engine-room of decision-making, however, was not in committees at all. The big decisions were hammered out either directly between Cameron and me, or with the two of us accompanied by George Osborne and Danny Alexander. Cameron and I met on a more-or-less weekly basis throughout the lifespan of the coalition, and often more regularly than that, while meetings of the four of us were only a little less frequent. The Civil Service, because it cannot see a process without labelling it, soon came to call these meetings 'bilats' and 'quads' respectively. In the bilats, Cameron and I could – and would – discuss any issue under the sun, while the quads tended to be reserved for economic matters and were the chief forum for ironing out the details of budgets and autumn statements. While other ministers floated in and out of the quad meetings, depending on the nature of the discussions – most notably David Laws and Oliver Letwin, the Lib Dem and Conservative ministers responsible for policy – by and large they remained a forum for Cameron, Osborne, Danny and me to argue the toss over the key decisions affecting the economy.

The quad meetings were always open and frank – very few officials and advisers were present – and were largely conducted in good faith and remained constructive long after coalition cooperation in other departments had broken down. That's not to say they didn't have their stormy moments. Governing in the aftermath of an economic heart attack was far from plain sailing, and every grisly decision, every pound of public money saved or cut, had to be discussed and debated, often at great length. But it was here, in the matter of the government's economic policy, that the gap between the public's perception of how the coalition operated and the reality was perhaps greatest.

The prevailing view was essentially that George Osborne was the exclusive author of all the coalition's economic policy, whereas the truth involved a great deal of toing and froing between the two sides. While that clearly did immense damage to the Liberal Democrats – allowing Labour to accuse us of meekly going along with 'Osbornomics' – it also distorted the public understanding of how their government actually functioned. However much Danny Alexander and I slaved away in the government boiler room to settle the details of numerous budgets, as long as George Osborne was the government's principal economic messenger, he was always bound to be viewed as its principal author, too. To be fair to George Osborne, he and his Treasury team were far more open towards Danny, me and David Cameron than Gordon Brown as Chancellor ever was to Tony Blair as Prime Minister. This was perhaps shaped by the realisation that he simply couldn't speak in the House of Commons on behalf of the government without our consent, but it also spoke well of George Osborne's supple intellectual gifts as a highly effective Whitehall negotiator.

The reality of how things worked is most dramatically illustrated by the internal negotiations leading up to the 2012 budget, which became known as the 'omnishambles budget'. We were nearly two years into the coalition's term and the economy was still in a perilous state. There was precious little evidence that our economic strategy was working – growth was flat and tax receipts were down – so a successful and well-received budget was a priority. The negotiations over the budget were tense, with a huge amount of time and energy devoted to one big transaction: Danny and I were determined to see a major uplift in the personal allowance, the amount that every individual can earn tax-free; Osborne, however, did not want to make this the central component of the budget because, at that time at least, it was widely regarded as a totemic Lib Dem policy and it would consume most of the money available to the Treasury in the budget. He eventually conceded, reluctantly, but only in exchange for something that he knew would be politically painful for the Liberal Democrats to accept: a cut in the top rate of tax, which he wanted to reduce from 50p to 40p.

Discussions became so fraught that at a quad meeting in Cameron's flat, three or four days before the budget, I vetoed the entire thing. We later settled down to a compromise that the top rate would only come down to 45p, and with a year's delay before it was implemented. Given that the top rate of tax under Labour had been considerably lower – 40p – for much of their time in office, and given the landmark achievement of raising the starting point of income tax so dramatically (from £8,105 to £9,205, the equivalent of a £220 tax cut for millions of people on low and middle incomes), it seemed like a fair outcome to me.

Yet it was entirely overshadowed by the furore surrounding the so-called 'pasty tax', in which VAT would be applied to heated food. The Treasury had, in fact, been pushing for a much wider package of VAT reforms that included taxing sandwiches and other lunchtime snacks. I told Osborne outside David Cameron's office, after one of our meetings late in the process, that I thought this was mad and he should get rid of all the proposals for VAT on food. If he started hitting people on food, I argued, particularly the food people eat on their lunch breaks, he would be roundly criticised. Besides, it was clearly regressive, insofar as it would impact on poorer families the hardest, and I could not accept it. Thankfully, Osborne saw sense and rethought the proposal – though, bafflingly, he kept in the heated-food element, which rebounded on him spectacularly.

In the event, the budget was a calamitous failure, with the Chancellor's showpiece measure – the cutting of the top rate of tax from 50p to 45p – backfiring badly (he was accused, predictably, of being out of touch, having cut taxes for the wealthy at a time of austerity); the big Lib Dem achievement of the largest rise ever in the income-tax personal allowance was largely lost in the media coverage; and a number of unnecessary and politically toxic measures tucked away in the small print were branded as a 'pasty tax', a 'caravan tax' and a 'granny tax'. The whole thing unravelled disastrously, damaged George Osborne's standing and left the public's faith in the coalition's economic management, and therefore the viability of the coalition itself, very fragile indeed.

The following year, the budget negotiations were equally tense, not least because the economic situation had barely improved. We expected the Office for Budget Responsibility to downgrade our growth forecasts, meaning that there would be no money to pay for a further uplift in the personal allowance (once again my party's top priority), and that we risked missing our own targets on deficit and debt reduction. In effect, Plan A was not working. Osborne's solution was to expand the cuts to departmental spending in 2015/16 by an extra £3bn, to £13bn in total, which would include cuts to the NHS, something that both parties had vowed solemnly not to do. The NHS money was to come from underspends in its budget, with Osborne's argument being that if the Department for Health wasn't spending the money, then it clearly wasn't needed. Osborne wanted to use the extra departmental savings not only to help meet the deficit target, but also to raise the personal allowance and cut the standard rate of income tax by a penny – a proposal that came completely out of the blue. I was struck at the time that both David Cameron and George Osborne appeared to be so willing to shave money off the NHS, given the prominence they had placed on their promise in the 2010 general election not to cut the NHS budget. At any rate, I thought the whole thing was barmy and blocked it, telling them it was impossible to justify cutting the NHS to pay for tax cuts. I offered to have a no-frills budget, even if it meant not making any advance on the personal allowance, rather than embark on such an unpalatable course of action.

In order to meet the debt target, Osborne also wanted to bring forward about £13bn of cuts to 2016/17, which would have been an extraordinarily gory thing to do. On the Monday morning, nine days before budget day, Cameron and Osborne brought in Sir Nicholas Macpherson, the long-standing Permanent Secretary to the Treasury, to the quad meeting, and he warned, in effect, that if we did not meet the debt-target deadline, then it would do great damage to the fiscal credibility of UK plc. Therefore, he argued, we absolutely had to make the extra cuts. Cameron said very little. Osborne was careful to let the Permanent Secretary do the talking. I bluntly said no. I insisted that we stick to the fiscal plan, even if it meant extending the timetable. I saw no merit in the government chasing its tail, fiscally speaking. If our original deficit-reduction plan was going to take a little longer than envisaged, rather than randomly cutting billions of pounds more from public services to meet an arbitrary deadline at the end of the parliament, we would just have to be open about the slippage in our timetable. I simply didn't believe the apocalyptic predictions that we would find ourselves on the rack in the bond markets, and I intensely disliked the way the Conservatives were using the Treasury to pressure me into accepting what was, essentially, an ideological and not an economic case. Eventually they relented. We pushed back the timetable of the cuts by another year, and the world kept on turning.

In order to make it a meaningful budget, and to create space for the increase in both the personal allowance and for a new Conservative proposal of a cut in employers' National

Insurance contributions for firms taking on new staff, Osborne's elegant solution was to bring forward Lib Dem minister Steve Webb's plans for a simpler and more generous 'single-tier' state pension. This policy came with a £5.5bn National Insurance increase, which could be recycled to pay for these other measures.

The following spring, in 2014, we had another significant behind-the-scenes Treasury-related row, this time over RBS bonuses. The bank, which at this stage was 81 per cent state-owned, was proposing to pay some of its highest-paid staff excessively generous bonuses worth up to twice their salaries, including a number of high-value staff based in the US. I was clear from the outset that I couldn't accept this, but when I registered my opposition I was met with a wall of resistance. I received a volley of breathless warnings, from officials at the Treasury, from UK Financial Investments (the body established by Alistair Darling to manage the public stake in the stricken banks) and the then chair of RBS, Philip Hampton, a decent man whom I'd asked to come to see me in my office. Time and again I was warned about the spine-chilling consequences if we blocked the bonuses: there would be mass resignations; the board would walk out; the value of RBS would collapse; I would be personally to blame if the bank wasn't returned to the public at good value and in good time. Essentially, the response was that this just had to happen.

I dug in my heels. Chris Saunders, my long-standing and hugely experienced economics adviser, who played a pivotal role in all the major economic decisions I was party to in government, provided me with all the evidence I needed to reject the decision. After one particularly scratchy meeting I had with David Cameron on the subject, George Osborne came to see me. He had one more go at persuading me, but when I then wrote to him a detailed letter explaining why I wouldn't budge, he relented and said he'd go away and try to do what I wanted. He later texted me to say that if he was able to hammer this out with RBS, he didn't want anything in the press saying I had forced him to do so. I told him I'd happily keep our disagreement quiet, as long as the right decision was taken. Besides, this was formally a decision to be enacted by UKFI, not by ministers. Gallingly, the decision was splashed across the *Financial Times* shortly afterwards, with George Osborne given all the credit for blocking the bonuses.

What was revealing about these episodes was how fixed group-think can become in all institutions, not least in an organisation as powerful as the Treasury. With hindsight, it seems remarkable to me that I had to deploy such stubbornness to reject such patently daft ideas as taxing British food and rewarding American bankers with fat bonuses. Yet, at the time, I was almost entirely isolated. I don't for a minute think that George Osborne, David Cameron, the Treasury, Sir Jeremy Heywood or the RBS chairman were either malign or unintelligent in their approach to these questions. It's just what the received wisdom was at the time. I cannot think of a better example of the merits of proper checks and balances within government, proper scrutiny of policy ideas, which is so often absent in one-party governments. The politically inept Conservative budget of March 2016, in which Osborne yet again proposed a package of multibillion-pound giveaways to some of the wealthiest in society while proposing to cut benefits for the disabled, simply confirmed the hubris of unchallenged one-party decision-making in Whitehall, as well as the consistent tendency of the Conservatives, when left to their own devices, to favour the rich over the poor.

The political tragedy, for the Liberal Democrats at least, is that none of this was remotely visible to the British public at the time. Indeed, in the case of RBS bonuses, the inverse of the truth was disseminated to the press. My efforts – in terms of party political advantage at least – might as well never have occurred. Instead, the mismatch between the optics of power and the mechanics of it was so entrenched that it allowed my opponents to make two diametrically opposed arguments about me: to many on the left, I was presented as a sell-out, sitting meekly at the side as the Conservatives ran amok; to many on the right, and in particular the true-blue brigade on Cameron's backbenches, I was a pantomime villain, a fox in the Tory hen-house, frustrating and confounding them at every turn and stopping the government from being the full-blooded Thatcherite fantasy they believed it could, and should, have been.

As the increasingly unflattering gap between the reality of coalition government and the caricatures of the Lib Dem role in it took root, my team and I searched for ways to try to bring to light the dynamics of the quad meetings. One idea we pushed repeatedly was to allow cameras in to film a quad meeting – although the Conservatives always resisted, for the equal and opposite reason that it would betray the carefully constructed image of untrammelled authority that they sought to convey. We eventually got them to concede, towards the very end of the parliament, to a news feature that ITV's political editor, Tom Bradby, was producing on the Lib Dems and my role in the coalition. Even then, we could only get agreement from the Conservatives for the ITV team to film a minute or two at the beginning of one of our meetings, in return for our consent that they would also film the PM in a meeting of the full Cabinet. In the end, Tom produced an astute report, a key theme of which was that people did not know quite how much authority the Lib Dems exerted across Whitehall. This only served to remind me that when we succeeded in pulling back the curtains of the coalition even just a little, it had a positive effect on how the role of the Liberal Democrats was viewed. But by then, of course, it was far too late.

What these particular travails in government reveal, however, is a far bigger problem than who gets the credit or takes the blame for any one policy. One of the reasons why modern politics is misfiring as badly as it is – and certainly why the Liberal Democrat contribution to the coalition was rarely recognised – is that the perception of how power is wielded is often so different from the reality. I adhere to the core liberal principle that all power is best administered as openly and accountably as possible. Secret power may sometimes be necessary – our safety would be jeopardised without the secrecy of the intelligence services – but it should always be the exception, not the rule. Where people try to exert influence or power without being open about it (corporate lobbying is an obvious example), there should be the maximum amount of transparency about who is trying to influence whom, and to what end. Openness keeps our politics clean.

Yet too often who pulls the strings and who claims to pull the strings are quite different. Ministers may make an announcement because a newspaper proprietor or editor has told them it will get them some good publicity. Or they might seek to take credit – as the current Conservative Government does on a regular basis – for something initiated by another party or a previous administration. Or they might blame an unpopular decision, which they privately support, on the European Union or some international convention. Most commonly of all, ministers will routinely assert that they are personally taking decisive action on a matter of public concern, when in truth it is their special advisers or civil servants in Whitehall who have suggested the course of action to them. Politicians often act as mouthpieces for people with the real ideas, the real will to act, who rarely emerge in the bright light of day. The apocryphal image of a foul-mouthed political spin doctor ordering some hapless minister to go out and pretend they're in charge of some unfolding crisis may be a little wide of the mark, but it nonetheless reveals an enduring truth. Those who present themselves as being in power may very often be acting at the instigation, or even under the authority, of someone else who is really in charge.

There is nothing wrong or new in this. Power and influence are by nature multi-layered. There are thinkers and doers, decision-makers and communicators, planners and orators, all of whom have power, but play different roles. Civil servants, in particular, wield considerable influence over decisions that affect every aspect of society – from local planning to taxation, from building regulations to the case for war – but they act, or at least should act, accountably to those who have political authority derived from a democratic mandate. That has always been the case. Nor do people expect politicians to come up with all their policies themselves. Being open to the advice and proposals of others is, in many ways, a virtue. What is new, however, is that this now takes place within the context of increasing public impatience with the opacity of power.

As we have all become more empowered as consumers, as information technology has enabled us to exploit and enjoy information with the click of a button in a way never before seen in history, it is jarringly anachronistic that we are still expected to accept who wields power over us in the same old way. As consumers, we live in a digital age. As citizens, we are stuck in an analogue era. To make matters worse, decision-makers themselves are trapped in a fatal pretence: that they are in complete control, when everyone knows they are not. The days when British prime ministers could claim that they controlled all they surveyed, that the votes of the House of Commons could shape the destiny of citizens and nations alike, are long, long gone. Yet there is still a lingering whiff of empire in everything that Westminster and Whitehall does. From the macho guffawing in the House of Commons to the puffed-up way in which government press releases regularly declare a new dawn, the self-importance of power brooks no compromise with the more mundane reality: that governments are, in truth, less in charge than ever before.

Globalisation has rendered all governments more reactive, more passive in the face of wider economic and financial forces. Supranational governance – most especially in the

European Union – means that decisions that were once taken unilaterally by governments are now the subject of compromise and horse-trading with other governments. Judicial oversight and an increasingly litigious culture have clipped the wings of governments, too. And the sophistication of single-issue campaign groups, plus the vigilance and hyperbole of the press, have had a cowing effect on everyday government decision-making. And yet – far from recognising these new limitations – politicians still play to the gallery, over-claiming what they are capable of, overstating their influence over events. Michael Gove's schools policy, effectively a ramping up of the Academies programme set in train under Tony Blair and Andrew Adonis, was described breathlessly by the right-wing commentariat as a 'revolution'. Iain Duncan Smith lauded his introduction of Universal Credit as 'the most radical redesign of the benefits system this country has ever seen'. Gordon Brown notoriously declared that he had 'ended boom and bust'. I wasn't immune to this hyperbole myself: I claimed that my ill-fated attempt to revamp our creaking political system was 'the biggest shake-up of our democracy' since the Great Reform Act of 1832.

Since politicians keep claiming they possess gravity-defying powers, it is hardly surprising that people demand that politicians provide instant solutions when things go wrong. As I went around the country visiting constituencies and holding public meetings, I would constantly be asked what I was personally going to do about every local issue under the sun – from potholes and roadworks to local planning decisions and fly-tipping. I remember once, at a public meeting at a school in Newquay while I was Deputy Prime Minister in 2011, being asked by irate local residents how I personally was going to stop underage drinking and antisocial behaviour in the town centre.

In short, attitudes towards power have become hopelessly knotty and contradictory: as consumers and private individuals, we have an unprecedented amount of power, choice and autonomy over our own lives; as political citizens and subjects, however, we are subject to an opaque form of government, unrepresentative parliaments, over-claiming politicians, and an infantile public discourse that assumes that politicians should have all the answers. No wonder populists and firebrands of all stripes are doing well – they can puncture the pretensions of those in power without taking any responsibility of their own, and declare that they offer honest answers where other politicians make implausible claims.

The problem, ultimately, is this: too often, the theatre of power is organised to obfuscate exactly what goes on in government. Left to their own devices, governments would happily restrict most of their interaction with the public to the choreographed settings of Downing Street and the Chamber of the House of Commons. Neither, sadly, holds governments to account in a particularly exacting way. The press pack is, understandably, at the mercy of what governments choose to divulge to them and cannot reasonably be expected to have expertise in all the areas of government activity. The House of Commons is strong on rhetoric, insults, one-liners and a lot of braying – but pretty hopeless, with the exception of some Select Committee investigations, at getting under the skin of government power. Even when it does, the flattering parliamentary majorities that governments invariably receive under our electoral system ensure that those in power remain unruffled by parliamentary scrutiny.

Of course, the reason why the political establishment generally dislikes greater transparency in government is that it risks lifting the lid on the way in which power is really administered. In this respect, the introduction of the Freedom of Information Act by Tony Blair in 2000 was a strikingly forward-thinking thing to do – much though he now claims to regret it. In my time in government, I witnessed a remarkable change of heart by the Conservative Party high command in its attitude towards Freedom of Information (FOI). At the outset, there was broad agreement that the Act should be extended. Tom McNally, the wonderfully wise and loyal leader of the Lib Dems in the House of Lords whom I appointed as a minister in the Ministry of Justice, successfully overcame Ken Clarke's initial reservations about the inconveniences of greater transparency. Tom and Ken got on so well that Tom remarked that it was the only topic on which they strongly disagreed. In the end, we managed to agree to extend Freedom of Information requirements to a growing area of government activity.

Simon Hughes, who replaced Tom in the Ministry of Justice later in the parliament, managed to push the boundaries a little further, such that, by the end of the parliament, the government had committed to make Network Rail subject to FOI requests. Simon wanted to go further, attempting to update the code of practice that gives guidance on how public authorities interpret FOI legislation, which, although rather technical, would have given people the power to ask questions about private-sector contractors who provide public services on behalf of local authorities. Many services, including transport, bin collections and health services, are subcontracted, but powers to scrutinise these contracts are extremely limited. This attempt at opening private subcontractors up to public scrutiny was ultimately blocked by a combination of the Civil Service and senior Conservatives, neither of whom wanted to see the Act extended. Had Simon got his way, I know he would have wanted to go even further, and expand the powers to cover all private organisations that provide what the public consider to be vital services, such as water companies, the National Grid and even housing associations.

At the same time, Francis Maude – who appeared to harbour a slightly irrational dislike of the Civil Service itself – was making great and welcome strides in using information technology to release huge dollops of data, from traffic flows to statistics on childhood obesity, which had traditionally been kept under lock and key in Whitehall. He rightly received plaudits from around the world, and from the IT industry in particular, for overseeing a greater release of government data than under almost any other government. Yet, as the number of FOI requests began to pile up – many of which they considered vexatious – the mood among Conservatives changed sharply. Michael Gove, especially, would launch into colourful rants around the Cabinet table against the temerity of campaign groups and journalists who sought to find out who decided what, and how, in Whitehall. He believed that a safe, secret place for internal government debate was vital to good governance, and that the push for accountability and transparency had overstepped the mark. The fact that he simultaneously paraded himself at the time of the Leveson Inquiry as the great defender of press freedom was an irony that went unnoticed.

In 2015, the Conservative Government appointed a technical panel to review the workings of the Freedom of Information Act. The panel included some of Westminster's most conservative insiders, such as Lord Carlile of Berriew and Jack Straw, which gave rise to concern that it would recommend a significant reduction in FOI rules. While much of what was at stake here is fairly mechanical, it nonetheless acted as a weathervane for the wider principle: how is power made transparent to the wider public? How can the powerful be held to account for the decisions they take? The fact that the government eventually backed off from introducing major restrictions to FOI shows, perhaps, that the trend towards greater transparency is now unstoppable.

What I hadn't appreciated at the start of the government was that the symbols of power are there for a reason: in making the powerful appear powerful, they provide a vital signal to the public – a projection of what is going on behind closed doors. In 2010, the public had no frame of reference for what a Deputy Prime Minister in a coalition government does. In the absence of anything that visually demonstrated my authority, an impression soon formed that I was, in fact, bereft of authority. Not having a recognisable location for my office made it impossible to give the public a memorable image of where I was, what I was doing and what my purpose in government was. Sitting next to Cameron at Prime Minister's Questions became a particularly powerful image that reinforced the very worst caricature of me: that I sat docile and mute while Cameron did all the talking. About halfway through the parliament I considered moving a few yards sideways and sitting on the Lib Dem benches. I eventually decided that making such a move late in the parliament would look a little petulant. That fear was confirmed by the reaction to the one time I did decide to miss a big parliamentary occasion – the 2014 Autumn Statement – when I chose to head to Cornwall instead, to announce one of the infrastructure schemes contained within it. My absence looked churlish, and was presented as such.

Once I had grasped the importance of having a recognisable backdrop against which I should appear as Deputy Prime Minister – an equivalent to the shiny black door of Number 10 – I attempted in vain to rectify it. I began hosting regular press conferences in Admiralty House. This was not without its presentational challenges. At a 2011 press conference that I held jointly with Mark Rutte, the Dutch Prime Minister and an old friend of mine, we stood side by side answering questions, oblivious to the fact that hanging behind us was a vast painting depicting the navies of our respective countries furiously shelling each other in an eighteenth-century sea battle. I also took advantage of an enforced office move in 2012 – the walls of my original room in the Cabinet Office were stuffed with asbestos – to relocate a few yards further up Whitehall to Dover House, home of the Scotland Office. Dover House had a spacious entrance with an under-used staircase, which I hoped could become a serviceable backdrop for my greeting of official visitors. In the event, I barely used it much at all.

If I came late to understanding the iconography of power, it was something the Conservatives clearly understood from the outset. While they were, at first, genuinely enthusiastic about coalition, they were always extraordinarily protective of prime-ministerial space. There may have been two of us at the top of the tree, but there was never to be any confusion in the public's mind as to which of us was top dog. Number 10 would sometimes go to surprising lengths to make sure that Cameron's image as the government's commander-in-chief was protected. At the Nato summit in Cardiff in 2014 I was walking out of the building to watch a fly-past with other leaders, while talking with Mark Rutte, when all of a sudden one of Cameron's special advisers appeared. She grabbed me by the elbow and told me I was not permitted to join the photo call. When I tried to insist, she firmly led me away. I was offended and impressed in equal measure.

Cameron's office was also protective of Number 10 itself. My team always met enormous resistance if we wanted to host even the most piffling event or reception in the building, so much so that we eventually gave up and started hosting receptions in nearby Admiralty House instead. Childishly, they never wanted me to appear in front of the famous Number 10 door, either. Even at the very end of the government's term, when I wanted to give a statement on the doorstep of Number 10 after the final coalition Cabinet meeting, my team had to organise it in a cloak-and-dagger way, ducking and weaving so that the PM's team did not know that I would be making remarks to the press pack waiting outside.

Perhaps Cameron's defensiveness around his prime-ministerial image was in part a consequence of the circumstances in which the government began its life in office. We had come into power surfing a wave of public clamour for a 'new politics' – a new era of cooperation, after thirteen long years of the Blair–Brown wars – and with the MPs' expenses scandal a very recent memory. In that climate, I had briefly become the poster boy for this new way of doing things, so much so that when Cameron reached out to the Liberal Democrats with his 'big, open and comprehensive offer' to form a government, he began by explicitly referencing the public's appetite for 'new politics'. Admittedly, I was soon brought crashing down to earth, but for a few weeks in the spring and early summer of 2010 there was little to distinguish David Cameron and me in the public pecking order of the new government. I remember telling Cameron that the moment I felt the public really understood that he was their Prime Minister was when he delivered his statement to the House that June, apologising to the families of the victims of the Bloody Sunday massacre. I had helped him with the statement, and he delivered it with real gravitas. From around that point onwards, the balanced ticket that we both represented at the outset gave way to a clearer hierarchy in the public's mind: Prime Minister first, Deputy Prime Minister second.

While the Conservatives clearly understood the importance of the symbols of power, and ensured that they possessed them, I honestly don't think it was the case that, when these decisions about plumage and presentation were made, they were knowingly trying to take advantage of the Liberal Democrats' unfamiliarity with power. They didn't hoodwink us. We just behaved differently. The trappings of power were important to them, and they were not important enough to us. As relations between the two sides of the coalition became more hard-headed and transactional, though, the tug of war about how decision-making authority was administered became more intense. George Osborne revealed a less attractive side of his complex character in a protracted argument he and I had about the terms on which Lib Dems in government could commission advice from civil servants without relaying that advice to Conservative Secretaries of State. My team felt – rightly – that in a coalition government both parties should be able to explore preliminary policy ideas with the help of officials, without immediately sharing them more widely. Given how trenchant the Conservatives had become about protecting the 'private space' within government, free from Freedom of Information requests, I assumed they would understand that both political parties deserved a little 'private space' in which to work up their own ideas in government. Osborne was, by turns, petulant and underhand in his remorseless efforts over several months to frustrate the plan. In the end, I managed to get my way – but, as he well knew, it came so late in the parliament that it was of little practical use. What this odd *Yes, Minister* episode shows – two of the most senior members of a government locked in an impenetrably petty procedural feud – is the significance that the Conservatives attached to the mechanics as well as the trappings of power. It is what they live for.

The bigger issue remains, though. Much as I fear that the modern pressures on politicians and their families will lead to a hollowing-out of the political class, so I also fear that the opacity of government will only deepen the widespread scepticism of the public towards the powerful. We live in an age where deference – for good or ill – has disappeared. Hierarchy is subverted by new technologies. Authority is questioned at every turn. Whether we like it or not, power needs to be explained and justified; it cannot simply be granted like a blank cheque. Decisions need to be communicated, not simply handed down. Secrecy can no longer linger unchallenged. The worst the future could hold for British politics is a new political elite stuffed full of party political hacks working over the heads of the British people behind the battlements of Whitehall. We are perilously close to that predicament already. The best the future could hold for British politics is a political class representative of the diversity of British society, working in an ever more transparent relationship of trust and accountability to the people. Which future occurs is still hanging in the balance.

So political success relies on persuasive storytelling, and public trust in politicians relies on an accurate representation of power. But the perception of politics, critical as it is, is quite different from its underlying purpose: changing things for the better. Given the pressures and constraints faced by any politician or government, let alone by the coalition, the vital question is this: how does change actually come about?

CHAPTER 4

The Virtue of Compromise

Change doesn't happen with the stroke of a pen. A government minister, no matter how powerful or influential, cannot simply decree that a policy will become law. For a major reform to come into being, it has to overcome many hurdles – some institutional, some financial, some political. The canny politician has to mobilise public opinion, persuade colleagues, assemble a parliamentary majority and navigate the machinery of Whitehall. He or she also has to build and win a financial case and get the private sector, local government, trade unions, non-governmental organisations and other third parties on board. They have to put time, energy and political capital on the line. And even then, if they have succeeded in all of that, the momentum for change can dissipate in an instant. Political winds can alter direction, new urgencies can intrude, and support that has been painstakingly pieced together can disappear overnight.

Making change is not easy: it is most definitely an art, not a science. As junior partners in a coalition and having been out of power for decades, the Liberal Democrats had to learn quickly how to get things done in a system that can resist change at every turn. The coalition government was, of course, a unique experiment in British politics with some unusual features, not least the need to secure agreement across the leadership of two political parties. Unsurprisingly, then, much of the significant change that came about during the coalition involved trade-offs and compromises: what could one side get, in exchange for giving the other side something?

Sometimes, as we shall see, that involved a straight policy swap. On other occasions, it involved forensic haggling about the substance of contentious new policies. When we wanted a tax on plastic bags, for instance, and the Conservatives resisted, we compromised by allowing a number of exemptions from the tax for smaller chains, shops at airports and, somewhat bizarrely, 'ultra-biodegradable' plastic bags that degrade within days (a type of bag that Owen Paterson insisted be exempted, despite the fact that it doesn't exist). On another occasion, as we were debating proposals for Internet porn filters, the argument even came down to the exact nature of the tick-box that would pop up on someone's screen when they turned on their computer. The Conservatives wanted the box labelled 'I do not want to allow adult content' pre-ticked, while we wanted a more permissive box to be pre-ticked (we are liberals, after all). Eventually we reached a grand compromise: no box would be ticked, and computer users could choose their own filters.

Whilst this toing and froing sounds a little unseemly, most of the time it was conducted in good humour. The main disadvantage, especially in the latter stages of the parliament, was when disagreement on a particular policy led to gridlock and a failure to take a decision. But the need to strike compromises also had important advantages: having to justify one's ideas in the face of scrutiny from a sceptical coalition partner forced both parties to be more thoughtful and creative; and the challenge of finding agreement between two parties ensured that extreme or excessively partisan policies rarely survived. Moderation invariably triumphed.

Perhaps the best example during the coalition government of a change that came about through a straightforward policy swap was the introduction of universal free school meals for infants. It is a policy whose inception was intimately bound up with one of the most infuriating, yet creative characters in the government, Michael Gove, who moved from ambivalence to hostility to acceptance of a policy for which he was both an unwitting co-author and a serious obstacle.

In the early days of the government, Gove was one of the most prominent public advocates for coalition. When we went for a meal near my home in Putney very early on in the parliament, I found him to be charm personified. He was generous, witty, collegiate and very smart. Over dinner, I tried to persuade him that the A-level system provided too narrow an education, which was neither good for pupils nor beneficial for the economy. We should do something radical, and broaden the curriculum prior to specialisation at university. He didn't agree – but he disagreed with amusing verve and flair, over a couple of bottles of wine.

A little over three years later, our relationship had soured to the point that he banned Lib Dem special advisers from physically entering the Department for Education, hid on one occasion in the toilet to avoid speaking to David Laws, and let loose his somewhat unhinged advisers to brief against me, and even against Miriam, in the press. On one of the last occasions I spoke to him in government, I asked him to come and see me in my office. He was keen to be accompanied by his assistant, but I insisted we meet alone, as I wanted to deliver a blunt message. Once we were alone, I asked him how he would react if someone on my behalf wilfully lied about his wife in the newspapers? (Miriam had, ludicrously, been accused in the *Mail on Sunday* by one of Michael Gove's advisers of seeking a Whitehall contract for a children's book charity – the contract had in fact been decided by Number 10.) He mumbled that he thought he 'knew what had happened'. I was livid.

Shortly afterwards, I told David Cameron that I wasn't prepared to waste my time working with Michael Gove, and that David Laws would do so on my behalf (hence Gove's concealment in the toilet). Given how much Number 10 clearly loathed Gove's principal adviser at the time and were as exasperated as I was by his occasional public outbursts, this didn't seem to come as much of a surprise to Cameron.

But even before the personal relations had soured, policy disagreements had started to accumulate. At the beginning of the government I was encouraged by what I thought might be an exciting confluence of Liberal Democrat and Conservative priorities in education: Gove's support for an extension of Tony Blair's emphasis on greater school autonomy; and our emphasis on promoting social mobility through the implementation of radical funding reform such as the pupil premium, something I'd written about well before I was even an MP and a policy that David Laws had very much made his own. At first there seemed to be genuine enthusiasm from Gove, too, to forge a new cross-party approach. Yet, almost exactly two years into the government, as I was leading the government delegation to the UN Sustainable Development Summit in Rio in June 2012, Michael Gove announced out of the blue that he wanted to return to a traditional two-tier O-level system. David Laws called me very early in the morning in my hotel room in Rio to discuss our response. We decided it should be immediate, so I did a couple of TV interviews making it clear that such a regressive turning back of the clock would not take place on my watch. From bonhomie in a Putney restaurant to policy disputes across the Atlantic – the contrast couldn't have been greater.

There ensued numerous other policy disagreements, from an attempt by the Conservatives to increase childcare ratios in nurseries – the number of children each trained member of staff can look after at a time – to Gove's unceasing effort to divert money away from needy mainstream schools to Free Schools. Given this fractious context, it would require a lot of effort to ensure that the Department for Education that Michael Gove controlled would successfully implement the provision of free school meals for all infants. Unlike the raising of the personal tax allowance, for example, it had not been discussed at the start of government, or enshrined in the

Coalition Agreement. In opposition, however, David Laws had strongly advocated the policy. It seemed common sense that children would perform better in class in the afternoon if they weren't hungry, and even more so if they had eaten a healthy and nutritious lunch. Research also showed that as many as four in ten children officially categorised as living in poverty were still not eligible to receive free school meals – and that a universal provision would be disproportionately beneficial to those on lower incomes. The policy captured a growing mood for improved school meals, following the campaigning work of Jamie Oliver, and gained the support of a host of charities and campaign groups. But it would also require significant funding and so it was not something we immediately pursued in office.

Ironically, its origin as government policy can be traced to a holiday that Michael Gove himself took in Marrakech, where he stumbled across Henry Dimbleby, the co-founder of the Leon restaurant chain and a healthy-food campaigner. As a result of the encounter, Gove commissioned Dimbleby and his business partner, John Vincent, to produce a report on how to raise the standard of school food. This became the School Food Plan, which was published in the summer of 2013 and was welcomed heartily by the Education Secretary. Buried in it was a recommendation to introduce free school meals for primary-school children, although at the time of publication there was no expectation that the government would be able to find the money to introduce such a radical policy.

Later that summer, as the conference season approached, Oliver Letwin and David Laws began the annual process of agreeing which government policies each party would announce that autumn. As ever, any spending commitments would have to be agreed as part of the autumn budget statement, and Osborne had a rabbit he was determined to pull from his hat: a tax cut for married couples, where one of the spouses stayed at home. In reality, the amount a couple would save was relatively puny, but Osborne saw it as a symbolic gesture to warm the hearts of traditional Tory voters as well as the editorial teams at the *Daily Telegraph* and the *Daily Mail*. Knowing this was an unpalatable policy for us – it was a sop to married couples where one stayed at home and the other worked, while doing nothing for working couples, unmarried couples, single people or widows – he proposed a deal: the policy's price tag was £600m; if we would agree to it, he would find a similar amount for a policy of our choosing.

We considered raising the personal allowance further, but decided not to because that was something we felt should happen in any event in each budget. We also considered using it to fund discounted bus passes for eighteen- to twenty-one-year-olds, in order to help them get to training, work or education, but the technicalities proved problematic. Then David Laws suggested that we should take a look at the free school-meal proposals and work out what we might be able to do with £600m. Given the recent spats with Gove and his team over O-levels and childcare ratios, and certain as we were that he would object to a policy that imposed more obligations on Free Schools and academies, the proposal was worked up without his knowledge. David Laws and our education adviser, Matt Sanders, drew up the policy with the help of a couple of civil servants in the Department for Education. Together they worked out that the money would be enough to extend the policy to all children in the first three years of state primary school in England, although it would need to be accompanied by some extra capital to help schools adapt their kitchens. We took the proposal back to Cameron, Osborne and Letwin and they agreed to the trade-off – and also agreed to keep the move to themselves, including keeping it from Gove. David Laws eventually informed Michael Gove at a later stage. To his credit, Gove said he was happy for officials to continue to work on the policy in private and he also agreed to keep it confidential, even from his own team of political advisers, so that it wouldn't leak.

Those advisers, predictably enough, took this rather badly. Not only had their authority been undermined and their permission circumvented, but their own department and party leadership had worked against them, while the policy itself challenged the very basis of their Free School project, requiring, as it did, supposedly autonomous schools to comply with the legislation. Soon the papers were peppered with specious stories planted by Gove's office about the diversion of resources from other areas of the education budget, implementation difficulties and budget overruns – all of which were nonsense. The implementation was remarkably smooth, not least because David Laws oversaw it in minute detail. By the time the policy came into effect at the start of the next school year in September 2014, he could practically recite the lunch menus for each of the 17,000-odd state primary schools in England. And today over a million more small children eat a healthy meal at lunchtime every day at school.

While trade-offs of this nature may have been a more conspicuous feature of the coalition than of single-party governments, all governments – including single-party ones – go through a huge amount of internal horse-trading to implement their plans. In our case, it was sometimes a cumbersome way of taking decisions, but with a healthy majority in Parliament, it at least meant that when agreement between me and the Prime Minister had been reached, we would rarely waver from a decision and could ensure that it was put into practice (even against the wishes of a senior minister): the contrast with the endless zigzagging and U-turns of the single-party, Conservative government after the 2015 election speaks volumes.

One significant difference between the coalition government and other single-party governments, though, was the way in which its founding text – the Coalition Agreement – was treated, unlike most policy documents or election manifestos, with the reverence normally reserved for tablets of stone. The fact that the Liberal Democrats, despite being the smaller party in the coalition, succeeded in implanting a greater share of our manifesto commitments into the Coalition Agreement than the Conservatives made our attachment to it all the firmer.

The importance of the Coalition Agreement in providing a blueprint for change was perhaps most clearly illustrated by one of the coalition's biggest reforms of all, the raising of the personal tax allowance – the delivery of which, once again, required numerous trade-offs and much brinkmanship before it actually happened.

'I would love to take everyone out of their first ten thousand pounds of income tax, Nick. It's a beautiful idea, it's a lovely idea. But we can't afford it.' This was how David Cameron reacted during the first televised leaders' debate in 2010, with a somewhat dismissive wave of his hand, towards what eventually became by far the biggest tax reform of the coalition years.

I had insisted that the raising of the income-tax allowance should feature prominently in the Coalition Agreement, given that it was one of the key policies the Lib Dems had campaigned on during the 2010 general election. Danny Alexander successfully inserted a commitment in the Coalition Agreement that the policy 'should take priority over other tax cuts'. The Conservatives, however, were reluctant to agree to commit to delivering the policy in full, for fear of detracting from their own tax policies. As George Osborne repeatedly made clear to Danny and me in meetings of the quad, the Conservatives regarded the policy as a Lib Dem 'ask', for which we would need to make concessions elsewhere. In the early stages of the government he insisted that, according to the wording of the Coalition Agreement, the £10,000 threshold was merely a 'longer-term policy objective', which meant that the Treasury was not duty bound to deliver it.

I was nonplussed at how churlish the Conservatives were towards what was a patently popular policy, but I was naturally happy to champion tax cuts to low- and middle-earners as a Liberal Democrat achievement. But as soon as Osborne realised its immense public appeal, he changed his tune. During budgets and autumn statements in Parliament he revelled in the pantomime atmosphere of the Chamber – more similar to Gordon Brown than he would ever care to admit – and used the tax cut to burnish his progressive credentials and taunt the opposition benches. And he wasn't the only Conservative to notice its popularity. Not long after the Conservatives hired the Australian political strategist Lynton Crosby in November 2012 to mastermind their 2015 election campaign, we found the tax cut emblazoned across Conservative leaflets in Lib Dem constituencies. Later, they adopted the raising of the personal allowance as their major tax pledge for the 2015 election. It spoke to exactly the audience – aspirational voters – that the Conservatives were seeking to target. No wonder the Conservatives furiously sought to deny Danny Alexander's revelation that George Osborne had once told him, 'You look after the workers, we'll look after the bosses.' It was clearly said as a joke, but it revealed a deeper truth: loath as they might have been to admit it, the Conservatives recognised that coalition brought balance to the government that it otherwise would have lacked.

Raising the personal allowance was a major liberal achievement and one that I am immensely proud of. To deliver it, we had to rely on Conservative support. We didn't own the machinery of the Treasury – so through endless brinkmanship and a few straightforward policy swaps, we persisted until we got our way. Since it was not their idea in the first place, the Conservatives were initially reluctant to help. But then the merits of the measure and its popularity trumped their concerns. In an act of shameless if effective political plagiarism, they ended up trying to make it their own. So we may have sparked an unseemly scramble for public ownership of the policy, but without doing so, we would never have been able to get it done, and today millions of taxpayers would still be paying more tax every month.

In this instance, widespread public approval of a popular tax policy helped to carry the day. In other cases, the pressure for change was entirely driven by forces outside government altogether – not so much from the public, but from the effect of unforeseen 'events'.

Governments are often remembered more for how they react to the unexpected than for their record in delivering their own policy programmes. Harold Macmillan's famous, if apocryphal statement, 'Events, dear boy, events', when asked what his greatest challenge was, is engraved on the hearts of all government ministers. Invariably, unexpected events are viewed with unmitigated alarm in government, as tripwires designed to show up politicians as flat-footed or incompetent. But my experience was that events – from the riots in the summer of 2011 to the bombing of Libya, from sluggish tax receipts to the revelations of Edward Snowden – could also act as the spur for significant change and reform.

Before June 2013, no one had heard of Edward Snowden. Then, beginning on 5 June, *The Guardian* published a series of explosive revelations about the extensive reach of US government-sponsored electronic surveillance, based on a cache of documents that Snowden had assembled while working in a National Security Agency subcontractor's facility in Hawaii. The initial reaction was a classic establishment spasm: condemnation, denial, fury. There was no doubt that while his intention was to blow the whistle on what he perceived to be unethical behaviour, Snowden's actions provoked deep concern about the impact they could have on counter-terrorism operations by revealing details of previously secret capabilities. But the whole security establishment, backed by Number 10, the Home Office and all Conservative ministers, focused exclusively on the man and not the ball, working themselves up into a lather of indignation at his personal conduct, rather than grappling with the wider issues that his revelations clearly raised.

In the immediate aftermath of those revelations, there was a distinct sense of relief in Whitehall that no newspapers other than *The Guardian* appeared to be exercised about them, and that the public reaction was fairly muted. The lack of wider press coverage had more to do with old-fashioned Fleet Street rivalry – every newspaper is loath to give publicity to the scoops of another – than any objective appreciation of the issues at stake. Public indifference was also unsurprising: issues of privacy and civil liberties are traditionally of immense interest to a minority of people, but seem esoteric or irrelevant to the everyday concerns of many voters. So, initially at least, there was a distinct feeling that Whitehall had dodged the Snowden bullet: there was no great public clamour for change, no great pressure in the media for reform, either.

I, however, believed from the outset that the Snowden revelations had simply exposed something that I had long felt to be the case: that the laws and rules governing the deployment of surveillance techniques, and the manner in which surveillance powers were held to account, were being outpaced by huge technological change. I was determined to use the controversy surrounding the Snowden revelations to reopen a debate that urgently needed addressing: how to rebalance the twin needs of security and transparency in an electronic age?

That very spring, a couple of months before the Snowden revelations emerged, I had blocked the so-called 'Snoopers' Charter' – Theresa May's Communications Data Bill – because it proposed sweeping measures to retain data from all individuals in Britain, without any meaningful evidence that it was either necessary or that it would actually work. I recognised that the laws governing the ability of the police and security services to access communications data needed to be updated in order to reflect the immense pace of technological change, but I felt it was a flawed bill that encroached unnecessarily on the privacy of millions of law-abiding citizens without any evidence or consensus, even among the security industry, that it would make us safer. It seemed like a crude, blunderbuss solution to a complex problem – a scheme dreamed up by Whitehall officials who were used to ministers signing their ideas into law, no questions asked.

My decision to kill off the Communications Data Bill in the spring of 2013 had caused real ructions within the security establishment, so much so that neither side of the coalition had any appetite for new surveillance legislation. The Home

Office quietly shelved its plans for a new data dragnet. When the Snowden revelations came a few weeks later, my dilemma was how to persuade Whitehall to get beyond the arguments over the Comms Data Bill, and shift the dead weight of convention and secrecy in the Home Office towards a more grown-up appraisal of the surveillance powers of a modern state.

Knowing that the Conservatives would never voluntarily sign up to reform, I tried to persuade Cameron to set up an independent expert review into surveillance. Cameron wasn't interested in the least – surveillance was a Pandora's box: you never knew where a review might lead.

Then two events occurred in quick succession that combined to create the opportunity and impetus for reform. The first was a ruling of the European Court of Justice that the powers by which the UK and other member states required Internet and phone companies to hold on to business records for twelve months were unlawful. This knocked out police access to phone records, which had become the bread and butter of serious organised-crime investigations. Second, senior security officials came to see me to explain that, in light of the Snowden leaks, US technology companies had begun closing down some of the collaborative channels that had previously allowed us to track terrorism suspects. I became convinced after many long hours of discussion with the intelligence agencies – whose professionalism and adherence to the rule of law always impressed me immensely – that a failure to enact new legislation would jeopardise crucial transatlantic data-sharing that was vital to our own safety.

What emerged from these twin setbacks was an emergency bill, the Data Retention and Investigatory Powers Bill, known – once it had passed into law as an Act – by the unfortunate acronym DRIPA. There were dire warnings of what would happen if we didn't act quickly before the summer break. The bill could only proceed with my agreement, and I was only going to recommend to my MPs that they support it if there was a wider commitment to far-reaching reform. Crucially, in accepting the need for the emergency DRIPA legislation, I argued that it should contain a so-called 'sunset clause', meaning that its provisions would automatically expire at the end of 2016. This put a sell-by date on the new powers, and meant that the next government effectively had its hands tied: it would have to legislate afresh for a whole swathe of surveillance powers, and give Parliament the opportunity to debate it in full. Theresa May came to accept this on behalf of the Home Office because, still smarting from our disagreement on the so-called Snoopers' Charter, she viewed the new 2016 deadline as an opportunity to make the case in a new parliament for the wider powers that the Home Office had always hankered after. The stand-off between me and the Home Office had, in effect, been deferred by two years.

The next step was to ensure that this interlude would be filled with authoritative studies, which would nudge government as a whole towards a new, more sensible settlement on the fraught issue of surveillance versus privacy. The reviews would serve as a prelude to the publication of new draft legislation, to be scrutinised by a joint committee of Parliament in the spring of 2016, followed by a substantive new bill. I asked David Anderson, QC, the government's independent reviewer of counter-terror powers, to conduct a full assessment of the UK's current surveillance laws, including those enshrined in DRIPA. Anderson was a breath of fresh air compared to his predecessor, Alex Carlile, who had taken a narrow and unimaginative approach to his remit. By contrast, Anderson was much more alive to the radically changing technological and political context in which surveillance powers are exercised. He understood that extensive reform was now unavoidable, to re-establish political and public confidence in the way in which secret surveillance powers are wielded.

I then commissioned Sir Nigel Sheinwald, a respected former UK Ambassador to the USA, to review how transatlantic data-sharing works. I explained to David Cameron that I simply didn't understand how, in the long run, we could make sense of the requirement for governments to keep their citizens safe in a borderless networked world, without doing so on an international basis. In order to get hold of data on the communications of legitimate UK-based suspects, there had to be a way to get that data from companies based overseas, many of them in California. But US data-protection law expressly prohibits US companies from sending data overseas, except through cumbersome diplomatic channels. Number 10 wasn't particularly interested in this issue and seemed to think it would be little more than a diplomatic exercise, so gave their consent to this idea with little thought about its significance.

Theresa May did understand its significance and was far more resistant. The Home Office was convinced that UK supremacy over the laws of other countries could simply be asserted in order to force the handover of data. They were cavalier about the consequences of that approach, which would have been to encourage every other country to assert the supremacy of their own laws in the online world, leading to the Balkanisation of the Internet into a series of 'national Internets'. In the event, Sir Nigel backed the creation of a new US–UK treaty – the first time there has been an official recognition that the arrangements between governments surrounding surveillance will need to be internationalised on a clear legal footing in the future.

Finally, I commissioned the respected defence and security think tank, the Royal United Services Institute (RUSI), to look at the effectiveness and appropriateness of our surveillance programmes. Crucially, the panel of experts that RUSI assembled ranged from former heads of the intelligence agencies to leading civil-liberties campaigners. If they managed to reach a consensus on how to move forward – how to enable the state to make proportionate incursions into the privacy of its citizens in order to secure their safety – then, I believed, we would finally be in a position to replace the existing legislation with a better alternative.

In the event, there was a remarkable convergence between the reports produced by Sir Nigel Sheinwald, David Anderson and RUSI: together, they acknowledged that the status quo was unsustainable; that greater oversight of the way in which intrusive surveillance powers were authorised by government was now necessary; that the case for a so-called Snoopers' Charter was unproven; that current UK legislation was past its sell-by date; and that a new formalisation of the way in which different jurisdictions organised their surveillance powers was needed. As a result, after the general election in 2015, Theresa May was forced to retreat from her previous version of the Snoopers' Charter, and acknowledged instead that reform was now unavoidable.

The legislation debated in Parliament in 2016 was a comprehensive account of the surveillance state, with previously secret powers formally avowed, and written in a form that – while far from perfect – was clearer than before. Key elements of the 2012 bill have been dropped, and the principle that judges rather than ministers should oversee phone-tapping has been conceded. There are, unfortunately, still serious shortcomings in the Home Office's approach, most especially the continued dragnet retention of vast quantities of people's data under a new acronym, ICR (Internet Connection Records). Without the constraints of coalition compromise – and in view of Labour's pliant, uncritical attitude – Theresa May and the Home Office have unsurprisingly taken the opportunity to recycle some of the measures I had rejected in government. But, forced by events, political pressure and independent expertise, they have at last lifted the veil on powerful surveillance capabilities that were previously hidden, and those powers will be held to greater account by judges and by Parliament. Reform, even in the most secret recesses of the British state, is still possible – especially under the pressure of unexpected events.

These stories of Whitehall battles, clashing ministerial egos and fraught policy negotiations are incomplete without referring to the people who have to make sense of it all in the first place: civil servants.

While it is fashionable for politicians to bemoan the inherent caution of Whitehall civil servants – Michael Gove provided regular entertainment at the Tuesday morning meetings of the Cabinet, with his florid, if unreasonable condemnations of the Civil Service – their insulation from the political madhouse of Westminster serves as a crucial counterweight in our democratic system. The vast majority of civil servants I encountered in my five years in office were hard-working, thoughtful and driven by a quiet, if fiercely held belief in public service. The senior civil servants who ran my private office – Calum Miller, Chris Wormald, Lucy Smith, Philip Rycroft – were unfailingly loyal, discreet and devoted to sound policy development, as were the teams of officials they led on my behalf. The flaws of Whitehall (like any great bureaucracy, it has plenty of them) are systemic, not personal: the tendency for bright, young and wholly inexperienced officials to hold great sway over key areas of public policy for short periods of time, before being moved up to the next rung of the ladder, creates discontinuity and immaturity in policy-making. The over-centralisation of power in the Treasury leads to daft policy gyrations: from the failure to regulate the banks, to micromanaging them; from lax fiscal policy, to overzealous contraction; from the underfunding of capital projects, to a bevy of white elephants.

Above all, perhaps, it is the Balkanisation of authority across Whitehall that is responsible for dysfunctional decision-making. Some departments, notably the Treasury and the Foreign Office, are regarded as the Oxbridge colleges of Whitehall. Others, notably the Department for Culture, Media and Sport or the Department for Communities and Local Government, are snobbily derided as red-brick departments. Each department develops a strong identity of its own – lofty at the top, chippy at the bottom – in the Whitehall pecking order. Understandably enough, discussions between Whitehall departments are as much a trial of strength for the civil servants who are involved as they are about sensible collective decision-making. In the paperwork I read late at night at home, officials would regularly describe arguments about a policy decision as if they were a chess game of complex manoeuvres between different departments. Since my role in government was precisely to avoid getting sucked into their baronial rivalries, I gave short shrift to any advice whose sole purpose was that I should put a particular department in its place.

At the same time, both David Cameron and I would frequently bemoan how difficult it was to get a particular department to produce recommendations or enact a decision, even when demanded by both sides of the coalition. This reluctance to respond to instructions or requests from the top of government was exacerbated if the Secretary of State in charge was particularly difficult, if there were tensions between them and the Prime Minister or me, or if the Secretary of State had been in post for such a long time that they were convinced they knew best. The effect of this could be debilitating in the face of the twenty-four-hour media circus. While the stately pace of decision-making in government is, in many ways, a useful antidote to the fickle daily demands made of politicians in the press, it can also come across as being out of touch with the reasonable public expectation that action should be taken rapidly.

In late 2012 and early 2013, for example, *The Times* printed a number of compelling accounts of Afghan interpreters who had assisted British forces in Helmand Province and who were worried that they would be subject to retribution from the Taliban, once British forces had left the country. It was obvious to me – as I imagine it was to anyone who had read the same articles – that the government should move swiftly to provide reassurance that these interpreters would be treated fairly, if need be by relocating them and their families to the UK. Given that we were talking about just a few hundred people, the numbers were minuscule in the context of overall migration flows. I duly demanded an early discussion in the

National Security Council and asked the Home Office and the National Security Adviser to prepare proposals as swiftly as possible. Instead, it took weeks and weeks of haggling to drag a grudging Home Office to come up with a plan that, in the end, was so convoluted it barely helped anyone.

Another instance of sloth-like decision-making in government related to careers advice and guidance. Shortly after the coalition came to power, a decision was made to scrap the network of Connexions offices that had been established by the previous government, because, by and large, they were not providing high-quality careers advice and guidance to youngsters across the country. While this was harsh on those centres that were doing a better job than most, it was not an unreasonable measure as long as something more effective was swiftly installed as a replacement. Little did I realise at the time that Michael Gove had a personal bee in his bonnet against any publicly organised careers advice and guidance of any description. So once the Connexions service was scrapped, nothing happened. Hundreds of thousands of youngsters were left in limbo without any properly organised support – other than that provided by individual schools – to make excruciatingly difficult decisions about their future educational, vocational and professional futures. Apparently, according to Gove's orthodoxy at the time, any requirement imposed upon schools to provide meaningful careers advice and guidance was regarded as a breach of the sacrosanct autonomy of schools. The push to spread 'Academy' autonomy to schools had become a weird dogma, which risked depriving youngsters of exactly the kind of help they needed to make the difficult journey from the world of education into the world of work.

Strikingly, it was not just my opinion that this was wrong; it was also the opinion of Number 10 and, most especially, David Willetts, the Conservative minister in the BIS department at the time who shared some responsibility for educational outcomes for school leavers. Yet, month after month and year after year, the non-cooperation of just one department in Whitehall prevented the government from doing what was patently needed. It wasn't until the very fag-end of the coalition that Gove's successor, Nicky Morgan, finally introduced a new approach to careers advice and guidance, which went some way towards filling the vacuum that had opened up in the previous four years.

Needless to say, the principal fault in both cases did not lie with officials – the failure of Number 10 to assert its will over two obstreperous Secretaries of State was a far greater problem – but they both illustrate the mismatch between the need for swift action and the reality of constipated decision-making within Whitehall. I regularly found myself squeezed uncomfortably between the wish to react rapidly to reasonable public demands for action and the reality of cumbersome decision-making in government, stuck between the politics of a digital age and the analogue arrangements of Whitehall.

The truth is that the British Civil Service is both a Rolls-Royce and a Morris Minor. It contains some of the most gifted individuals I've ever had the privilege to work with and some of the most dotty practices imaginable. When the businessman Sir Philip Green carried out a review of government waste shortly after the 2010 general election, he said that if he ran his company the same way as Whitehall operates, 'the lights would be out'. Given the subsequent revelations about his own spectacular mismanagement of the now-defunct BHS, his conclusions should be treated with caution. Nonetheless, he found billions of pounds wasted in Whitehall as a result of bad contracts, lack of coordination between departments, vague accounting, unsupervised spending and a culture of poor money-management. He found departments spending anywhere between £8 and £73 on a box of paper, and printer cartridges being bought for £86 in one place and £398 in another. When he tried to figure out how much the government spends on travel costs, he reported: 'We were initially advised that the annual travel spend for central Government was £2bn; the second estimate was £500m; the third estimate was £768m. A thorough review revealed that the actual spend was £551m.'

Whitehall, like any government machine, is congenitally disposed to hoarding power. Over the course of decades, ministers and mandarins have centralised information and decision-making – sometimes deliberately, sometimes accidentally. And the process almost never runs in reverse. Citizens' rights have been slowly altered by the quiet proliferation of laws that increase surveillance and store data – some of which ends up on laptops and data sticks that get lost. Executive authority has steadily increased, at the cost of a neutered Parliament. The increasing role of the judiciary as a check on government prerogative is deeply resented by decision-makers, as is the pesky intrusion into their deliberations by Freedom of Information requests. Despite a rich vein in government rhetoric in favour of devolution and decentralisation, England remains the most centralised country in Europe, bar Malta. We still have one of the most centralised tax systems in the developed world, with around 95 per cent of all taxes raised in cities like London, Sheffield, Birmingham and Liverpool going straight to the Treasury, rather than being kept and spent locally (though this may change, if local business rates are fully localised in future). Balkanised, centralised and largely unaccountable to Parliament: our system of government, just as much as our system of politics, is in chronic need of wholesale reform.

There is no hard-and-fast way to make change happen in government. Change is a combination of poetry and prose. Without the poetry of clear values, big aspirations and a belief in your own ideas, change is stillborn. But without the prose of persistence, procedural guile and compromise, change remains all rhetoric and no substance. Above all, making good decisions always involves some give-and-take. From tax policy to school lunches, from the surveillance state to porn filters, the coalition government showed that there is virtue in compromise. No one party ever has a monopoly of wisdom, and single-party governments often suffer from a mixture of hubris and a fixation on their own hobby-horses. Messy though it no doubt was at times, the coalition government proved over half a decade something that had never been proved in Whitehall before: sometimes two heads are better than one.

The challenge for mainstream politics, of course, is that the rising tide of populism on both left and right rejects the very idea that positive change can be effected through government at all. The problem that faced the Liberal Democrats in government – scepticism that we were able to get anything done, as a smaller party in coalition – was compounded by a wider public cynicism towards all claims about change from all governments. In the end, if mainstream politics is to mount a fight-back against the political nihilism of Trump, Le Pen, Farage and others, it must demonstrate the ability of governments to bring positive change to people's everyday lives. And for that, far-reaching reform of the dysfunctional institutions and rules of British politics will first be needed.

Yet, as I learned the hard way, there is nothing as difficult as reforming politics itself. Of all the things that need changing, the hardest change of all is this: taking power away from the powerful.

CHAPTER 5

Taking Power from the Powerful

Britain is a country still dominated by powerful people and powerful groups with powerful vested interests – in business, in the media, in politics. Breaking up vested interests and dispersing power lies at the heart of liberalism, and in twenty-first-century Britain – as well as the rest of the Western world – that challenge is as urgent as ever. But taking power away from powerful vested interests is the third rail of British politics: touch it and you get one hell of a shock. Our attempts to introduce a more representative voting system, a democratic House of Lords and curbs on the influence of big money in politics all encountered ferocious resistance.

It is important to explain why reform was, and remains, necessary: we have an arcane and deeply unrepresentative Parliament; it is not only demographically unrepresentative of the public at large, it also bears little resemblance to the democratic will expressed at the ballot box. The general election of 2015 produced the most unrepresentative result of all: the Conservatives won a majority of the seats in Parliament, and hence formed a majority government, yet they only secured 37 per cent of the votes cast – and just 24 per cent of all eligible voters. Half of Scottish voters chose a party that was not the Scottish Nationalists, yet the SNP came away with fifty-six of the country's fifty-nine seats. They did so with just under 1.5 million votes, whereas the Liberal Democrats got 2.4 million votes and just eight seats – the same number as the Democratic Unionists, who got just 184,000 votes. Supporters of UKIP had perhaps even more right to feel aggrieved, as they returned just one MP despite winning 3.9 million votes. The Greens got the same return – a solitary MP – despite hauling in 1.2 million votes. The Lib Dems received 299,000 votes per seat won, whereas for the SNP it took just 26,000 votes, the Conservatives 34,000 and Labour 40,000.

The election result was a kaleidoscope of colours, but the government was true blue. Why? Because we have an electoral system designed for the days when elections were a straight fight between two major parties: Labour and the Conservatives. In 1951, the two major parties accounted for 97 per cent of all votes cast. In 2015, that figure was 67 per cent. One-third of all voters now choose an option other than the red team or the blue team, yet they do so in a system – First Past the Post – designed to perpetuate a duopoly. First Past the Post means that the MPs in Parliament are determined by 650 individual races across the country, in which the winners can sneak in with as little as a quarter of the vote. It not only favours the two big parties, but those, like the SNP and the Democratic Unionist Party, whose support is highly localised. Parties like the Lib Dems, UKIP and the Greens, which have wide but often shallow support across the whole country, suffer disproportionately.

The result, inevitably, is that political parties focus all their resources on a small number of local areas where they think they might be able to nudge into the lead, neglecting vast swathes of the country where they don't stand a chance. A voter located in a 'safe' seat in which there is no realistic challenge to the incumbent MP is ignored and overlooked at election time. As a result, we don't actually know how much real support each party has, because First Past the Post forces voters to make a 'tactical' choice based not on their personal preferences, but on those parties they believe stand a chance of winning in their constituency. If you are a Labour voter in a constituency in which the Liberal Democrats and the Conservatives are the only real contestants, you are forced to vote for a party as a second-best alternative to your real preference, rather than 'waste' your vote on a party that has no hope of winning. For decades, Liberal Democrat leaflets have featured bar-charts demonstrating to voters that their preferred party cannot possibly win. Are you a voter who supports Labour in North Cornwall? They have no chance of winning, so the only way to stop the Tories is to vote Lib Dem. Are you a Conservative voter in Leeds North West? Tough: they can't win, so the only way of keeping Labour out is to vote Lib Dem. Equally, the Lib Dem vote has been suppressed in plenty of races where our opponents have made the same case against the party.

In many Scottish races in 2015, Labour, Conservative and Lib Dem candidates were making the case to their constituents that they were the unionist candidate most likely to beat the SNP, so they called on voters to put all other differences to one side. Meanwhile, Conservative central office was posting letters from David Cameron to tens of thousands of Lib Dem voters in the South-West of England that essentially said, 'I know you're a Lib Dem, that's okay, we've worked with them very well for five years, but if you really don't want Ed Miliband in charge, with Alex Salmond pulling the strings, then on this occasion please lend us your vote.' It was a devastatingly effective tactic.

These are the bizarre contortions that parties and voters are forced to go through. We have no idea what the result of a general election would be if people voted with their hearts, as opposed to voting against the party they least want to win. No wonder, then, that so many are disillusioned with politics and argue that the people in charge do not represent them. For the vast majority of people, that is demonstrably true.

Not only is this unfair, but it incubates political volatility: the eruption of anger and disillusionment expressed in the EU referendum was, in part, because many blue-collar workers in traditional Labour seats in the North and the Midlands had been overlooked for so long by the Labour Party – forced by the electoral system to concentrate its efforts in marginal seats elsewhere. Those voters understandably took the opportunity to register their anger by voting against the status quo. A more representative Parliament at Westminster would contain a significant contingent of UKIP MPs reflecting the section of the population who wish to turn the clock back and who reject the pace of change in a modern, diverse Britain. For that matter, a more representative Parliament would also contain a contingent of hard-left MPs, a mainstream centre bloc composed of liberals, social democrats and liberal Conservatives, as well as a smaller Conservative Party. The fact that the electoral system suppresses these different political currents, robbing disaffected voters of an authentic voice, only aggravates their sense of grievance and frustration. Democracy is built on a system of safety valves in which everyone's voice can find expression somewhere. It is deeply unhealthy that the voice of many people who do not believe in the established division of power in Westminster are overlooked altogether by the anachronistic electoral system.

If all this makes the House of Commons a misshapen democratic chamber, the House of Lords is an affront to the very principle of democracy itself. The Upper House is the only unelected chamber of its kind in Europe and, at more than 800 peers and counting, the second-largest parliamentary chamber in the world, behind China's National People's Congress. The American Senate, by comparison, has 100 members, the French 348 and the Indian 250. Even North Korea has a measly 687. Every year or so the Lords grows more bloated still, for which I am as guilty as any other party leader. During the coalition years I appointed several new peers, in order to bring Lib Dem representation up to a level close to our standing in the country (although, given the kicking we took in the 2015 election, we are now somewhat over-represented).

Some argue that the House of Lords is an enhancement to our democracy – a bastion of wisdom and expertise that can keep governments in check and scrutinise legislation, while rising above the electoral fray. It is certainly true that there are many brilliant minds and compassionate hearts on the red benches, and many experts in everything from law and medicine to the arts and the art of war. It is also true that the Lords regularly forces the government to rethink half-baked or rushed legislation. But it has also become a gilded retirement home for former politicians – around a quarter of its members are ex-MPs who either lost their seats or gave them up of their own volition, and a good few more are former party advisers. Rather than rising above the electoral fray, the Lords increasingly votes in massive blocs along party lines, while many of the non-aligned 'cross-benchers' rarely show up at all. The Lords is more often than not a chamber in which peers obey the party whip as much as, if not more than, in the Commons. The Electoral Reform Society worked out that between 1999 and 2009, Conservative peers voted against the Labour Government in 97 per cent of whipped votes. Labour peers voted against the coalition government in 99 per cent of whipped divisions between 2010 and 2015.

Some Lords supporters have even argued that the Upper House helps to redress the representational imbalance in Parliament, since the appointment structure enables leaders to fill in gaps in diversity. I certainly tried to make sure that my own appointments were broadly balanced between men and women, and with a mix of faiths and people from black and ethnic-minority backgrounds, as well as people from the different regions of the United Kingdom. But let's not kid ourselves. The average age of the barons and baronesses is seventy. Women make up about a quarter of the House, a slightly lower proportion than in the Commons. Little more than 5 per cent are from ethnic minorities. The House of Lords is no beacon of diversity.

David Lloyd George once described the House of Lords as 'a body of five hundred men chosen at random from amongst the unemployed'. And that was a hundred years ago. The reality is that the House of Lords was past its sell-by date at the time of the First World War. The fact that the only significant change since then is a near doubling of its size should be a source of great shame for a nation that prides itself on being a champion of democratic enlightenment. The people who make the laws should be chosen by the people who are subject to those laws. Simple as that.

Then there's the hollowing-out effect of big money on party politics. Without large amounts of money, political parties can't compete. They can't hire and retain talented staff. They can't carry out the research necessary to devise policies. They can't produce the leaflets and posters they deploy in campaigns. Those letters from David Cameron that were sent to Lib Dem voters in the South-West were part of a hugely expensive and sophisticated Conservative targeting campaign. The Conservatives received more than £15m in donations in the first quarter of 2015, compared to £3m for the Lib Dems. They were able to pepper individual voters in marginal seats across the country with specific messages designed to maximise the Conservative vote and suppress that of their opponents, all at great cost. The Liberal Democrats fought back by doing the same, but we couldn't come close to competing with the Conservatives' bulging war chest. Financially, it was David versus Goliath. We may not be in the American realm of 'super-PACs', expensive TV ads and billion-dollar elections, but make no mistake: in British elections, money talks.

While a limited amount of public money is available to support opposition parties in Westminster (money that George Osborne pettily proposed to cut, in his first Autumn Statement after the 2015 election), the reality is that significant private funds are now needed for political parties to operate properly and compete in elections. The Conservatives raise a huge amount of money from fund managers in the City of London. Labour are reliant for the vast majority of their money on a small handful of trade unions. Directly or indirectly, this ends up influencing the decisions those parties make. When I raised the idea in coalition of introducing an additional levy on properties worth more than £2 million, to help deal with the deficit, David Cameron refused not because he objected to the idea itself (in fact the Conservatives have ended up taxing higher-value property in any event, through Stamp Duty reforms), but because, as he put it, Conservative party donors 'would not wear it'. Indeed, in 2012 Tory Treasurers Lord Fink and Michael Farmer sent a letter to big donors and wealthy home-owners warning them about the mansion tax, dubbed 'Ed Balls and Vince Cable's homes tax', and stating: 'The Conservative party are clear that a homes tax will not happen on our watch.' It then invited them to join one of the party's various forums for wealthy backers, at a cost of between £2,000 and £5,000. Likewise, the support of the big trade unions played a pivotal role in Ed Miliband edging out his brother in the race for the Labour leadership in 2010, and in the election of Jeremy Corbyn in 2015. Union bosses have never made any secret of their determination to influence Labour Party policy.

The Liberal Democrats have relied on a small number of wealthy, altruistic individuals for financial support. Most are genuinely liberal or pro-European people who are donating in order to support a party that shares their values, but the party has been caught up in funding scandals, too. Shortly before the 2005 general election, the party was approached by a wealthy businessman called Michael Brown, who handed over around £2.4m from his company coffers to help with the campaign. While the party carried out its due diligence and was subsequently cleared of any wrongdoing by the Electoral Commission, Mr Brown turned out to be a major conman who later skipped the country in an attempt to evade justice.

An old-fashioned, elitist and unrepresentative Parliament; a skewed voting system; an unelected and anti-democratic House of Lords; and an unhealthy relationship between political parties and money. Our democracy is a disgrace. It needs cleaning up from top to bottom. So that's what we tried to do.

It might seem like a lifetime ago now, but when the coalition government took office there was a palpable desire for large-scale political reform. The previous summer, the news had been dominated by the MPs' expenses scandal, the aftershocks of which still shuddered throughout the general-election campaign. British politics had been discredited, as the banks had been in 2008. Opinion polls showed not just widespread distrust of the political class, but a huge appetite for change. Indeed, the fact that people were so distrustful of the established order was one of the principal reasons David Cameron was unable to get the Conservatives over the line in the election, despite facing a tired and unpopular Labour Party that was clearly on the way out. He may have been a fresher face than Gordon Brown, but a summer of stories about Conservative MPs in the shires claiming money from the taxpayer for moats and duck houses hardly made the Conservative Party feel like a breath of fresh air.

The Liberal Democrats, by contrast, had long championed political reform as a matter of principle. Notwithstanding passionate debates about the virtues of different electoral systems echoing in Liberal Party conference halls down the years, it was not an enthusiasm traditionally shared by the public at large. By the time I stood up onstage in front of the television cameras for the first leaders' debate on 15 April 2010 and called for politics to be done differently, however, it suddenly struck a chord. We stood for a 'new politics' and it was clear that was what a very large number of people wanted, too. So much so, in fact, that both Labour and the Conservatives felt obliged to embrace a certain amount of reform as well: Labour included the Alternative Vote system in its manifesto, and both parties championed reform of party funding and an elected House of Lords.

As such, when we sat down to negotiate a coalition deal with the Conservatives, we felt we had a window of opportunity to deliver a wide-ranging set of political reforms, including changing the voting system, bringing democracy to the House of Lords, introducing fixed-term parliaments of five years (ending the right of prime ministers to call elections at times of their choosing), party-funding reform to limit the influence of big donors, and a power of recall so that constituents could vote to chuck out corrupt MPs without having to wait for the next election. The Conservatives acquiesced to most of these reforms pretty easily, although as the talks wore on, it looked like the whole deal might collapse on the crunch issue of voting reform.

First Past the Post is enshrined in the DNA of the Conservative Party, not least because it has consistently delivered Conservative majority governments, even as their share of the popular vote has steadily declined. However, when it became obvious that we simply wouldn't join a government at all without a commitment to a referendum on voting reform, their appetite for immediate power outweighed (rightly, as it turned out) their fear of losing power, through whatever electoral reform might ensue. With their agreement to a referendum on the Alternative Vote – a fairer voting system whereby voters rank candidates in order of preference, and MPs need at least 50 per cent support in order to be elected – on the fifth and final day of negotiations the glue of the coalition deal was set.

In the early days of the coalition there was a clear symmetry to the government's narrative that spoke to the mood of the time. the Conservatives brought an emphasis on balanced budgets; the Liberal Democrats brought political reform; and we shared (or so I thought) a commitment to both. To that extent, we clearly answered the two biggest crises facing the country at the time. It felt to me, and to many in both parties, like the right government at the right time, offering renewal on the two fronts where it was most needed: the battered economy and the tarnished reputation of politics. It made sense, then, that I would take on direct responsibility for delivering the government's constitutional reform agenda, while the Conservatives would focus on the fiscal overhaul. I was (very) fleetingly the most popular politician in the country, riding a wave of support for the sort of change that I cared about deeply, and which was in the DNA of my party. The prospects for lasting political and constitutional change seemed, finally, to be unstoppable.

Of course, it all turned out quite differently.

The most important day in setting the tone of the five-year coalition parliament was, without doubt, 20 October 2010. It was then that George Osborne announced the government's Comprehensive Spending Review. Governments, I have learned, can do many things at once – go to war, build schools and hospitals, argue amongst themselves, and so on – but they are rarely remembered for more than one principal purpose. And that purpose, after October 2010, became fiscal discipline above all else.

The Comprehensive Spending Review, in which George Osborne outlined his intention to drastically cut government expenditure in order to reduce the deficit, established the core purpose, the core motive, of the whole government: to restore balance to the nation's shattered finances, and stability to an economy that was dangerously fragile. While the Liberal Democrats made sure that the pace and scale of deficit reduction remained sensible and did not lurch in an unduly ideological direction – the Conservatives, attached to the idea of a smaller state, wanted deeper and faster cuts to public spending – we strongly supported the overall push for fiscal balance. But I don't think any of us foresaw at the time how much the narrative of austerity would blot out all other government ambitions.

Austerity was a more powerful story, for one clear and compelling reason: it affected people's real lives. In its shadow, the public mood for political reform was lost. The media's appetite for it waned dramatically.

Worst of all, despite all the agreements and manifesto promises, it gave the two old establishment parties the cover they needed to retreat from change. In that early window of opportunity, when the appetite for political reform was still real, we had succeeded in delivering two not unimportant reforms. The first was fixed-term parliaments of five years.

I made clear to David Cameron from the outset that this had to be delivered straight away. It was not only wrong in principle to give the Prime Minister of the day the power to play cat-and-mouse with the British electorate, by setting the date of an election at his or her whim, but I was not prepared to have the rug pulled from under us halfway through the parliament just because it was to the electoral advantage of the Conservative Party. (It is ironic that some Conservatives who objected to the Fixed-term Parliament Bill at the time later invoked it to resist the calls for an early general election in the wake of David Cameron's resignation, meaning that to all intents and purposes a new government was imposed on the country by 199 Tory MPs who backed Theresa May as his successor as leader of their party. In fact the legislation allows for elections to be held earlier in exceptional circumstances – and the bombshell of the EU referendum clearly qualified as such.) The other early step forward had been the legislation to bring about the referendum on the Alternative Vote, otherwise known as AV. The legislation passed relatively easily, such was the axiomatic importance of the referendum to the creation of the government in the first place.

When the referendum took place the following spring, however, it did so in a political climate completely altered from the heady days of May 2010. Capitalising on public indifference to reform, as people became ever more concerned about the money in their pockets and the security of their jobs, the strangulation of electoral reform became a shared endeavour by both the Conservative and Labour parties. For the latter, it was a sin of omission: a failure to campaign actively for a reform it claimed to support. Indeed, the AV system was deliberately chosen to appeal to the Labour Party, as it was the system to which they had specifically committed themselves in their manifesto. In an extraordinary irony, a government composed of Liberal Democrats and Conservatives was debating a reform that was the preference of the Labour Party alone (the Liberal Democrat preference was for the Single Transferable Vote system, a far purer form of proportional representation). Ed Miliband paid lip service to the reform, but was too bewitched by the prospect of doing damage to the Liberal Democrats, in the wake of the furore around tuition fees, to commit his troops seriously to the cause of reform in the referendum. He elevated short-term party advantage over both the long-term interests of the country and, oddly, of his own party, too: it is quite possible that AV would have provided the Labour Party with a backstop against the onslaught they suffered in Scotland from the SNP.

For the Conservatives, it was very much a sin of commission: Conservative donors, MPs and activists fought a brutal and highly personalised campaign, taking advantage of my unpopularity over the coalition compromise on tuition fees, all under the watchful eyes of David Cameron and George Osborne. I vividly remember, one Saturday morning when we were visiting my parents in rural Oxfordshire, my father showing Miriam and me a leaflet that had been put through their letter box. It was a crude, personal attack on me, with the infamous picture of me holding the tuition-fees pledge card and the headline 'AV leads to broken promises'. 'What's that got to do with electoral reform? I think it's appalling,' my father said. Around the same time, David Cameron joked – a little too gleefully for my liking – about how much he enjoyed the campaign broadcast by comedian Rik Mayall as his venal politician alter ego Alan B'stard – complete with smarmy smile and posh drawl – in which he mocked the broken promises that the 'No' campaign claimed would flow from the introduction of AV.

In the end, the somewhat herbivorous campaign in favour of electoral reform stood little chance against the much more carnivorous aggression of the 'No' campaign. A mixture of public indifference, scaremongering fibs and deliberate char-acter assassination did the trick, and the case for reform was lost by a huge margin of more than two to one. In short, we had lost that precious window of opportunity to deliver significant political reform. The dream of electoral reform was crushed.

If the Comprehensive Spending Review was the key date in setting the overall narrative of the government, then 5 May 2011 – the date of the referendum on AV – was when the relationship between the two coalition parties changed for good. Until that moment there had been a sense of shared endeavour and a considerable amount of personal goodwill between the two sides. In my initial conversations with David Cameron, he had seemed personally ambivalent about electoral reform (though he turned sharply against it, the moment it became obvious his party would not countenance it). Senior Conservatives such as Michael Gove had been openly flirting with the idea of supporting AV. Odd as it might seem now, there was even excited chatter in parts of the Conservative-supporting commentariat that the coalition might evolve into a lasting realignment of British politics, such was their early enthusiasm for it. So the sheer personal ferocity of the attacks during the campaign took me aback. I instantly saw that they would be highly effective – but I felt then, and still feel now, that they were wholly unnecessary, as the 'No' side would have won comfortably anyway without seeking to further bash my battered reputation.

Shortly after the referendum result, as Danny and I sat with David Cameron and George Osborne in the Prime Minister's small office, I told them I was dismayed at what they had done – it was self-harming to the government as a whole to hammer the standing of a coalition partner so early in the parliament. Staring awkwardly at their shoes, they claimed, somewhat implausibly, that they had little control over how the campaign had been run and were at the mercy of unscrupulous Labour street-fighters like John Reid, who had calculated that the best way to discourage Labour voters from voting for AV was to make me the target of their campaign.

There is little point in getting exercised about personal attacks in politics – they're a fact of life, which indignation will do nothing to alter. When it was revealed that George Osborne and his team had arranged for various stories to appear in news-papers towards the end of the 2010 general-election campaign about me, Miriam and our life in Brussels, it was irritating, but it neither surprised nor offended me. From the Conservatives' point of view, they were understandably desperate to avoid their dream of a majority slip away and would do anything to stem the rise of the Liberal Democrats at the time. What was striking about their behaviour in the AV referendum, by contrast, was how short-sighted their tactics were. From that moment on, sentiments of personal generosity and goodwill gave way to an increasingly transactional relationship between the two coalition parties. That undoubtedly made it much harder for the Conservatives to get their way in the coalition, which in turn helped to provoke their right-wing backbenchers into disowning and seeking to undermine the coalition for the remainder of the parliament.

The death of House of Lords reform was a much longer and more arduous affair, although with the benefit of hindsight, it is clear that the early window of opportunity for House of Lords reform had closed before the laborious cross-party work on reform even began.

All three major parties had committed in their manifestos to reforming the Upper House so that it was at least partly elected, and the coalition's Programme for Government com-mitted to 'establish a committee to bring forward proposals for a wholly or mainly elected upper chamber on the basis of proportional representation'. It may have been couched in the language of committees and proposals, but the unam-biguous intention was to proceed with Lords reform. So I set about trying to build consensus around a new structure for the Upper House, and chaired meetings of representatives from all the main parties for months on end – gathering convivially around the oversized wooden meeting table in my Whitehall office. Given the clarity of their respective manifesto commitments, and the patent nonsense of having a second chamber without a democratic mandate, I naively thought it was only a matter of time before an agreed blueprint would emerge. Instead, the whole process became an exercise in artful procrastination.

Notwithstanding the commitment to reform by the leaderships of both Labour and the Conservatives, in reality the discussions sank into a morass of disagreements about the right proportion of elected peers, the fate of unelected bishops, the electoral system, the timetable of elections, the system of remuneration, and so on. Lord (Tom) Strathclyde, the Conservative Leader in the Lords, was a charmingly roguish adversary throughout. It was obvious to me that he was utterly unconvinced of the need for change, but he went through the motions of pretending that he did, with a wink in his eye. In many ways, I found his mischievous insincerity about reform much more palatable than those who professed earnest interest in reform without the slightest intention of acting on it. I tried to meet the Conservatives halfway, agreeing that some unelected peers would remain and that the elections would be phased in over the course of three elections. At one stage I fleetingly considered breaking the logjam by putting the proposal to a referendum, something that Paddy Ashdown advocated at the time.

But the electoral mandate for Lords reform already existed – it had been in each party's manifesto – so I tried using raw political leverage instead. Lords reform was something the Liberal Democrats cared about, and it was umbilically linked to other constitutional reforms that the Conservatives cared about just as much, notably the reduction in the number of constituencies from 650 to 600. This was something the Conservatives were convinced would give them a political advantage, with some pundits predicting the change would be worth as many as twenty extra MPs to them at an election. I was in favour of reducing the number of MPs as part of a package of political reforms to improve democratic account-ability, but not in isolation. Why on earth should we reduce the number of democratically elected parliamentarians in the Lower House, if they were not prepared to improve democratic accountability in the Upper House? And why on earth would we gift the Conservatives a political advantage when they were dithering about honouring their agreement with us on every other aspect of the political reform agenda?

The back and forth over Lords reform and constituency boundaries dominated the summer of 2012. I became increas-ingly frustrated that the basic deal that had underpinned the creation of the coalition – economic *and* political reform – was being unpicked by the Conservatives. More widely, as the Conservatives became ever more alarmed at the rise of UKIP, the pressure steadily increased on their backbenches to shift sharply to the right, and Cameron and Osborne were coming under attack from their own side for being, in the memorable words of Conservative MP Nadine Dorries, 'arrogant posh boys'. As the economy continued to flatline, the collaborative spirit of the early part of the coalition gave way to a series of draining spats, as the Conservatives repeatedly sought to throw red meat to their restive backbenches. Time and again, George Osborne sought to unpick the green policies that Chris Huhne and then Ed Davey had put in place, to satisfy his backbench MPs' opposition to onshore wind and other green technologies. They demanded that we take needlessly provocative 'action' against the trade unions, even though industrial relations were remarkably quiescent at a time of unprecedented public-sector cuts. There was little evidence in favour of these reforms – other than breathless demands made in the *Daily Mail*, which increasingly served as the new yardstick of Conservative policy-planning in government.

Early in July, Cameron, Osborne, Danny and I had what turned out to be a significant dinner together – without any assistants or officials present – in the Prime Minister's flat. A host of mutual grievances had accumulated on both sides of the coalition, so as we shared a meal around his family dining table, we methodically went through all the areas where we had reached an impasse – energy policy, trade-union reform, Lords reform, and so on. Danny and I also warned Cameron and Osborne against becoming too fixated on the debt-target timetable – we had taken stringent measures to start reducing public spending and felt they should be given time to work. We were alarmed at the prospect of the Conservatives chasing an artificial timetable towards ever-steeper cuts because growth and tax receipts had not yet materialised. This foreshadowed the major argument we had about the trajectory of government cuts at the subsequent budget the following spring, which I described earlier.

Most importantly, I made it clear to Cameron and Osborne that I felt we were sharing power with a party that was quite different from the one we had entered into government with in the first place: a compassionate, moderate Conservative Party was one we could do business with; a Conservative Party dancing to the tune of their angry right-wing backbenchers was quite another. I didn't need any lessons on the importance of holding steady in the moderate centre ground – many people within my own party were highly critical of what we were doing in coalition and wanted to take us in a more traditional left-wing direction. In the same way that I was upholding the centre-ground bargain at the heart of the coalition, I expected Cameron and Osborne to do the same. They weren't the only ones facing restive MPs. They couldn't duck and weave to satisfy their own backbenchers and the wild-eyed demands of the right-wing commentariat, without sacrificing the basis on which we had chosen to govern together.

In essence, I wanted them to understand that they needed to make a choice: pander to their own right wing, in an attempt to secure their internal party position; or hold fast to the deal they had struck with us, to secure the survival of the government as a whole.

For a short time, at least, I think the meeting had a positive effect. Cameron and Osborne glimpsed their own political mortality. They needed the Lib Dems in order to govern, and they saw that we would not sit quietly on the sidelines while they chased their own tails. The next morning we had a political Cabinet meeting in Downing Street and everyone, universally, agreed that we would reassert the value of coalition government and try to reset the clock on our economic strategy in the autumn. Michael Gove was refreshingly frank. He said that the Conservatives had to understand how bitter the Lib Dems felt that Tory donors had funded a personal campaign against me, and that we had to understand how angry the Tories were that the NHS reforms had effectively been subcontracted to a Lib Dem party conference (a policy motion at our spring 2011 conference led directly to a pause in the passage of the legislation and a large number of amendments to it).

Yet, only a few weeks later, the last attempts to reform the House of Lords finally hit the buffers: on 10 July, a combination of bolshy Conservative backbench MPs and specious arguments from the Labour Party against the timetable for the reform bill meant that the plan was effectively killed in Parliament. There was no majority in the House of Commons to proceed with the bill. I told Cameron – as I had repeatedly told him on previous occasions – that in the event of the House of Lords reform bill being stymied by Conservative MPs, I would withdraw Liberal Democrat support for the linked issue of reform to constituency boundaries. It is a tribute to his good humour that the only time in five years when he ever raised his voice in anger was during the telephone conversation in which I informed him of this decision, from my office in the House of Commons.

Once again, the early window of opportunity for reform had been lost. The huge amount of time and effort I had devoted to Lords reform turned out, in the end, to be wholly fruitless.

To witness the opponents of reform from within the Lords piously complain today that an unelected House of Lords is getting far too big has only reminded me of the peculiar double standards that overshadow the whole place.

By the time we began meaningfully to explore the contentious issue of party funding reform in 2012, I had more or less given up hope that radical reform was at all possible. Nonetheless, I asked David Laws to oversee the process and he dutifully went through the motions in a series of meetings with representatives from the Labour and Conservative parties, discussing how we might cap the influence of big-money donors and trade unions. I had become bloody-minded by this stage. I didn't expect us to get very far, despite the commitments in both Labour's and the Conservatives' manifestos, but I wanted the other parties to say that to our faces. They duly did.

The problem – as with the entire constitutional reform agenda – was that what was at stake was the very essence of political self-interest: power. Our parliamentary system, outdated as it is, reinforces a two-party system, giving the two larger parties a shared, vested interest in maintaining the status quo. Without an overwhelming public clamour for change, they dug their heels in. That clamour had existed – in the wake of the MPs' expenses scandal – but only for a fleeting moment.

Recognising a window of opportunity and using it to push change through quickly is important, regardless of what sort of reforms you want to enact, but if what you want to change involves taking power away from the powerful, it is essential. Often, these windows exist in the early part of a government's life, when its mandate is strongest and its opponents are weakest, and before the internal wars of attrition that come to characterise most administrations have set in. Tony Blair has stated his regret that he didn't go further and faster on public-service reform in the early part of his premiership, when he was at his strongest and before the infighting of the Blair–Brown turf wars took over. It is a lesson that David

Cameron and George Osborne clearly tried to act on. In the wake of their surprise election victory in May 2015, they took advantage of the disarray of the Labour and Liberal Democrat parties to announce a dismantling of tax-credit support for millions of low-income working families, an assault on Housing Associations, a menacing review of the BBC, a plan to give English MPs different voting rights from other MPs, an intention to limit Freedom of Information rules, a reversal of most support to green-energy companies, and a tax giveaway to dead property millionaires – not to mention an attempt to hold a vote on fox-hunting once again.

Of course, this raises the question: could we have achieved more if we had acted more boldly in the first few months of government? Perhaps. Not only was the public appetite for reform much stronger, but so was our political position. There was more goodwill inside government, and neither party wanted to be the first to jeopardise a government that was, at that stage, still uncertain to last the course. The conventional wisdom is that the AV referendum took place too early, making it the first opportunity for the public to give a bloody nose to the government, the Liberal Democrats and me personally. Perhaps it was actually too late.

The fact that the British political system appears to be so immune to change – and so in hock to the vested interests of the two larger parties – will only strengthen the hand of populists who argue that real change requires more extreme action. The more the vested interests in Westminster set their face against overdue reform, the more ferocious the reaction to mainstream politics will become. But the failure of the coalition to bring about wider political reform also raises questions about how plural, multi-party governments operate. It is most likely, at some point, that Britain will have another coalition government – the fragmentation and volatility of politics points that way, as I shall explore. And the smaller parties in coalitions are invariably keener reformers than the larger, established parties with which they share power. In order to make future coalition governments a success, the ability of smaller parties to survive the experience of coalition and to promote their own reforms will be crucial. But is it actually possible? Do smaller parties fare better in other coalitions elsewhere? Or is successful coalition government – as those who condemned the Lib Dem decision to join the coalition in the first place believe – simply an idealistic fantasy?

CHAPTER 6

Burgemeester in Oorlog

'I'm going to be completely honest,' Sweden's Deputy Prime Minister and Green Party leader Åsa Romson told the assembled press, her eyes red raw with emotion. 'Recently, we've been having difficult discussions within the party . . . about the perception of reality.'

And then she couldn't hold it in any more. Her lips trembled. Tears slipped from the corners of her eyes.

'In the last couple of weeks,' she said, choking back further tears, 'I've been convinced that this is the best way to help the local Green Party politicians actually do something.'

It was November 2015 and Romson was holding a joint press conference with her senior coalition partner, Prime Minister Stefan Löfven, leader of the Social Democrats, to announce a U-turn on their government's open-door policy towards Syrian refugees seeking safe haven in the country. From now on, refugees would only be granted temporary residence, in line with other EU countries. For Romson and the Greens, it was a painful compromise and, she later admitted, a 'terrible decision'. Nonetheless, it was one she stood by, arguing that the consequences of leaving government would have been even worse. Six months after her tearful press conference she resigned as party leader.

Åsa Romson appeared to me to be a good person placed in an impossible position. She had no other choice. Her tears were the tears of sincere distress, a refreshingly human moment of anguish in the dehumanised world of politics, an expression of the agonising collision of one's highest ideals with harshest reality.

One refrain politicians hear over and over again from members of the public and the press is 'Why can't you stop bickering and learn to work together instead?' The remorseless tribalism of party politics is held in contempt, politicians are told. Endless point-scoring between politicians puts ordinary people off politics altogether. Why can't politicians, just for once, put the national interest first? And yet, when the compromises of coalition government are made – and stable coalition is impossible without them – this plea for cross-party cooperation often turns sour. This especially seems to be the case when the smaller party in a coalition is from the progressive, more idealistic wing of politics. In Ireland, for example, where smaller parties within a coalition are referred to as 'punchbags for heavyweights', one such punchbag was the Irish Green Party, which went into coalition with the larger, centre-right Fianna Fáil in 2007. The Green Party had been on the up, increasing its vote share in three consecutive elections, and in coalition managed to secure a number of policy achievements. However, it also compromised in a number of areas and struggled in particular over the action needed to tackle the country's enormous financial crisis. Unlike the Lib Dems, the Irish Greens pulled out of the coalition early, before the 2011 election. It didn't make much difference. They still got hammered, losing every last one of their seats.

The Irish Greens and Fianna Fáil were succeeded in office by a new coalition of Fine Gael and the smaller Labour Party. Labour's Eamon Gilmore had led the party to its best electoral performance in ninety-nine years, securing thirty-seven seats, including eighteen in the capital city, Dublin. He then became Tánaiste, or Deputy Prime Minister. I worked closely

with him during my time in office – we occasionally compared notes on our similar political predicaments – and he
always struck me as a decent guy determined to do the best
for his country. In office, his popularity plunged and he was
eventually overthrown as leader by an internal party putsch.
At the subsequent general election in February 2016, Labour
plummeted to its lowest-ever share of seats, just seven, and
6.6 per cent of the vote.

In the Netherlands, the current junior coalition partner is,
at the time of writing, the Labour Party – the PvdA – led by
former Greenpeace campaigner Diederik Samsom. Samsom
became leader in 2012 after something of a stratospheric rise
to prominence, leading his party into government that autumn.
He is widely regarded among the Dutch commentariat as
charismatic, thoughtful and good-humoured. In office, he is
being torn apart by opponents and voters alike for selling out
his principles.

Painful coalition experiences for smaller parties are not confined to Europe. In Trinidad and Tobago in 2010, the centre-left
and broadly socially liberal Congress of the People became
junior coalition partners to the centre-right but similarly named
United National Congress, led by the country's first female
Prime Minister, Kamla Persad-Bissessar. Five years later the
junior party lost all but one of its seats.

And to prove the experience is not exclusively limited to
parties on the left, the right-wing New Zealand First party
entered government for the first time in its history in 1996,
after the country's first election under a proportional representation system. The government collapsed mid-term and the next
election ended in disaster for New Zealand First.

In each of these cases, the smaller party was accused of
selling out, of betraying its supporters, of valuing the trappings
of power above its principles. In each, the leader of the smaller
party had faced a choice: take the opportunity to put those
principles and policies into practice, at the cost of compromise
with a party with which they disagreed; or allow a minority

government, or a government of other parties, to exercise power without their influence.

The Dutch, as ever, have a pretty pithy way of describing this dilemma: *Burgemeester in oorlog*, which means 'to be a mayor in wartime'. Under the Nazi occupation, Dutch mayors could either resign and be replaced by a stooge; or stay and become compromised. Neither choice was a vote-winner.

When the Liberal Democrats entered into coalition with the Conservatives in 2010, I assumed that compromise would be easy to understand, and easy to accept, in light of the circumstances we faced. The election had been indecisive: if no one wins, no one rules on their own. The country was also in the middle of an economic firestorm and urgently needed a government that could govern. It was an arithmetical fact that the only coalition capable of doing so was a combination of the Liberal Democrats and the Conservatives. After all, a combination of Labour and Liberal Democrat MPs would still have been eleven seats short of a majority in the House of Commons. To get a majority in the House of Commons you need 326 seats, although you could just scrape by with 321 because the Speaker, his deputies and the five Sinn Fein MPs do not vote; there were just 315 Labour and Lib Dem MPs combined. That meant we would have needed the support, formal or otherwise, of some combination of Northern Irish MPs (of which there were twelve, excluding Sinn Fein), Scottish Nationalists (six), Plaid Cymru (three) and the Green MP, Caroline Lucas, to form what the press had dubbed a 'rainbow coalition' or, less generously, 'a government of the losers'. At one point in the topsy-turvy discussions I had with Gordon Brown in the sleepless aftermath of the 2010 election, he started scribbling the numbers of a possible 'rainbow coalition' on a small piece of paper with a thick felt-tip pen. This would have been a perilous way to run a government at the best of times, but during a period of massive economic uncertainty it would have been impossible.

There was also no evidence that Labour was anywhere near capable of imposing the iron discipline that such a fragile and ramshackle multi-party coalition would have demanded. Even as I was listening to Gordon Brown's somewhat frenetic case, senior figures including Jack Straw, David Blunkett and John Reid were taking to the airwaves arguing that the Labour Party should go into opposition instead. I said to Brown that the numbers just didn't stack up and that a rainbow coalition would barely last a few months. Having now experienced the stresses of a two-party coalition, I reckon even that prediction was generous – it wouldn't have lasted more than a few weeks.

The only other options available to us would have been to allow the Conservatives to govern as a minority government, either with our loose support in what is known as a 'confidence and supply' arrangement – in which we would vote with them on budgets and Queen's Speeches, to ensure the government did not collapse – or with no such arrangement, leaving the government's viability to be questioned at every major vote. I was instinctively against a 'confidence and supply' arrangement, which struck me as the worst of all worlds: responsibility without control; supporting a government, but not steering it. And I never seriously considered the latter, which seemed just as bad: months of protracted political uncertainty would only exacerbate the economic difficulties facing the country, before the Tories called another election later that year.

If that were to happen, we had no doubt that the Lib Dems would be crushed and the Conservatives would win an outright majority. We had little money left to fight another election and the Conservatives would have a clear (and well-funded) message to our voters: 'We know you voted for the Lib Dems last time because you wanted change, but we really need a stable government now, so vote for us.' Having refused to step up to the plate and govern, we would risk being seen as part of the problem rather than part of the solution. During one of the lengthy late-night discussions of the Liberal Democrat parliamentary party, in which we weighed up our options after the 2010 election, Tim Farron persuasively reminded colleagues that of all the invidious choices we faced, we should seek to avoid a second snap election at all costs.

Yet, while the realities of parliamentary arithmetic seemed obvious to me, they were by no means obvious to everyone. To this day I am asked why the Lib Dems 'chose' to go into government with the Conservatives rather than Labour. In the end, that simply wasn't the choice before us. Rather, it was a choice between governing in the only combination available or not governing at all.

Given this background, it is not surprising that from the moment the coalition was formed, every compromise we made was decried by someone, somewhere as a betrayal. By contrast, when the Conservatives made concessions or struck compromises, they did not face similar criticisms. On welfare cuts, tax policy, Internet security, the environment, fixed-term parliaments, industrial policy, Free Schools, Europe and much else besides, the Conservatives were forced by coalition to drop, reverse or dilute numerous manifesto commitments. In private, they often did so with barely disguised enthusiasm – Danny Alexander and I were both struck by the alacrity with which the Conservatives ditched their headline-grabbing Inheritance Tax cut, which had been at the centre of their 2010 election campaign. It was obvious to us that they were relieved not to have to go through with such a spectacularly profligate policy, in the face of the fiscal crisis we had to deal with. But when the Prime Minister struck a compromise with me or jettisoned one of his own policies, it would be described more often than not as another example of Lib Dem restraint on his true vigour, rather than an indication of weakness – the charge invariably levelled at the Lib Dems.

From the outset, much of the Conservative supporting press decided that the best way to promote their interests was to depict the coalition as an illegitimate mongrel government in which the birthright of the Conservatives to rule was being frustrated at every turn by pesky Lib Dems. It was a ruthlessly effective depiction of the Conservatives as honest, strong and true, and of the Lib Dems as perfidious, underhand and weak.

The frustration of the right-wing press was understandable: the whole point of coalition government was to anchor our policies in the centre ground and not let the Conservatives pull it to the right. When the *Daily Mail* published a front-page quote in May 2012 from David Cameron – 'I'd govern like a true Tory if it wasn't for the Lib Dems' – Lib Dem party activists wore the phrase as a badge of honour, plastering it all over their leaflets and Facebook pages. The personal vilification of me, while hysterical at times, was also far from unexpected. After all, I'd had a taste of it during the 2010 election campaign itself. At the height of our surge in the polls after the televised leaders' debates, the attacks from the right-wing press went so overboard that a countermovement started on Twitter. Using the hashtag #nickcleggsfault, sympathetic Twitter-users tweeted comic examples of things for which I was personally to blame, from the volcanic-ash cloud that grounded British planes in April 2010, to the decision by Walkers to use blue instead of green for the packaging of their cheese-and-onion crisps.

Sadly, the Twitterati no longer came to my defence once I assumed high office. While I was unsurprised to be vilified by the right, I had vaguely hoped that Britain's progressive forces would at least recognise, and perhaps give credit for, what the Lib Dems were trying to do in government: restrain the Tories, enact liberal policies and put the country on an even keel after the economic heart attack of 2008. No such luck. Our compromises were treated unforgivingly on the left as a betrayal of progressive values, an act of wilful complicity with the enemy. I soon found that newspapers whose hearts beat on the left were as vitriolic as those on the right. On occasion, the strength of feeling was quite bizarre. Barry Gardiner, a Labour MP, once spat the word 'quisling' at me in the Chamber of the House of Commons with red-faced ferocity: the word derives from the wartime Norwegian leader Vidkun Quisling, who collaborated with the Nazis. His colleague Andy Burnham, meanwhile, led a group of demonstrators outside my constituency office. Student activists occupied the office itself, frightening the living daylights out of my constituency-office team. A large protest group occupied the street outside our home in Putney. In May 2014 the Labour Party even spent tens of thousands of pounds producing a three-minute party political broadcast depicting me, in Hammer Horror style, as 'The Un-Credible Shrinking Man'. In a spectacular act of political self-indulgence, the Labour Party had clearly decided that their priority was beating up the Lib Dems rather than training their guns on the Conservatives. The Conservatives, in turn, couldn't believe their luck.

The moment that captured most clearly the perversity of Labour's vilification of the Lib Dems came in the early hours of election night in May 2015. After a sleepless night in our flat in south-west Sheffield, during which the brutal scale of the Lib Dem collapse became painfully apparent, Miriam and I arrived at the vast indoor sports centre in the Don Valley at around 4 a.m. for the results of my constituency count. The sports centre was also the venue for the counts in the other four Sheffield seats, which were all held by Labour, so the place was full of red-rosetted activists who were following the BBC coverage of the night's events on cinema-sized screens in the centre's main hall. At one point, as my team and I waited glumly for my narrow victory in Hallam to be declared, an enormous cheer went up – the loudest I would hear all night. I tried to see what all the fuss was about: the BBC had just announced that Vince Cable had lost his seat in Twickenham. But he had not lost to his Labour opponent, Nick Grant – he had lost to a Conservative, Tania Mathias. Labour activists were cheering at the most left-wing member of the government losing his seat to a Conservative. Unbelievable! A short while later, they were stunned into silence by the news that Ed Balls had lost his seat in a nearby constituency, also to the Conservatives. Nothing better illustrates the political blindness that Labour vilification of the Liberal Democrats had brought about: if the Labour activists who had poured into Sheffield Hallam to try to unseat me had spent a fraction of their time helping out their own side, Ed Balls might still be in Parliament today.

And so, sadly, the left merely ended up doing the spadework for the right: the more we were castigated for selling our soul to the devil, the more that centre-ground and progressive voters felt we were no longer standing up for them. As progressive forces wallowed in recrimination, the Conservative Party reaped the rewards. It turns out that, after five years of being called a party of sell-outs, traitors and weaklings, some of it sticks.

I have no doubt that our own errors and miscalculations played some role in fostering the attacks on us, notably the manner in which we changed tack on the issue of tuition fees. But if I am right that our experience as a smaller party in coalition was not a one-off but part of a wider pattern, corroborated by the experiences of other such parties around the world, then tuition fees must have served as the occasion, rather than the underlying cause, for the way we were attacked. Besides, our mistakes cannot reasonably explain the wild-eyed intensity of the rage we provoked on the left.

Much of that animosity can also perhaps be explained by the complex historical relationship between Labour and the Liberal Democrats. There are members of both parties who believe that the future of progressive politics in Britain relies on the Labour and Lib Dem parties uniting forces against the right; clearly, to them, the Lib Dem–Conservative coalition was intolerable in principle. The future of a possible realignment of the centre-left is examined in more detail in the next chapter. But I believe there was something still deeper at play.

In very general terms, the motivations that account for the decisions made by voters can be divided into those based on 'interests' and those based on 'values'. 'Interest voters' base their electoral choices primarily on an assessment of which party seems to be offering the best deal to them, their family, their community or any other group of which they consider themselves a part. Low taxes – appealing to the straightforward interest people have in keeping more of their own money – is a classic enticement for such voters. Such voters are, in general, pretty pragmatic about politics, sceptical about politicians, and unmoved by grandiloquent claims that governments can change the world. Crucially, they are also fairly unsentimental about what it takes for political parties to hold on to power, and readily understand that the practice of power can be an imperfect, muddy science of give-and-take – as long, that is, as their vital interests remain largely protected.

'Values voters', by contrast, base their electoral choices primarily on a judgement as to which party best represents their world view. They regard the act of voting not just as an expression of their own needs, but also as an expression of the kind of society they wish to inhabit. An appeal to social equality, for instance, is a strong values-based appeal, even to voters who may themselves be well off and untroubled, personally, by high rates of inequality. Yet it matters to them that the position of others in society is improved for the better. Often, such voters will have far less patience with compromises that take parties away from the ideological path to which they subscribe, regardless of the motives for, and merits of, the compromise. For many 'values voters', the compromises that come with governing – in coalition or on your own – are not a price worth paying if it comes with a sullying of the values they hold dear.

Of course these are caricatures: no one is a pure 'interest voter' or a pure 'values voter'. We all have a world view that we want to see reflected in our politics, and interests that affect our pockets, our families and our communities. But it seems likely that many who see themselves on the values end of the spectrum, particularly younger voters, vote for parties of the idealistic, progressive left: liberals, social democrats, greens, socialists. That is not to say that there are no idealists on the right, but by definition conservatism is an ideology of preservation and conservation (the clue is in the name) rather than of lofty change.

Naturally, the right has its own betrayal myth, but it is different in one important respect: for the left, betrayal comes from those who take power and sully their ideological purity with its compromises; the right have no problem at all with power. Its problem comes not from having power, but from power being wielded by the wrong people. According to the suspicion that lurks in parts of the right, foreigners, socialists, left-wing academics, pencil-pushers in Brussels, immigrants and intellectuals running the BBC are all interlopers challenging the settled order of life in Britain. The left, which is born of the disempowered, is suspicious of those who seek and wield power. The right, which is born of the already empowered, is suspicious of those who seek to subvert the established order.

For both, a newcomer in the corridors of power, like the Liberal Democrats, is an unwelcome challenge to the politics they prefer.

Beyond the ideological reflexes of voters on the two opposing sides of the political spectrum, there may be something even more profound within our social psyche that elicits such a hostile reaction to the politics of compromise. In her classic work of cultural anthropology, *Purity and Danger*, Mary Douglas proposed the theory that societies reject as dirty or polluting anything that crosses cultural boundaries. That is why, she argued, pigs and shellfish get a hard time. They are neither one thing nor the other: pigs have four legs and cloven hooves but don't chew the cud; shellfish live in the sea but have hard shells. They are, quite literally, neither fish nor fowl. They are abnormal, and therefore deemed to be impure. That is one of the reasons, Mary Douglas concluded, why shellfish and pigs are banned in the tradition of kosher. They just don't fit. Later in life, she recanted this explanation of kosher rules, admitting that she had misinterpreted the theological basis for them. Nonetheless, her wider point about the importance of demarcation in society still stood:

> I believe that ideas about separating, purifying, demarcating and punishing transgressions have as their main function to impose system on an inherently untidy experience. It is only by

exaggerating the difference between within and without, about and below, male and female, with and against, that a semblance of order is created.

Douglas's theory built upon the thinking of Claude Lévi-Strauss, the French structural anthropologist, who proposed the theory of binary opposites. According to Lévi-Strauss, meaning derives from the relationship between things rather than from the things themselves, and above all through relationships of opposition: we understand something to be black because it is the opposite of white, and vice versa; in the same way we understand concepts such as male/female, dirty/clean, sacred/profane, left/right only through their binary opposition to one another.

The work of structural anthropologists is not uncontroversial and cannot be 'proved' in the strictly scientific sense. Nonetheless, it may help explain why people from different sides of the political spectrum unite with such ferocity in rejecting any person or party who muddies the political waters and messes up the neatly bifurcated political map with which they feel familiar.

The difficulty of accommodating more than two sides to an argument is obvious enough in the everyday language used to portray politics. News reports of political disputes invariably lead with one voice or argument and then include a response from an opposing voice. Third- or fourth-party voices are rarely heard. The very language of debate – phrases such as 'on the one hand, and on the other', 'there are two sides to every story', 'the other side of the argument' – does not easily lend itself to three-, four- or five-sided arguments. The confrontational architecture of the House of Commons and our winner-takes-all electoral system only reinforce the two-sided choreography of our politics. Elections themselves, of course, also boil down to a binary opposite: continuity versus change. In the end, once the blizzard of policy promises from political parties has been showered on the electorate, a simple choice remains. One lot will say that it is better to stick with what you've got, not to rock the boat. Another lot will say it's time for a change, throw the rascals out.

The difficulty of being a third voice – an interloper in this polarised choice – is stark. In the 2015 general election, the Lib Dems were in effect condemned to saying a little bit of both: advocating continuity for many of the things we had done in coalition, not least to avoid derailing the economy; at the same time, advocating change. But saying a little bit of both doesn't get you very far, especially in an election campaign as polarised as the 2015 campaign. The Conservatives, as the larger coalition partner, were far more plausible in presenting themselves as a party of continuity and stability. Labour, as the opposition, were clearly the party of change. Our dilemma was that we could never present ourselves as the more plausible party of either. Portrayed as a party of neither the left nor the right but of the centre ground, of neither continuity nor change but of 'moderation' and 'restraint', we were simply not a compelling answer to the question that came to define the election campaign: do you stick with a Conservative-led government, or do you take the gamble on Ed Miliband, knowing that there was a good chance he might be dependent on the support of a resurgent Scottish National Party?

True, there were Lib Dem seats that were always likely to be lost – the ones in Labour-facing urban constituencies in places such as London, Manchester, Burnley and Redcar. These had been won in 2010, mostly with small majorities, at the depths of Labour's unpopularity. These areas contained voters most likely to feel betrayed by the coalition, and holding on to these seats against a Labour Party no longer tarnished by power was always going to be a struggle. Our fate in Scotland – we lost ten seats – may also have been exacerbated by the unpopularity of our association with the Conservatives, but it cannot be entirely explained by it. After all, Labour, which had nothing to do with the coalition, was also reduced to a single seat, having won forty-one seats five years earlier.

However, the majority of the fifty-seven seats we were defending were in places where our main challengers were the Conservatives. At the beginning of the six-week campaigning period in 2015, we felt it was entirely possible that we could pip the Tories in as many as thirty English and Welsh seats. At that point, the question people were wrestling with seemed to be: 'What sort of government can keep the country on-track?' Our argument that the country needed a moderating force – to compensate for either excessive cuts from the Conservatives or economic irresponsibility from Labour – seemed both relevant and resonant. But as the campaign wore on, the mood changed. The combination of an increasingly confident Nicola Sturgeon, growing public doubts about the credibility of Ed Miliband, a hopelessly belated reaction from the Labour Party to the fears of their reliance on the SNP, and hours of TV news coverage and column inches devoted to precisely that hypothetical scenario had a simple and overwhelming effect: it turned a multi-party contest into a binary choice, Labour–SNP vs Conservative. With millions of English voters deeply unsettled by the thought of Ed Miliband in Number 10 and the Nationalists pulling the strings, the Conservatives were let completely off the hook, since there was no meaningful scrutiny of the scenario that eventually came about: a Conservative majority.

The Conservatives, meanwhile, were busily throwing the kitchen sink at Lib Dem-held seats, bombarding not just swing voters, but traditional Lib Dem voters too with emails, telephone calls, letters and leaflets. As they grew more confident that their fear campaign was working, the Conservatives firmly parked their tanks on our lawns, with Cameron paying personal visits in the last few days of the campaign to David Laws's constituency in Yeovil and Vince Cable's in Twickenham, contributing no doubt to the marked – and late – swing in their favour.

As the Conservatives tightened their grip on our constituencies, I mused to Jonny Oates, my long-standing chief of staff, confidant and friend, about ten days before the election itself, that the only thing I could say that would make a material difference to the outcome would be to dismiss, under all circumstances, the possibility of entering into a coalition with the Labour Party. Conservative canvassers were able to corral wavering Lib Dem voters into their corner by pointing out that I had not ruled out a coalition with Labour – as indeed I hadn't. Putting a complete distance between ourselves and the perceived risks of a Labour-led government might have been a tactic that could have helped keep some of those voters onside. But this was something I could never say because it would have been incompatible with the very identity of the Liberal Democrats as an independent party.

In the end, then, we were beaten in all three types of seat we had set out to defend: SNP-facing Scottish seats; Labour-facing urban seats; and Conservative-facing English seats.

No one could have predicted in 2010 that Scottish nationalism would be the tail that would wag the dog of British politics five years later, but come 6 May 2015, every Scottish seat bar three belonged to the SNP, with Labour, Conservatives and Lib Dems reduced to just a single MP each. It was a tidal wave that crushed all before it. Indeed, every election in recent times has been dominated by issues that no one had anticipated in the election immediately before: in 2001, no one talked about Iraq, yet the invasion of Iraq overshadowed the election of 2005; in 2005, no one talked about a crisis in our banks or MPs fiddling their expenses, yet both loomed over the 2010 campaign; and in 2010, no one discussed Scottish nationalism, yet the fear of Scottish Nationalists holding the rest of the country to ransom became an abiding concern for many English voters in 2015, masterfully exploited by the Conservatives. The claim that the seeds of the electoral fate of the Liberal Democrats in 2015 were all sown by the act of entering into coalition five years previously ignores the force of these unexpected events. It could just as plausibly be argued that, even if we hadn't entered into coalition in 2010, we still wouldn't have been the answer to the anxieties playing on voters' minds in 2015. We clearly would not have ended up losing so many seats as we eventually did, but in a merciless 'safety first' campaign, I doubt very much that a Lib Dem party that had been idling away on the opposition sidelines for five years would have emerged as a significantly more attractive option to voters.

As it was, there were a number of things that I misjudged during our time in coalition: the scale and suddenness of the loss of support of aspirational middle-class voters, not least because of the decision on tuition fees; the remorseless vilification of much of what we did in large parts of the press; our struggle to replace lost voters with a new coalition of centrist support, to name a few. All of these misjudgements and more played a role in shaping our fate. But none of them on their own explain the precipitate decline in the party's fortunes. I suspect that even if no mistakes had been made in coalition – a state of perfection unknown to the messy world of politics – we would still have struggled to insert ourselves in the polarised choice on election day.

Shortly after the election, Miriam and I had dinner with Tony and Cherie Blair. With his characteristically clear and unsentimental understanding of how power works, Blair set out the diagnosis pithily: the kind of politics you were trying to create just doesn't work in the system we have, he said.

Of course, there are exceptions to every rule. In 1999, the Scottish Liberal Democrats, led with great skill by Jim Wallace, found themselves in a position to form a coalition government with the larger Labour Party. Far from being crushed, when the elections came round again four years later, they returned exactly the same number of MSPs, seventeen, and were in a position to continue the coalition. The differences between that coalition and the Lib Dem–Conservative coalition in Westminster were, however, just as significant as any similarities. For a start, the Lib Dems in Scotland were in coalition with a party of the centre-left rather than the right, and the electoral system in Scotland encouraged the Labour Party to hold back in its attacks on the Lib Dems at the time. David

Whitton, a former special adviser to the Labour First Minister Donald Dewar, admitted as much when discussing the 1999 election: 'During the election campaign our attention focused on the SNP and to a lesser degree the Tories. It's fair to say we went soft on the Liberals knowing they were likely coalition partners.' No such mercy was shown by the Conservatives towards the Lib Dems in 2015.

Another party that entered coalition as a left-leaning junior partner and emerged relatively unscathed was the German Green Party – Die Grünen – which entered government in 1998 with the Social Democrats. Led by the charismatic Joschka Fischer, who took the post of Foreign Minister, they used their first-ever experience in government to boost their credibility as a serious governing force. Along the way they faced the usual criticism of compromising their principles, particularly when they supported military intervention in Kosovo. However, they also achieved significant policy victories, such as phasing out nuclear power and introducing civil partnerships. The government eventually collapsed, not because of Green fright, but because of splits within the Social Democrats. Far from being punished at the ballot box, at the 2005 election the Greens won more seats than they had before. But again, this rare tale of junior-party coalition success came when both partners were broadly of the centre-left.

Other examples are perhaps more instructive. Democrats 66, or D66, are a Dutch social liberal party, committed first and foremost to radical political reform, which has spent five terms in government as junior coalition partners since its formation in 1966. The life of D66 is one of peaks and troughs. They seek to govern, but do so knowing that coalition is followed by decline, opposition followed by resurgence. They were most recently in government between 2003 and 2006, only to be smashed at that election to their lowest-ever share of the vote – just 2 per cent. But time and again D66 have managed to bounce back, and in 2014 they topped the polls in the European elections.

The Free Democratic Party, or FDP, are a German economic liberal party that has been a fixture of power in Germany for most of its post-war existence. As junior coalition partners to either the right-of-centre Christian Democrats or the left-of-centre Social Democrats, the FDP have spent more time in power than either of their larger competitors – more than four decades in total since 1949. They secured this position of semi-permanent power by carving out a centrist niche in Germany's multi-party proportional system, streamlining their ideological approach in the process so that they owned a small but distinct part of the pro-enterprise German political landscape. This role has allowed them to assume power more often than not, but it is not without its risks. At the most recent federal elections, in 2013, after four years in coalition with Angela Merkel's Christian Democrats, the FDP suffered a brutal collapse at the ballot box, shrinking from nearly 15 per cent of the vote to less than 5 per cent and losing every single one of its ninety-three seats in the Bundestag in the process.

A similar path to that of Die Grünen was trod by Margrethe Vestager, leader of the Danish Social Liberals – Radikale Venstre – in 2011, when she led them into power with Prime Minister Helle Thorning-Schmidt's Social Democrats. Vestager assumed the role of Economic Minister (equivalent to our Chancellor of the Exchequer) in the coalition, a role that enabled her to present herself as a figure of immense power in the government. Fleetingly, she was even regarded as more powerful than Thorning-Schmidt. However, unlike Die Grünen, Radikale Venstre could not sustain their advantage. With Vestager leaving the government in 2014 for a role as a European Commissioner, the party slumped at the 2015 election, losing half its votes and nine of its seventeen seats.

Whichever approach the Liberal Democrats may choose to take in future, one lesson is clear: life is perilous for smaller parties, no matter what choices they make. Considering the factors that affected the 2015 general election, it is quite possible that the Lib Dems would have declined even without the taint of coalition, if not so sharply. What happened in Scotland was a phenomenon that had very little to do with the political choices of the Liberal Democrats in Westminster. Perhaps what is telling, though, is that the Liberal Democrats increased both our percentage of the vote and the number of seats we won throughout the late Nineties and Noughties, in an era of majority governments where the outcome of elections was fairly obvious from the start. It may be that when an election is predictable, more voters are prepared to lend a smaller party their vote, secure in the knowledge that it won't change the likely government of the day. Admittedly when the 2010 election took place – anticipated to be the closest in nearly two decades – we increased our vote share again (though, alas, not our seat count), but this may have been an exceptional case. The truth is that the performance of smaller parties at general elections often has a great deal to do with factors well beyond their control.

On entering government I felt, at least in the early days, that we had to go out of our way to demonstrate that coalition itself was a viable form of government, especially given the uncertain economic circumstances of the country and the hysterical warnings that a hung parliament would lead to chaos and instability. So at the outset, my approach was one of loyally promoting the coalition as a whole. This had the virtue of keeping the attack dogs on the right largely at bay, but our own voters and voices on the left understandably thought we had lost our identity. Later I tried another approach: asserting our own identity within government more forcefully, while keeping the coalition show on the road. This had the virtue of shoring up what little support we still had, but it inflamed the attacks from the right, while the left still complained that we weren't going nearly far enough. Every compromise was still a betrayal, and each approach still enraged the right or the left – and usually both.

Ironically, if the Conservative–Liberal Democrat coalition had been on the ballot paper in 2015, my guess is that we would have won with a handsome majority. The coalition had served the country well. It had provided strong, sensible, sane government at a time of crisis. Disraeli was wrong: the coalition was more popular than he might have predicted. It just wasn't on the ballot paper, so people couldn't vote for it.

One way smaller parties in other countries seek to ensure that the prospect of a coalition *is* on the ballot paper is by pre-announcing the coalitions they are prepared to form. Ahead of Ireland's general election in 2016, the Labour Party was quite open about its intention to continue governing with Fine Gael. In Trinidad and Tobago, the Congress of the People campaigned as part of a four-way coalition with the United National Congress and two smaller parties, even giving itself a name: the People's Partnership. This may have the advantage of presenting up front to the electorate the compromise necessary to govern – but pre-empting the choice of the British people by picking a side before a single vote has even been cast would be out of kilter with the nature of British politics, and certainly out of step with the independence of the Liberal Democrats. The subsequent defeat of the Labour Party in Ireland suggests it is a tactic that doesn't work anyway.

Whatever the circumstances in which the opportunity for power-sharing may arise in future, I remain of the view that progressive parties should always seek to take it. If progressive parties are frightened off from assuming power because of the risks to themselves, they will only let down the people they seek to serve in the first place. Politics is about changing lives. If, by shunning power, you let your opponents simply occupy power in your place, then you let down the very values that reformist parties believe in. As it is, we spent the five years before our demise at the 2015 general election investing in the education of the youngest and the poorest children in our society; breaking down the institutional discrimination against those with mental-health problems; allowing gay people to marry, so that all love is valued equally; ending the detention of children behind bars in asylum cases; cutting taxes for ordinary working people; creating millions of new apprenticeships for young people; overhauling our pensions system; helping the renewable-energy industry to employ thousands of people; and much, much more. And we did so while working with our coalition partners to pull the British economy back from the brink of an economic catastrophe, saving untold jobs and livelihoods in the process. That is the point of politics.

I hope that my successors will find more forgiving circumstances in which to govern and will meet greater understanding for the role of compromise. Maybe it won't be accepted until it has been tried a few times. I guess I had the honour and the disadvantage of going first. After all, Dutch mayors are a lot more popular these days.

But if progressive parties are to have any hope of gaining power, in coalition or otherwise, and if the politics of reason and compromise is to respond successfully to the rise of nationalism and populism, then it seems clear to me that some kind of realignment of British politics itself will be required first. The question now is: what form should that realignment take?

CHAPTER 7

Was Roy Right?

I met Roy Jenkins only once, at a meeting of the European Movement in Nottingham in the late Nineties. I was a wet-behind-the-ears political ingénu in my early thirties and he was an elderly man not long for this world, but he still carried himself with a rare gravitas. I was pretty overawed. I asked a couple of deferential questions – I can't remember what, I was just trying to appear as self-assured as possible – and he patiently answered in return.

Roy Jenkins is a hero of the liberal left for two reasons. The first is that he was the most liberal Home Secretary of the twentieth century, who, in just under two years in the Home Office in 1966 and 1967, oversaw the end of capital punishment and the legalisation of homosexuality and abortion. Indeed, in the words of the renowned political scientist Vernon Bogdanor, he was 'the only really liberal Home Secretary that the Labour Party has ever produced'. The second is that he was the chief proponent of an argument that has beguiled Liberals, Liberal Democrats and many Labour modernisers for decades: that the future of progressive politics lies in the realignment of the centre-left.

Jenkins was one of the Gang of Four – alongside Shirley Williams, David Owen and Bill Rodgers – that broke away from the Labour Party at the height of its civil war in 1981 to form the Social Democratic Party, which later merged with the Liberals to form the Liberal Democrats. Throughout the latter part of his career, Jenkins advocated cooperation between Labour and the Lib Dems and championed electoral reform, in the hope that it would usher in a new ascendancy of the centre-left. He made a seductively simple argument: the Conservatives had dominated Britain's government in the twentieth century because of the divisions between Liberals/Liberal Democrats and the Labour Party. If only the centre-left would get its act together and coalesce, the latent progressive majority in Britain would prevail.

Throughout my career I have shared Roy Jenkins's passion for electoral reform, civil liberties and Europe, but I have dissented from the view that Labour and the Liberal Democrats are somehow estranged partners who are destined to fall back into each other's arms. I disagree with the notion that British politics would benefit from being reduced to two American-style centre-left and centre-right blocs. Instead, I retain the more traditional liberal attachment to choice, pluralism and diversity in UK politics. The creation of a coalition with the Conservatives was consistent with this belief: compromise across party lines is a natural corollary of the pluralist politics that the Liberal Democrats have long advocated.

Indeed, genuine pluralism is the opposite of realignment. The former implies a shifting combination of coalitions, in which parties maintain their independence but act to follow the will of the electorate as best they can. The latter is arguably just a glorified term for two or more parties ganging up together to hammer a common enemy.

No wonder, then, that those who have been – and remain – the most trenchant critics of the creation of the coalition in 2010 are often disciples of Roy Jenkins. For them, understandably enough, the coalition wasn't just a one-off innovation they disliked; it was a threat to the very purpose to which they had dedicated much of their political careers. One of the most outspoken critics of the coalition within the Liberal Democrats, Matthew Oakeshott – or, rather, Baron Oakeshott of Seagrove Bay – started his political career working for the great man himself, as an assistant in Roy Jenkins's parliamentary office in the 1970s. Later he became Jenkins's special adviser during his second stint in the Home Office. During the coalition years, Matthew revelled in his status as an ally of Vince Cable, who was also a Labour special adviser in the 1970s, and used this status to call repeatedly for me to be toppled and for the coalition to end. It was never clear to what extent he was speaking with Vince's authority, but I suspect it was far less than he liked to suggest. Politically, Matthew Oakeshott was a somewhat cartoonish character. His occasional public appearances in dark glasses gave him a sinister demeanour entirely in keeping with his reputation in Westminster as an insatiable schemer. But he was at least consistent in his views: he loathed the coalition from the outset and never wavered in his wish to see it undone.

Despite his rather cack-handed machinations, I always respected his basic stance, and that of people like him. It at least had a coherent logic to it. In many ways, I found Matthew's disgruntlement a lot easier to understand than those who enthusiastically applauded the creation of the coalition at the outset, but subsequently claimed they'd known all along it was going to be a disaster; or those who say that the coalition wasn't the problem, but rather the way in which we conducted ourselves within it. Everyone is wiser after the fact.

Nonetheless, having tested – perhaps to destruction – the sort of pluralism that allows parties as far apart ideologically as the Conservatives and the Liberal Democrats to work together in government, I have found myself returning to this question. Was Roy Jenkins right all along? Should liberals like me abandon the idea that we can govern across the political divide, and instead focus on building an anti-Conservative majority? Most pressingly, will the shock waves of the EU referendum lead to a new alliance amongst progressive, internationalist parties seeking to provide stability to a country rocked by the economic and political turmoil engendered by the Conservatives and UKIP?

To understand someone's political choices, you have to understand their political journey. Roy Jenkins's journey took him from a small mining town in Wales, to Oxford University and then to the Cabinet. He rose through the ranks of the Labour Party in the 1950s, a time when the tensions between its moderates and its radicals were beginning to emerge. He sided increasingly with its modernising wing over its socialist left. This rift came to a head over the issue of Europe, which led to the pro-European Jenkins quitting the frontbench in 1960. Despite this, he returned to a ministerial position in 1964 and just over a year later found himself in the Home Office, where he enacted his famous liberal reforms. He subsequently became Chancellor of the Exchequer, only to be turfed out of office by the electorate in 1970. Had Labour won the election that year, it is quite possible that he would have succeeded Harold Wilson as Prime Minister. They didn't, and he didn't.

In opposition the Labour Party swung to the left, and in 1972, once again, Jenkins quit the frontbench over the issue of Europe. He returned to government in 1974 and then lost to Callaghan in the 1976 Labour leadership contest. The next year he packed his bags for Brussels, leaving Parliament to become Britain's first and only European Commission President. He spent the remainder of the 1970s growing increasingly disillusioned with a Labour Party that was lurching to the left under the influence of the so-called Militant Tendency, until he finally severed his ties and, with the Gang of Four, formed the SDP. He later became a Liberal Democrat when the SDP and the Liberals merged, and a Member of the House of Lords, from where he advised Tony Blair on electoral reform. His recommendations might have been implemented, were it not for the fact that Blair won a stonking majority in 1997 and no longer felt the need to pursue them.

Jenkins's political journey, then, was one of a man who found himself mired in the infighting of the British left and who felt compelled by a mix of frustration, pragmatism and intellect to pursue the creation of a new, modern and progressive alternative to tribal socialism. Many of his friends and supporters within his generation of Liberal Democrats trod a similar path.

By contrast, the political journey for my generation of Liberal Democrats – Danny Alexander, David Laws, Norman Lamb, Jo Swinson, Lynne Featherstone, Ed Davey and others – took place in a wholly different context. Our views were formed not just by the harsh injustices of 1980s Conservatism, but by the rise and fall of New Labour between 1997 and 2010. During those years, liberal reformers rallied around their opposition to New Labour's disregard for civil liberties – ninety days' detention without charge, ID cards, mass databases and surveillance, a seemingly endless parade of new laws governing every corner of British life – and their attachment to centralisation. Furthermore, whilst I am a southerner by birth and education, my whole political career has been rooted in the Midlands and the North: as the first Liberal parliamentarian, an MEP, in the East Midlands since the 1930s, and then later as the sole non-Labour MP as far as the eye can see, in South Yorkshire. The arrogance with which local Labour Party bosses governed these one-party states provoked in me an intense dislike of the Labour machine.

But my earliest political instincts, like everybody's, can be traced to my upbringing and my education. While neither of my parents were card-carrying political devotees of any particular persuasion, their own experiences and those of their parents instilled in me, my brothers and my sister a strong, if ill-defined respect for the importance of politics. My father's father was a medic, writer and long-standing editor of the *British Medical Journal*. My father's mother hailed from Russian aristocratic roots. Her family, like those of so many 'White Russian' émigrés who ended up in either Paris or London, was split, shunted and scattered across Russia, the Baltics and

Western Europe by revolution and war. People with that kind of experience intuitively know that political ideas can have profound consequences.

My mother was born in Indonesia, as were two of her three sisters, since her father worked for Shell in Java, then a major Dutch colony. As a young girl, she endured several harrowing years with her mother and two sisters in a Japanese women-only prisoner-of-war camp. My mother did not tell me or my siblings much about her experiences until we were adults. Like so many people who have witnessed the horrors of war, she saw little point in disturbing our childhood innocence with images that would have been impossible to explain. When *Tenko*, a series about the experience of British, Dutch and Australian women prisoners in a Japanese camp, was screened on British television screens in the early 1980s, I remember asking my mother whether it bore any relation to reality. She said only that the scenes in which courageous prisoners addressed and faced down their tormentors were inconceivable: no one had been allowed to speak to the prison guards, ever.

We were a garrulous, boisterous family – there was nothing morbid about the legacy of my parents' backgrounds, but it established in us a barely articulated awareness of recent history and the role of politics in shaping our world. In particular, there was an unspoken recognition, more apparent in hindsight than it ever was at the time, that Britain was a place of comparative stability and solidity, which had largely been spared the violent upheavals that had taken place elsewhere. In common with the children of many families thrown together by immigration and flight from conflict, my siblings and I inherited an affection – perhaps a little sepia-tinted – for British traditions of fair play, the rule of law and political moderation.

Unsurprisingly, then, I developed a keen interest in the Second World War as a young boy. I remember reading an illustrated history book about the siege of Stalingrad at an unhealthily young age. I was also of a generation marked by the threat of nuclear war. The US TV film *The Day After,* an apocalyptic depiction of a nuclear conflict between the West and the Soviet Union, first screened in 1983, made an immediate and chilling impact on people of my age. In my final year at the Buckinghamshire boarding school where my younger brother and I were educated, I shared a dormitory with a pupil whose parents had sent him to school in Britain from Hawaii. He was convinced that he would never see them again, as the Soviet Union would be bound to strike the naval base in Hawaii first. So I asked our history teacher – a bespectacled man with an old-fashioned, disciplinarian bearing – if he would give a special lesson on the Cold War, so that we could understand what was going on and see if my Hawaiian friend's fears were well founded. Our teacher obliged, and the lesson was terrifying. He got a large map out and, with the aid of a long wooden stick, explained where the 'warm-water ports' were, how the Soviets would get to them through Central Europe, the range of their nuclear arsenal and where they would strike first, including Hawaii. My poor friend wept into his pillow all night long.

Our history teacher made two further observations that I can remember: the first – made to our classroom of eleven-year-olds – was that he thought we would all be dead by Christmas; the second, made to my mother, was that he thought I would be Prime Minister one day. He never quite explained how on earth one could follow the other.

But it wasn't until more than a decade later that my appetite for politics really sparked into life. I was in the middle of my postgraduate studies at the University of Minnesota when the seminal political moment of the late twentieth century took place: the fall of the Berlin Wall on 9 December 1989. For people of my generation, who had grown up with nuclear annihilation hanging over our heads like the sword of Damocles, it was an extraordinarily powerful moment – a great release from years of apprehension and a new beginning. All of a sudden, anything seemed possible. Huddled around a radio with my fellow student from the Cambridge–Minnesota Fellowship scheme in our freezing basement apartment in a suburb of

Minneapolis, I remember weeping as I listened to the news on NPR, the public-service broadcaster. As we heard descriptions of ordinary Germans taking pickaxes to the Wall, my mother called me on the phone and said, 'Isn't this amazing? Isn't this just amazing?' I have never experienced such a palpable sense of everything – absolutely everything – changing in an instant as I did then.

It was there, at the University of Minnesota, that my intellectual journey towards liberalism really took shape. As the Cold War was coming to an end, I spent months holed up in the university's library researching a thesis on 'Deep Green' politics. This was a movement that had become fashionable in the late 1980s, which argued that for the planet to be saved, sweeping, draconian measures were required. At their extreme, Deep Green advocates argued that the ends – saving humanity from itself – justified drastic means to tackle over-population and pollution, including strict curbs on individual choice and individual liberties. The more I read about Deep Green philosophy, the more I found it sanctimonious, illiberal and authoritarian. I turned instead to the seminal liberal texts of Isaiah Berlin, John Rawls and John Stuart Mill. I came to abhor the philosophies they railed against, namely those ideologies that would sacrifice privacy and liberty in the name of a greater good. I was drawn to liberalism because it says there is something sacrosanct about the individual: that we will progress as a society if we trust individuals to use their talents and creativity, rather than empowering the state to dictate what is good for them.

The optimism of liberalism appealed to me, too. Growing up in the 1970s and 1980s, my generation was browbeaten by domestic politics in Britain. I have vague memories of the Winter of Discontent: of blackouts, candles hurriedly lit around the house, and pictures on the TV of rubbish piling up in the streets. The news bulletins were dominated by two deeply unappealing protagonists: the angry political machine of the Labour Party and trade-union bosses; and the unfeeling response from Margaret Thatcher and rows of grey-suited ministers from the Conservative Party.

Labour seemed like a party of angry men – and they were almost always men – who cared more about themselves than about the collateral damage they caused to people's everyday lives. You can hear faint echoes of Labour's Militant movement in the language of some of its leaders now: invariably talking at you, rather than to you. Theirs is a world divided into 'us' and 'them'. You are either with us or against us. A comrade or a sellout. Every utterance is shot through with grim-faced certainty about how society must be ordered. That sort of Labour politics is progressive only in the strictest sense that it believes in the progress of society by challenging the status quo. But it is progress according to a fixed blueprint, defined from the top down, by politicians who think they know best.

When Tony Blair came along, I felt optimism and relief. I was chuffed to bits to see the back of the Conservatives, but even then I didn't vote for Labour. Blair was youthful and exciting, but the Labour Party was still a machine. Despite its shiny new gloss, it was still propelled by the same vested interests in the trade unions. Blair had a positive, forward-looking agenda, which was a welcome change after nearly two decades of increasingly inward-looking Conservative rule. But back in 1997, New Labour showed little interest in the genuine empowerment of communities. It still believed that good governments did good things to people, rather than empowering them to do good things for themselves.

As New Labour's term progressed and I became involved in frontline politics, first as an MEP and later as an MP and the Lib Dems' Home Affairs spokesperson, the worst side of New Labour's disregard for civil liberties became increasingly apparent. The glee with which John Reid struck a series of snarling, tougher-than-tough poses during his time as Home Secretary even had the effect of driving the Conservatives and the Liberal Democrats into the same corner in defence of civil liberties – unwittingly forging one of the early bonds that kept the later coalition together. For all New Labour's modernising, reforming zeal, it still treated people as numbers to be counted and organised, rather than as individuals to be encouraged to flourish.

Unlike many older Liberal Democrats, I didn't live and breathe the turmoil of the Labour Party in the 1970s, the SDP breakaway and the merger with the Liberal Party. Working in Brussels in the 1990s, I was also untouched by the hopes and fears inspired by the discussions between Tony Blair and Paddy Ashdown about a possible coalition prior to Blair's 1997 landslide. The potential realignment of the centre-left was not the great debate of my political life, in the way it was for Roy Jenkins, Paddy Ashdown and many others in the party. My political journey, and that of most of my generation of Lib Dems, reinforced the view that while the Conservatives were our natural opponents, the Labour Party were illiberal opponents, too. I saw a position of equidistance between the two big parties as an authentic standpoint, not just as electoral positioning. I believed in electoral reform as a means of unlocking real pluralism in British politics, not just as the enabler of a permanent Lib–Lab alliance.

The biggest decision of my political life was to lead my party into government in a coalition with our erstwhile enemies, the Conservatives. For many who had held out hope of a progressive alliance, it was a devastating blow. For others who simply felt far more affinity with Labour than with the Conservatives, it felt wrong. To me, it was neither of those things.

When I became leader of the Liberal Democrats in December 2007, I didn't expect us to have the opportunity to go straight into power at the next election. I was ambitious for the party and hoped to take us into government, but I imagined it would take two elections to do that. My focus for the 2010 election was on building up a bridgehead: increasing our number of seats and positioning ourselves as a credible force that would be ready to assume power as part of a coalition in a few years' time. Over two elections I hoped that, with a bit of luck, we could even double our number of seats, putting us in an even stronger position from which to become a partner in government.

The political circumstances at the end of 2007 were quite different from those of even a few months later. The financial crash had not yet happened. The Conservatives were not talking the language of austerity, but were instead describing how they would 'share the proceeds of growth'. Cameron was a 'compassionate conservative', hugging huskies and hoodies. That autumn Gordon Brown had considered calling a general election but hesitated, and his authority had started its long decline as a result. When the banks collapsed the following year, it reinforced the sense that Brown and Labour were on their way out and the Tories were on the way in. I felt that our electoral opportunity would come from taking advantage of Labour's unpopularity, while fighting a rearguard action against the Conservatives in the seats where they were our chief opponents, primarily in southern England.

I became especially focused on winning Labour seats in the North, in places such as Sheffield Central, the only other winnable seat in Sheffield, where my friend and ex-leader of the city council, Paul (now Lord) Scriven, was our candidate. Over many years, the Lib Dems had become the only real opposition to Labour in their urban northern heartlands, where Thatcher's legacy had destroyed the Tories' credibility. I held out hopes that we could gain as many as a dozen seats in big northern towns and cities. Of course, I didn't rule out the possibility of a hung parliament, but in 2009 when I asked Danny Alexander, David Laws, Chris Huhne and Andrew Stunell to prepare for possible coalition negotiations, I expected it would remain a paper exercise.

It has been assumed by many commentators that the mood amongst Liberal Democrats, as the results of the general election on 6 May 2010 came in, must have been one of euphoria. After all, we received the largest number of votes in the party's history: 6.8 million – 800,000 more than the high-watermark election of 2005. Yet my mood was anything but euphoric. Not only had we lost five seats overall, thanks to the perversities of the electoral system, but of the twelve northern seats we had hoped to take from Labour, we had won just two: Burnley and Redcar. Paul Scriven fell short in Sheffield Central by an agonising 165 votes. I was utterly deflated. I remember slumping in a fairly exhausted state, in the early hours of the morning, with Miriam in an upstairs balcony at Ponds Forge, the sports centre in Sheffield where my count was taking place. When we got on the train to London shortly after 7 a.m. with media helicopters buzzing overhead as they televised the progress of the train southwards, I wasn't caught up in the slightest by the excitement of possible coalition talks. Rather, I felt we had taken two steps forward and one step back. We certainly had less leverage than I had hoped we would, given the excitement at our prospects in the run-up to election day.

When I arrived at the party's Westminster HQ in Cowley Street, I was greeted by a crowd of tired party staff, who put on their bravest faces in order to cheer my arrival. In front of dozens of photographers and TV cameras, I insisted that we would do what I had said we would do throughout the campaign: allow the party that had won the most votes, and the most seats, to have the first go at trying to form a government. Now that the results were coming in, it was clear that meant the Conservatives, although I had no idea whether they would make any sort of serious approach to us.

Over the course of the next five days, I spoke to both David Cameron and Gordon Brown a number of times. My negotiating team met first with their Conservative counterparts, as we had said they would, but when the talks dragged on, we began parallel talks with the Labour Party, as demanded by many MPs in our parliamentary party. At that stage, I was not thinking about the outcome in terms of some grand realignment of the centre-left. For me, the decision was about whether or not it would be possible to form a government at all. I was aware that some senior Lib Dems who had long associations with colleagues in the Labour Party – Vince Cable with Gordon Brown; Paddy Ashdown with Tony Blair and Andrew Adonis – were in contact with them, in the hope that something could be agreed.

I had repeated conversations with Paddy throughout the negotiations, but any chance of governing with Labour seemed to be based on wishful thinking, rather than evidence that it could actually work. It speaks volumes about his loyalty and courage that in the end Paddy declared himself in favour of the coalition deal with the Conservatives in the final, decisive meeting of Lib Dem MPs and peers. He had devoted so much of his energy over many years to forging a new alliance between Labour and the Lib Dems, so the agreement with the Conservatives went against everything he had striven for. Yet he saw it was the only sensible outcome to the predicament in which we found ourselves. He told the meeting that at first he was so unhappy at the prospect of governing with the Conservatives that he had considered departing from the political stage, to spend more time in his garden and with his grandchildren, but that he had then read the draft Coalition Agreement and concluded: 'I have to say that it is magnificent. Amazing. Fuck it! How can I stay out of this fight? You know that I cannot resist a battle, not least in the company of friends.'

Moreover, throughout the negotiations it was clear that the Conservatives were prepared to bend to many of our demands and create a programme for government that contained the bulk of our own policies – three-quarters of our manifesto made it in – while shedding their more undesirable or unworkable ones, such as the cap on immigration and the Inheritance Tax cut for millionaires. Indeed, the Conservatives ditched both, without the slightest complaint. And it is worth remembering that, at the time, David Cameron was a Conservative leader who claimed to be a moderate centrist, pro-green and determined not to spend his time in office 'banging on about Europe'.

In the end, as we saw in the previous chapter, a coalition of any other sort was simply unworkable. With Labour having demonstrably 'lost' the election, a deal with Cameron's

Tories proved more palatable to the Liberal Democrat Party than an attempt to prop up Labour and reintroduce a Labour PM through the back door of Downing Street. The final decision, taken by thousands of Liberal Democrat members in Birmingham on Sunday 16 May 2010 to endorse or reject the coalition, was, in the end, an overwhelming vote in favour of entering into government.

There was one further significant consideration in choosing to enter coalition with the Conservatives: I was convinced that one of the principal reasons why people hadn't voted for us, in the numbers we had anticipated, was that we lacked credibility as a serious party of government. The election had taken place in unusually febrile circumstances. The eurozone crisis was a gathering storm, and people were anxious. In the days running up to polling day, images of riots on the streets of Athens were being beamed into British living rooms. As Greece slipped into chaos, the markets started turning their attention to the UK, wondering if we would be the next domino to fall. With the country in such a predicament, many people simply felt they couldn't afford to take a flutter on a third party that had been out of power for generations, however much they liked what they heard from us during the campaign. It was as if we were a feel-good option, a party to vote for when there was little at stake, but not one for serious times, when safety came first. That was why the shift away from us happened at the very end of the campaign: when people came to make up their minds, their pencils hovering over the proverbial ballot paper, many of them chose in the end to stick with what they knew. If we were ever to counter this – so my argument ran – and if we were ever to become a credible party of government, then we would need to show that we could govern in tough times, and finally put an end to the perception of us as a nice but ineffectual party of opposition. That, to me and the vast majority of my colleagues, was a more important consideration than whether we were supporting or shunning the Jenkinsite approach to centre-left realignment.

So that was our rationale at the time. I stand by the decision I took – and that the Liberal Democrats agreed collectively – and the reasons we came to the conclusions we did. But the disastrous result of the subsequent election five years later has rightly provoked a lot of soul-searching. In view of the drubbing we received in 2015, was it a mistake, after all, to have entered into coalition with the Conservatives in 2010?

For the country, absolutely not. I am more convinced than ever that providing the stable government necessary at a time of great economic turbulence was the right thing to do. In 2010, ours could have been the next national economic crisis in Europe, after the firestorms in Greece, Spain and Portugal. Of course the circumstances in each of these countries were quite different – and the fictional data upon which Greece's fiscal position had been falsely organised had no parallel in Britain. Conversely, the British economy was in many respects more, not less, vulnerable than other European economies because of our oversized banking sector, which was grossly over-leveraged and riddled with 'toxic debt'. I will never forget an official in Whitehall calmly explaining to me, shortly after I entered office, that the total liabilities of the British banking system in 2010 were close to five times the size of the whole British economy. The blood drained from my face as I realised that the slightest mistake, while defusing this ticking time-bomb, could upend the country and force us to go to the IMF with a begging bowl to bail us out of our troubles. What Britain needed, and what other European countries desperately lacked, was stability: a government that people at home and abroad could trust to do what was necessary to turn the economy around. And what we achieved was remarkable. Not only did we pull Britain back from the brink, but we also turned it into the fastest-growing economy in the G7, with more people in work than ever before – a record now carelessly cast aside by David Cameron's referendum on our membership of the EU and the resulting economic turmoil.

For the Liberal Democrats, though, there are very few straws to clutch at. We lost the support of millions of voters, many of whom felt we should not even have considered governing with the Conservative Party in the first place. But what about the effect on progressive politics more widely? Did the entry of the Liberal Democrats into coalition with the Conservatives in 2010 set back the wider fortunes of the centre-left in Britain, as has been claimed? Did that decision stymie Roy Jenkins's dream of a centre-left hegemony for good?

It seems incontrovertible to me that a progressive 'rainbow coalition' could never have worked, and indeed a chaotic and unstable government could have caused much deeper damage to the centre-left (not to mention the economy) than our coalition. It also seems clear to me that a Conservative minority government would have led inevitably to a second election in late 2010 or 2011, which would have resulted most probably in a Conservative majority government; in purely electoral terms, then, perhaps we would simply have reached our much-diminished state four and a half years sooner. More widely, though, it seems to me perverse to suggest that the present woes of the centre-left in Britain – in Labour as well as the Lib Dems – are all the fault of that decision to form a coalition in 2010.

For a start, Labour's woes are of its own making. Labour reacted in completely the wrong way to its defeat in 2010. Instead of taking a step back, coming to an honest assessment of why they lost, and slowly but surely building a new and coherent vision for the future, Labour opted instead for bitter tribalism. They threw angry and outlandish accusations at the Lib Dems, wallowing in a familiar conceit of the British left that a betrayal somewhere, by someone else, is the reason for their powerlessness, while doing nothing to win back the trust of voters who feared they were a risk to the economy. Labour went for several years without any meaningful policy positions – Ed Miliband's leadership was a masterclass in indecision – a deliberate tactic to ward off any internal dispute over the party's direction. Most tellingly of all, they allowed genuine opportunities for long-term progressive change to be squandered in favour of short-term tactical victories. When it came to the Alternative Vote, reform of party funding and democratising the House of Lords – all of which the Labour Party formally supported – they pursued little tactical victories rather than big reform. A party with a keener sense of the long-term needs of the centre-left would have recognised that all three measures could have weakened the Conservative grip on the levers of power for ever.

But of course the threat to progressive politics is no longer simply English Conservatism. Nationalism and populism – boosted by the EU referendum – are eating into its heartlands, undermining the very idea of a 'progressive majority' again being capable of wresting control of power nationally. Labour has been shorn of its Scottish heartlands by nationalist separatists, while the English nationalists of UKIP threaten its grip on its traditional white working-class base. It's unclear how Labour might ever gain another majority. With their opposition fracturing, the Conservatives are contemplating majority victories in 2020 and beyond, based on a new pendulum in British politics: no longer the pendulum of left vs right, but that of Scottish nationalism north of the border vs English Conservatism south of the border.

There is a very real prospect that we may be entering into a new pattern of British politics, where the fate of the centre-left is of marginal relevance compared to the curious interdependence of the SNP and the Conservatives. In the same way that Labour and the Conservatives have traditionally needed each other to define themselves, so the SNP and the Conservative Party now rely on each other to give their parties identity and purpose. Unlike the old Labour/Conservative rivalry, however, both the SNP and the Conservatives are content to allow the other to dominate in their respective domains of Holyrood and Westminster. It is an unholy political marriage of convenience.

Whatever one's political persuasion, it is self-evidently unhealthy to have a single party ruling the roost in Westminster without any meaningful challenge. Untrammelled power is bad for democracy. Complacent government is bad for society. The argument made by some Conservatives, in the wake of David Cameron's resignation, that only Conservative Party MPs should have the right to hand-pick the next Prime Minister of our country without the say-so of the electorate, even though a Brexit government is entirely different from the government elected in May 2015, shows the extent of their hubris.

In the wake of the EU referendum, the task for progressives of every stripe is simple: work together. We must put our differences aside and assemble a progressive challenge to the Conservatives. It means that we have to behave in a less tribal way. It means we need to be civil to one another. And it means we have to stop making the 'best' the enemy of the 'good', and start supporting each other's efforts to hold the government to account.

Prior to the referendum, the omens were not entirely promising. In October 2015, for example, the Conservatives tried to force massive cuts to Working Tax Credits (which effectively boost the incomes of those on low incomes) through the House of Lords, using a parliamentary procedure called a 'statutory instrument' – a tool for updating existing legislation. The Lords, where the government does not have a majority as it does in the Commons, were having none of it. A number of amendments were tabled, including one by a Labour peer that asked George Osborne to think again and make some changes to his plans; and another, melodramatically known as a 'fatal motion', by a Liberal Democrat peer that would have killed off the proposal entirely. The Lib Dems supported the Labour motion, which passed, but Labour did not support the Lib Dem motion, so it failed. Faced with the opportunity to kill off George Osborne's cuts to Working Tax Credits, Labour chose not to, because of their animosity towards the Liberal Democrats. This is the sort of petty tribalism that must be overcome, if progressives are to provide a serious challenge to the Conservative Government.

The referendum has changed everything. Even without the seismic decision to quit the EU, Britain is facing some significant dilemmas in the coming decades: how to reconfigure our economy to create sustainable growth while radically reducing carbon emissions; how to adapt our Health Service and social-care systems to the needs of an ageing society; how to increase social mobility so that the life chances of our children are not set by the circumstances of their birth; how to balance freedom and security in the Internet age; how to create a political system fit for the modern era. These are big issues that need big solutions. But they are all now overshadowed by the overarching dilemma of how Britain – a modern, open economy – can find its feet in the globalised world bereft of its economic and geostrategic anchor within Europe.

The responses in the immediate aftermath of the referendum from Michael Gove, Boris Johnson, Daniel Hannan and other Brexit Conservatives to the victory they secured suggested that they didn't really believe in many of the blandishments with which they seduced the electorate, particularly on immigration; and that they had no idea how to secure a new deal with the EU other than a vague, and naive, hope that the UK should be granted full access to EU markets without shouldering any of the obligations or responsibilities of the EU Single Market. So there is an overwhelming need for a new, progressive alliance – stretching from the Liberal Democrats, centrist Labour figures, perhaps even the SNP and some Greens, to liberal Conservatives appalled by the reverse takeover of their party by hard-line Eurosceptics – to address the intense social and cultural anxieties that propelled voters to back Brexit, while securing the best deal for the UK in Europe and the wider world.

There is another, inescapable conclusion to be drawn from the result of the EU referendum, which should also drive different parties towards a broader progressive alliance: the divisions in the UK are no longer reflected in the divisions between political parties. The referendum revealed a country divided between those – the young, the educated, the metropolitan, black and minority ethnic communities – who feel comfortable with the gyrations of a modern, globalised economy and a diverse society and those – older, with fewer skills and qualifications, especially white working-class voters in the North and the Midlands – who do not. This division bears almost no relation to the traditional left–right axis by which Westminster parties are traditionally organised.

So, to the extent that a political realignment is either likely or desirable in the aftermath of the EU referendum, it is not a realignment that can follow Roy Jenkins's blueprint, since his approach was based on a political landscape that no longer exists. Today, each of the major parties is itself a coalition of different ideologies and interests. The Labour Party contains hard-left socialists, Scandinavian-style social democrats, trade unionists, ban-the-bomb CND-ers, left-of-centre liberal academics, and many subsets of each. The Conservative Party houses diehard Thatcherites, landed gentry, cosmopolitan economic liberals, market-town Middle Englanders, UKIP-lite anti-Europeans, shrink-the-state libertarians and a host of other curiosities. The Liberal Democrats embrace a full ideological spectrum, from classical, free-market liberals at one end to interventionist social democrats at the other, while providing a home for secular humanists and nonconformist Christians, anti-war protesters and liberal interventionists, community-minded pothole-fixers and intellectual radicals. What congealed these various factions into parties for most of the post-war period was an underlying belief in an ideological spectrum that went from right to left, from private to public, from low tax to high tax, from the bosses to the workers, from a belief in the market to a faith in the state. One's location on this spectrum was the crucial, if not sole, determining factor in party allegiances. And in an electoral system where MPs only win by appealing to a broad range of local opinion within their constituencies, the expansive breadth of each mainstream party has made sense as a way of attracting the maximum number of voters. The tensions within each party, as well as the personalities that champion the different strands within them, may have meant that political parties have always been restless coalitions, but the electoral advantage of maintaining broad political churches has always outweighed the disadvantages of internal fractiousness.

Over the last two decades or so, however, something profound has happened to British society that is undermining the whole culture of political parties. The old left–right divide has diminished in significance, a relic of a twentieth-century ideological battle between capitalism and communism that started to crumble the day the Berlin Wall fell, and which now lies buried beneath the political rubble of the EU referendum itself.

Today, the old arguments of left versus right sound like distant echoes from a bygone age. In their place are complex and difficult debates between liberal and authoritarian models of governance, for which we are still struggling to find a clear language. Do we celebrate the chaotic freedom of the digital age or do we try to control it? Do we embrace the globalised world of open markets, free information and free movement or do we retreat from it? Do we accept an open, interconnected society with all its challenges and opportunities or do we try to restrict it, throwing up new borders, shunning new arrivals and keeping a close eye on every movement and utterance made by our citizens? The EU referendum threw all these questions and more up in the air – without, as yet, providing a clear answer as to what we should do about them. That is now the challenge for progressive parties of all stripes.

One of the most profound changes affecting domestic politics in recent years is the growing gap between our lives as consumers and our lives as citizens. We can buy anything we want, from anywhere in the world, at the click of a button, no longer limited by the shelf space on our high-street shops or the output of our local industries. Instead of a handful of television channels and mass-market newspapers, we now get our information from a multitude of different sources, curated by the idiosyncratic interests of our self-selecting networks on Twitter and Facebook, creating millions of self-contained online echo-chambers. As a result, we now live in our own bubbles, kings and queens of our own castles, our experiences of society and the world tailored to our needs and tastes, with a specificity previously unheard of in human history. And yet our political choices haven't changed. Trapped in ideological glasshouses that were built in a previous era, politicians speak a language of party affiliation that appears increasingly arcane in today's world.

One symptom of the malaise that political parties face is the long-term decline in party membership. In 1953 the Conservative Party had a reported membership of 2.8 million, while Labour claimed to have more than one million members. By the summer of 2015, the Conservatives had dwindled to fewer than 150,000 members and Labour to around 270,000. This does not mean that people aren't joining mass-membership organisations: the National Trust, for example, has more than four million members, and rising. And admittedly, in the last couple of years, two parties have bucked the trend: the SNP and the Labour Party. But what do they have in common? They have attracted people to a specific cause, a narrow mission, rather than a wider ideological franchise, a broad church. SNP membership quadrupled to more than 110,000 in the months after the case for Scottish independence was defeated at the referendum. The surge in Labour's membership over the course of its 2015 leadership contest – by 150,000 full members and a further 260,000 new associate members, who paid £3 for their right to vote in the election – was undoubtedly in large part caused by a wave of enthusiasm for Jeremy Corbyn's candidacy and his promise of a return to undiluted socialism after two decades of New Labour centrism. But undiluted socialism was only ever one element of the broad Labour coalition. As the new wave of grass-roots Labourites reassert a desire for ideological purity, a generation or more of progressive centrists have suddenly been alienated.

While Labour is struggling to work out whether it is still a broad church or a narrow, left-wing ideological sect, the Conservatives are more or less giving up on being a mass-membership party at all. At election time the Conservatives now operate as a highly sophisticated centralised messaging machine, delivering their appeal to voters directly from Conservative HQ through the letter boxes and Facebook timelines of millions of British citizens. Much as the ageing Conservative Party membership never had, or appeared to seek, much say in the policies of the party, so now they are largely irrelevant to the conduct of election campaigns. The Conservatives have become, to all intents and purposes, a virtual, ersatz political party run according to the whims of their leaders and the shifting tactics of their well-paid campaign consultants.

Another symptom of the decline of political parties is the increasingly presidential style of British politics. While fewer people now identify with or put their trust in the major political parties, many now base their allegiances instead on the personalities of those who lead them. I initially rose to national prominence in Britain's first-ever televised leaders' debate. In an electoral system where people vote for specific local candidates to represent them in Parliament, a televised debate between party leaders whose names do not even appear on the ballot paper might seem a little odd, but in 2010 the British public embraced the format enthusiastically: millions tuned in.

In many ways the hyper-personalisation of politics is well suited to modern consumerism, allowing people's unanchored allegiances to be transferred from one standard-bearer to the next. In Germany in recent years, the success of the governing Christian Democrats has relied heavily on the matriarchal appeal of Angela Merkel. In France's presidential system, political parties have long been subservient to the cult of the strong leader, since the days of General de Gaulle. American presidential politics is increasingly characterised by the rise of outsiders like Donald Trump, Ted Cruz, Ben Carson and Bernie Sanders, who play on a longing for individual authenticity, compared to the identikit conformism of mainstream party figures.

A further challenge to traditional political parties is the rise of non-partisan single-issue organisations. Campaign groups like 38 Degrees and change.org have harnessed online technology to become hugely effective lobbying operations, sharing petitions and calls to action on social media, and mobilising people to email their MPs in large numbers. It is an electronic form of direct democracy that kills stone-dead the notion that people are no longer engaged with politics. They are. It's just that they increasingly view political parties as part of the problem, not the solution.

Ultimately, the trend is clear: political parties, at least in the form that we have come to understand them, are increasingly out of kilter with the way people make their choices. As the gap between the two has widened, faith in politics, parties and politicians has dissipated. With the fixed points of the political order critically undermined, a volatile and unpredictable mood has taken hold. Jenkins-style realignment, by contrast, was an answer to a twentieth-century politics dominated by two giant parties of the left and the right and a significantly smaller liberal bloc. But that straightforward political line-up has disappeared for good, to be replaced by a more fragmented array of choices. When I stood onstage for the first leaders' debate of the 2015 election campaign, it wasn't just with the leaders of the Labour Party and the Conservatives; it was with the leaders of the Green Party, the SNP, UKIP and Plaid Cymru, too. It was an accurate depiction of a new, more plural politics that has only temporarily been obscured by the conventional one-party government that ensued.

In the short term, there are two significant groups of UK-wide progressives in Westminster with something in common: Labour moderates who reject the backward-looking ideology of Jeremy Corbyn's wing of the party; and Lib Dems who have lost influence in Parliament. In a sense, the latter's task is simple: rebuild. For Labour moderates, the challenge is existential: it looks highly unlikely that Labour can win a majority again in Westminster as long as nationalism remains so dominant in Scotland, and Conservatives so dominant in England. If Labour loses heavily at the next general election, its moderates could react by saying, 'I told you so', hoping that the internal party pendulum will swing back their way once the Corbyn-esque brand of idealistic socialism has been tested to destruction at the ballot box. Some moderate Labour figures believe, as I have heard from them myself, that they simply need to bide their time and wait for another great figure to come along and lead them out of the desert, in the way Blair did in the 1990s. Their assumption is that nothing has changed that can't be fixed by a charismatic leader. But messianic leadership of a broken tribe is generally a religious phenomenon, not a reliable political event. A new leader, whatever his or her gifts, will not be able to alter the fact that Labour's business model doesn't work in the deeply fragmented politics of Britain today.

In the end, there is little alternative to an honest form of pluralism that allows progressive parties to work together, but without diminishing their identities: a progressive alliance of parties able to provide the country with the leadership and stability it so desperately needs and will not receive from a riven Conservative Party. If need be, this could even take the form of a Government of National Unity. Such a government could step in, exceptionally, to help steer the country through the turbulent aftershocks of the EU referendum, which will continue to reverberate for years to come, both at home and in Europe more widely. Either way, the single most potent weapon to entrench that honest pluralism, foster that cross-party cooperation, while breaking the stranglehold that the Conservatives have on the levers of power, is electoral reform. Proportional representation would also pull at the deep contradictions within the Conservative Party, exposing the fault line that separates those Conservatives who believe in a modern, liberal state and those who long to turn the clock back to the certainties of the past.

In the long run, the only strategic answer for the Labour Party is to take the cork out of the bottle: to advocate electoral reform and embrace rather than shun the politics of plurality. One way or another, Conservative dominance at Westminster will come to an end. If, at that moment, every non-Conservative party were ready to work together to introduce a fairer voting system, then the opportunity for irrevocable progressive change would be great. And the British people would finally have the sort of genuine choice they clearly want, freed from the stifling and false choices presented by the old party blocs of today.

While I would certainly be happy to see progressive parties working together in an alliance or even a Government of National Unity, I still baulk at the idea that they must do so in some sort of permanent new composite arrangement. I fervently believe in diversity, choice and pluralism in politics. Big, self-serving blocs seem as undesirable in politics as they are in business. The little guy, the voter, the consumer, always gets taken for granted. So it should be the system that should be adapted to reflect changing public opinion – public opinion shouldn't be forced to adapt to fit into the system. After all, the whole point of democracy is putting people – not politicians – in charge.

These huge changes in our political culture and system cannot, of course, be fully understood without also understanding the single most powerful catalyst that has forced them to the surface in the first place: the anguished, torturous debate about the United Kingdom's place in Europe.

CHAPTER 8

History, Grievance and Psychodrama

My Dutch great-grandfather, Willem Van Dorp, was a chemist by training, a Francophile by taste and, a little eccentrically, a lover of circuses. He had stayed in the Netherlands during the war, unlike his daughter and granddaughters. While they were interned in a Japanese prisoner-of-war camp in Indonesia, he had endured the humiliation of Nazi occupation at home. In the summers immediately after the war, he would often take my mother on driving holidays across France in his clunky old Citroën. My mother described how, if ever he found himself behind a German car, he would always overtake it, as a matter of principle, refusing point-blank to sit patiently behind a German, even if they were on a hairpin bend halfway up a mountain.

Yet, like many citizens of the six founding member states, he saw the European Community as a means of moving on, of reconciliation, a triumph of peace over war – a turning of the page on an ugly and violent past. And, as my mother also pointed out, one of his closest friends was a German circus impresario who would bring his family circus to Amsterdam every year.

Similarly, for citizens of many southern member states – Spain, Portugal and Greece – European integration represented the triumph of democracy over fascism. A quarter of a century ago, when I first met one of Miriam's uncles, a rugged, weather-worn sugar-beet farmer from the vast plains of central Spain, I vividly remember seeing his chest puff up with pride as he talked about Spain joining the European Community. For him, joining the European project meant that Spain had arrived. It had a seat at the top table. Fascism and conflict were firmly condemned to the past – with its entry into the EC, Spain could hold its head up high as a modern, stable democracy.

The reactions of Miriam's uncle and my great-grandfather were typical of millions of people across the continent – positive, if visceral, emotional responses derived from a mixture of relief and pride in their countries' newfound peace and stability.

One of the reasons why the British political and media establishment consistently misunderstands developments in the rest of Europe is that it misunderstands this powerful emotional commitment to European integration itself. Roy Jenkins famously described how, as Chancellor, he asked officials in the early 1970s to prepare a speech that he wanted to deliver on the pros and cons of monetary union in the European Community. He was told there were no officials in the Treasury who could help, as none had sufficient knowledge of European economic affairs.

At the height of the eurozone crisis early in the last parliament, I attended a meeting with the Chancellor, the then Governor of the Bank of England, Mervyn King, and senior Treasury officials in George Osborne's oak-panelled official dining room in Number 11. It was asserted by some of those present that the eurozone would collapse in a matter of months, and that the only remedy for countries such as Greece and Spain was a temporary suspension of their membership of the single currency for at least ten years. In subsequent discussions around the Cabinet table, there was barely disguised glee amongst senior Conservative ministers as they breezily asserted that the eurozone would soon disintegrate because it was such a misguided project. I pointed out at the time that – regardless of the fiscal and monetary straitjacket that some weaker members of the eurozone found themselves in – Britain should not underestimate how much sacrifice would be made to sustain a currency union that had become integral to those countries' modern identities. Oddly, those Eurosceptics who condemn the eurozone because of its political motivations often miss the logical consequence of their own diagnosis: precisely because so much political effort has been vested in it, member governments are hardly going to give it up without a fight.

In many ways, the lofty disdain that characterises discussions in Whitehall today about the eurozone finds its origins in the attitude that Britain took to European integration in the immediate aftermath of the Second World War. When Winston Churchill addressed what he described as the 'tragedy of Europe' in Zurich, little more than a year after VE Day, he laid down a marker for pan-European cooperation, saying:

> But for the fact that the great Republic across the Atlantic Ocean has at length realised that the ruin or enslavement of Europe would involve their own fate as well, and has stretched out hands of succour and guidance, the Dark Ages would have returned in all their cruelty and squalor. They may still return. Yet all the while there is a remedy which, if it were generally and spontaneously adopted, would as if by a miracle transform the whole scene, and would in a few years make all Europe, or the greater part of it, as free and as happy as Switzerland is today. What is this sovereign remedy? It is to re-create the European Family, or as much of it as we can, and provide it with a structure under which it can dwell in peace, in safety and in freedom. We must build a kind of United States of Europe.

It was typical Churchill: powerful, colourful and bombastic prose designed to raise the sights of his audience towards a distant horizon. But this vision of a united Europe was missing one crucial ingredient. The United Kingdom. 'We British have our own Commonwealth of Nations,' he was quick to point out, before getting to his real point:

> In all this urgent work, France and Germany must take the lead together. Great Britain, the British Commonwealth of Nations, mighty America, and I trust Soviet Russia – for then indeed all would be well – must be the friends and sponsors of the new Europe and must champion its right to live and shine.

Friends and sponsors: in other words, happy to tell Europe to do as we say, but not do as we do.

That wasn't just the attitude of Churchill, but of the British establishment more generally towards European integration at its onset. We spent the 1950s standing on the sidelines watching the countries of Western Europe get on with it. When the pivotal Messina summit came in 1955 to discuss the formation of the Common Market, our position was neatly summed up by the Cabinet Office's Mutual Aid Committee, which reported that 'on the whole the establishment of a European Common Market would be bad for the United Kingdom and if possible should be frustrated. But if it came into being with us outside it we should pay an increasing price commercially. But even this would not outweigh the political objections to joining.' Those political objections were then listed, including the weakening of our relationship with the Commonwealth; that the Common Market would be counter to our 'worldwide' economic and political interests; it would lead to further integration; and it would remove our ability to protect British industry from European competition – objections that are eerily similar to the arguments put forward by those who supported Britain's exit from the EU in the recent referendum.

By the early 1960s, however, we had changed our tune entirely. In his 1946 speech, Churchill had called for France to recover its 'moral leadership' and become 'spiritually great'. By 1963 it was France, in the form of the imperious Charles de Gaulle, who was saying '*Non!*' to Britain, as we asked to join the six nations of the fledgling Common Market that we had snubbed a few years earlier. At a dramatic press conference in Paris on 14 January 1963 – an extraordinary moment of political theatre that all students of politics should watch – De Gaulle was asked why France opposed British entry. He responded by turning Churchill's preference for the Commonwealth against us:

> England in effect is insular, she is maritime, she is linked through her exchanges, her markets, her supply lines to the most diverse and often the most distant countries; she pursues essentially industrial and commercial activities, and only slight agricultural ones. She has in all her doings very marked and very original habits and traditions ... [T]he question ... [is] whether Great Britain can now place herself like the Continent and with it inside a tariff which is genuinely common, to renounce all Commonwealth preferences, to cease any pretence that her agriculture be privileged, and, more than that, to treat her engagements with other countries of the free trade area as null and void – that question is the whole question.

Britain and Europe, then, were star-cross'd lovers. We had rejected them once – and when we decided we really wanted to join them all along, they spurned us. It would take another decade until we finally got our wish to join the European Community.

What this illustrates is not only how ambivalent we were towards European integration from the outset, but also the feelings of deflation and defeat that led to the eventual decision to join. Unlike the attitude of the other member states, our decision to enter the European Community was no uplifting step towards a stronger national identity, it did not herald the dawning of a new era. For us, instead, joining the European project was an acknowledgement of the end of empire, greeted with a sigh, a shrug of the shoulders and a weary acceptance that 'If you can't beat them, join them.' It was the confirmation of our relative decline in the immediate post-war period, a pragmatic pounds-and-pence calculation of our new status in the world.

There was little poetry in the decision to remain within the EC in the referendum in 1975, either – the debate on the pros and cons was conducted as if the nation were comparing prices in a local grocery store; a cost-and-benefit analysis, little more. And so it has remained: a prosaic, hard-headed calculation of where our national interest lies in a turbulent world, rather than any poetic attachment to our European kith and kin. Four decades later, for better or worse, our national attitude towards membership of the EU is, as it always has been, pragmatic and lightly held, compared to the strong emotional ties of many of our fellow Europeans.

The ambivalence that lurked within the decision to join the EC more than four decades ago still colours our attitude to Europe today. That is why the pull of populist arguments against membership of the EU, of self-determination and hoisting the Union Jack, is so strong. They are arguments that draw on emotion – nostalgia for empire, pride in the English-speaking world, a yearning to 'take back control' – which British pro-Europeans struggle to match. It's significantly less uplifting to admit that we have to pool our loose change with the French and the Germans instead.

The stilted, listless campaign messages from David Cameron and George Osborne in the EU referendum – remorselessly bombarding an ever-more-browbeaten public with a volley of statistics – was both in keeping with the history of British debates about Europe and woefully inadequate in the face of the powerful, emotive messages from the Brexit campaign. On the day that George Osborne revealed his threat to impose a budget of £30bn of cuts and taxes if the country voted for Brexit, I sent David Cameron an email urging him to inject a stronger emotional tone into the Remain campaign during its final week. George Osborne was doing what he does best – crafting an aggressive, tricksy message for which he was accustomed to receiving uncritical acclaim from the right-wing press. But, as I pointed out to Cameron, such a message fell on fallow ground when competing with the emotional simplicity of Brexit's refrain, 'Take Back Control', which was enjoying the full-throated backing of the *Sun*, *Daily Mail* and others. I had seen George Osborne at work in campaigns before – Danny Alexander and I had restrained him from deploying aggressive, point-scoring messages in the Scottish referendum campaign in 2014 – and I was worried that the battle for people's hearts was being lost. I suggested to Cameron that an equally simple but more rousing refrain – 'Keep Britain Safe' (from recession, from the break-up of the UK, from climate change, from cross-border crime, et cetera) – should be deployed in return. He responded that he was more inclined to stick with their appeal to level-headed caution: 'Don't Risk It'. I did not pursue it further – not least because I believed, at the time, that the Remain camp would still win. In the end, of course, the heart won out over the head – not least because Britain's heart, when it comes to the EU, has never fully been in it in the first place.

Of course, any summary description of Britain's historical attitude towards European integration can quickly subside into caricature: we were not the only country to feel a sense of relative decline propelling us towards membership of the EC; Denmark (which joined the same day we did), Finland and most especially Sweden joined in large part because they realised that the generous Scandinavian welfare state could not be sustained in glorious isolation from the rest of Europe. Much of the Eurosceptic rhetoric in Scandinavia today is strikingly similar to that in Britain, hankering after a lost past, yearning for a return to Scandinavian exceptionalism. De Gaulle may have been right to underline Britain's unusual ties with America, our recent imperial reach and the vast trading links of a great maritime nation. But he deliberately exaggerated how particular they were to Britain, in order to justify his haughty veto of our entry into what was then a French-led club. In truth, founding member states like the

Netherlands share a very similar maritime and imperial past, as do more recent entrants into the EU such as Portugal.

Conversely, it would be just as easy to argue that other EU member states are more separated by history and outlook from the European mainstream than Britain is. Britain isn't alone in having a distinctive history. The whole Iberian peninsula, for instance, was largely untouched by the Second World War, immersed instead in its own internal strife. Spanish history was dominated for 700 years by Moorish occupation – as is still apparent in its cuisine, architecture and place names – which sets it apart from all the other major European powers. Britain, on the other hand, was intimately involved in the shifting sands of power within Europe over centuries – from the Spanish Succession and Seven Years War to the major conflicts of the twentieth century – invariably seeking to make sure that no single power dominated the continent. If the French or the Germans got the upper hand, Britain would intervene to restore the balance. Our job was not to lead Europe ourselves, but to ensure that no one else did. It is also fair to say that the emotional commitment to European integration felt so sharply by the generation of political leaders who had experienced the Second World War has given way to a more hard-headed, pragmatic attitude amongst their successors, not just here in Britain, but throughout Europe.

In other words, while I have no doubt that the psychological conditions in which Britain took the decision to join the EC more than forty years ago did set us apart, most especially from the war-ravaged countries of the mainland, there is not, as some would have us believe, something programmed into our DNA, as the inhabitants of an English-speaking island nation, that uniquely prevents us from taking decisions in common with our European neighbours. Indeed, the great successes of our past have often been achieved hand in hand with our neighbours, as much as through our own individual endeavour. If we acknowledge only a narrow version of our shared heritage, we misunderstand who we are – as the British National

Party comically revealed in 2009 when they published a leaflet attacking Polish immigration, which featured the image of a Spitfire, not realising that the plane belonged to the famous RAF 303 Squadron, made up of Polish airmen rescued from France before the Nazi occupation.

For my own part, I am immensely proud of the fusion of identities in my family, of being a European, but above all I am proud to be a British citizen: because Britain remains a country that brims with ingenuity. Our cultural impact far exceeds the sea-locked limits of our island home. We are a country with a pioneering spirit that leads the world in everything from computer games to wind power. We may not rule the waves any more, but we are still a world power of sorts, because we apply the confidence we have inherited from our history to the modern world of global culture and commerce, information technology and cutting-edge industry. This sort of patriotism – pride in being a self-confident, outward-looking, innovative nation – is strengthened, not weakened, by membership of the EU. Indeed, our very place at the centre of the 'English-speaking world' – the community of nations so regularly held up by Brexiteers as the natural alternative to our membership of the EU – will be jeopardised now that we are to leave. We carried more clout in Washington (as we did in Beijing, Brasilia and Mumbai, for that matter) precisely because we stood tall in our European back yard. We are world leaders in a global marketplace in large part because Europe enabled rather than thwarted it. Our relationship with Europe is not at odds with our national pride. It is a necessary ingredient *for* our national pride – and our departure from the EU will make us weaker, not stronger, in the affairs of the world.

Because there is another kind of national pride on the rise today: one based not on confidence but on fear; not on promoting our attitudes today but on protecting the inheritance of our past. To nationalists of this sort, Europe is a threat. Large-scale immigration is the flashpoint by which this fear is illuminated, a fear of having one's identity – one's customs, cultural practices, comforts, one's sense of home – threatened by changes beyond one's control. Whilst it may be true that the European Union is not the cause of the mass movement of people fleeing war and destitution in Syria, Iraq and Afghanistan, the sight of large numbers of desperate refugees flowing into a borderless Europe and the hopelessly chaotic response of European governments was bound to exacerbate the sense of powerlessness that fuels the politics of identity.

It is in this sense that the referendum represented a clash of two world views: one comfortable with internationalism, the other hankering for national identity; one reliant on the rationale of economic self-interest, the other drawing on a wellspring of popular anger at the status quo; one espousing the politics of reason and pragmatism, the other driven by the politics of grievance and anger. The fact that, in the end, the majority of British people voted to leave the EU does not mean that those strong feelings will somehow dissolve: until mainstream politicians are able to rediscover the ability to address their concerns, a significant proportion of the population will continue to be disenchanted with the current economic and political order. Indeed, the leaders of the Brexit movement have now placed themselves in a highly precarious position: having raised the expectation that leaving the EU is the answer to those concerns, they will now have to face the anger and frustration of millions of voters who will discover, in time, that there is no land of milk and honey awaiting us outside it.

Of course, the immediate reason for the referendum itself had a far more parochial source: the divided psyche of the Conservative Party. There is a deep and somewhat bizarre split in the Conservatives – a fault line between two starkly opposed parts of its identity. On the one hand, they are the defenders of home, hearth and heritage, the nuclear family, the King James Bible, village-fete Englishness and the absolute sovereignty of Parliament. On the other hand, they are free-market capitalists, admiring the great churn and innovation of private-sector dynamism and, crucially, sceptical that governments can ever 'buck the market'. They celebrate the constraints that markets impose on the sovereignty of governments and politicians. For decades the Tories have been at the forefront – not just at home, but across the world – of arguing for the relinquishing of national protections in order to unlock market forces. They have shown a supremely relaxed attitude towards the political sovereignty of the British economy. A straight line can be drawn from the privatisation of British Telecom and British Airways, through the 'Big Bang' deregulation of the City of London, and the welcoming of French and German companies to run everything from the electricity in our grid to the water in our taps, to George Osborne's undignified dash to China to implore them to build our nuclear power stations for us.

The actions of generations of Conservatives have exploded the myth that Britain retains any meaningful economic sovereignty of its own. Yet this is the same party that then goes berserk if Britain is outvoted in the EU Council of Ministers on technical amendments to the third widget directive. They have rubbed our noses in the idea that we have no alternative to being open to the world economically, while at the same time recoiling from the implications of that very openness. So it is little surprise that the Conservative Party has been dogged for years by a deep restlessness over our relationship with Europe. It is the two sides of the Tory brain at war with each other: Burke's little platoons versus the capitalist Big Bang; faith in the Mother of All Parliaments versus the disruptive realities of globalisation; a nostalgic belief in parliamentary sovereignty versus the wholesale loss of economic sovereignty. In some respects, there need not be any great conflict between a belief in turbocharged capitalism and social conservatism, but the European question shatters their peaceful coexistence – and it has been amplified by the relentless pace of globalisation and the digital revolution, pulling with ever greater force at the stitches that bind these two core parts of modern Conservatism together.

And the greatest irony of all? It was Margaret Thatcher, the Boadicea of the Conservative Party, the earth-mother they have never come to terms with slaying, who was the greatest pioneer of British openness to Europe. It was Thatcher who signed away the nation's patriotic birthright by signing up to the Single European Act in 1986 – which established the Single Market devised by Jacques Delors – by far the biggest surrender of national sovereignty by any British government in living memory. The Conservatives' most iconic figurehead is also the cause of their existential crisis.

The way this Conservative European psychodrama played out in coalition with the Liberal Democrats amounted to a five-year stand-off. Early on in the coalition, I asked William Hague – a skilled Foreign Secretary who frequently acted as an ally in behind-the-scenes debates over Israel and Palestine or the Middle East or China, where I would customarily push for a harder line than the narrow realpolitik espoused by Osborne – what the Conservatives' strategic principles were in the UK's foreign policy? He described the Conservative vision of a 'networked world', a web of multilateral and bilateral arrangements between governments, businesses, cultural institutions and private citizens. Britain, he argued, should not be fixated on its near neighbours, but should be casting its net as far and wide as possible. It was about Britain being open for business, revamping the government's UK Trade and Investment department, opening consulates in far-flung places and courting the world through a constant treadmill of trade missions and diplomatic outreach. He argued passionately, in a speech shortly after taking office in 2010, that 'influence increasingly lies with networks of states with fluid and dynamic patterns of allegiance, alliance and connections, including the informal, which act as vital channels of influence and decision-making and require new forms of engagement from Britain'.

I don't doubt that globalisation and the digital revolution have, in many ways, changed the dynamics of international relations. But to me the idea that we should downgrade leadership in our own European neighbourhood in order to spread our bets around the world is deeply flawed. I just don't believe that a fluid 'network' approach can provide the strategic anchor that Britain needs in the modern world. As power has shifted from West to East, as America's attention shifts from the Atlantic to the Pacific, as new powers in Asia and Latin America take their place at the world's top table, it seems obvious to me that a reliance on an ill-defined 'network' of relations will never provide Britain with the real clout we need. Yet that was the core of William Hague's argument then – notwithstanding his subsequent backing for our membership of the EU in the referendum – and remains the core of the argument of many Brexiteers today. Without a leadership role in the union of 500 million citizens on our doorstep, why should the Americans, or the Indians, or the Chinese, actually listen to us? We can't influence the rest of the world if we retreat from our corner of it – a view repeated to me over and over again by US decision-makers I met during my time in office.

I became increasingly frustrated with the erratic changes in Conservative foreign policy: early on in the coalition, it was deemed that the relationship with India would take precedence above all others – Cameron led a delegation to India little more than two months after the coalition was formed, to drive the point home; then it was decided that in fact China was the key relationship; towards the very end of the coalition, there was even a proposal that the government should issue a White Paper stipulating the priority we placed on our relations with the Gulf States, a proposal I irritably rejected on the grounds that the merry-go-round of shifting priorities was fast becoming a joke and would be seen as such, just a few weeks before an election.

It also became a bit of a running joke that, ahead of our regular National Security Council meetings – of which the Prime Minister was chair and I was vice-chair – Whitehall's senior security adviser would come to my office and ask me what I wanted on the agenda. I would always, like clockwork, tell him that I wanted a proper debate on Britain's long-term strategic interests in Europe and on our leadership role in European defence policy. He would dutifully write my request down, a bead of sweat appearing on his forehead, and then it would reliably disappear by the time the agenda was circulated to senior ministers by Number 10. I knew my request would never make it onto the NSC agenda – much as, I guess, a request from Number 10 to discuss leaving the European Convention on Human Rights would not have got assent from me – but I did the same every time in order to press the point. Nonetheless, it shows the scale of Conservative neuralgia on Europe that for five years we had detailed discussions on everything from cybersecurity to Boko Haram, from troop movements in Helmand to the situation in Zimbabwe, but not once did we have a strategic discussion in the National Security Council about our relationship with our nearest neighbours.

The one European initiative that did take place – sprung from Number 10 like one of Baldrick's cunning plans – was an 'audit' of the European Union competences that affected the United Kingdom. The intention, clearly, was that it would produce a picture of a monstrous European leviathan trampling on sacred British freedoms, which would provide the justification for the renegotiation of our terms of EU membership. In fact, as I safely predicted, having attempted a similar exercise myself some years earlier when researching a pamphlet I wrote as an MEP, it found the reverse: the reality of our relationship with Europe was much more mundane and less threatening.

I asked the ever-patient Lord William Wallace – whose wife, Helen Wallace, had taught Miriam and me when we were students together at the College of Europe twenty years earlier – to provide Lib Dem oversight over the whole process. I also insisted that a neutral panel of senior officials should be established to draw up the final conclusions in each policy area, to prevent Conservative special advisers from rewriting them to suit their political ends. To this William Hague agreed, and to his immense credit he policed the process from the Foreign Office in a meticulously even-handed manner.

In the end, two things happened: first, a ludicrous stand-off emerged between my team and the Home Office, because Theresa May's team tried to rewrite the conclusions pointing to evidence of a huge abuse of freedom of movement, even though the report from officials exposed no such evidence at all. Chris Grayling, the Conservative Secretary of State for Justice, and his special advisers similarly dug in their heels over the civil-justice section. Second, because the audit did not yield the conclusions the Conservatives had hoped for, the reports were smuggled out in the most innocuous way possible to attract the least amount of press scrutiny – carefully timed on each occasion so that they were published just as the Commons rose for the summer or Christmas recess. After months of toing and froing, the audit of EU freedom-of-movement powers was finally issued, with the content sticking rigidly to the facts. It was released on the final day that the House of Commons was sitting before the 2014 summer recess, alongside a host of other ministerial statements on newsworthy subjects – ranging from a report into the 'Trojan Horse' allegations in some Birmingham schools, to the announcement of an inquiry into the murder of former Russian spy Alexander Litvinenko – a tactic deliberately designed to minimise media scrutiny.

On the specific subject of a referendum on Britain's membership of the EU, the coalition government's position lurched from coherence to disarray within the five-year parliament. At its outset, David Cameron and I agreed that we should find some way to lay the issue to rest, so that it would not blight our time in office together. The result was the European Union Act passed in March 2011. In essence, it stated that if there was a future demand made of the United Kingdom to give up significant new powers to the EU, our response could only be agreed by way of a referendum. Both Cameron and I had suffered embarrassments on the issue of a referendum in the past: he by reneging on his 'cast-iron guarantee' to demand a referendum on the Lisbon Treaty, signed in 2007, which made various amendments to the EU's governing bodies, powers and voting procedures; in my case, because of the chaotic three-way split in the Lib Dems, which led to a smattering of frontbench resignations, that resulted from my attempt to impose a single position across the party on the ratification of the Lisbon Treaty. So we both grabbed at the chance to put the conditions for any future referendum on a statutory footing, beyond the reach of further party political gamesmanship.

So when David Cameron told me two years later that he had decided to tear up the legislation we had so meticulously agreed together and instead declare his intention, in the event of a Conservative majority government, to hold a referendum, I was utterly nonplussed. Not only was I well aware that senior members of his own party had serious reservations about this sudden genuflection towards his Eurosceptic backbenchers. Not only was it a direct contradiction of his own and William Hague's persuasive argument to the House of Commons in 2011 – the Foreign Secretary had stated that holding a referendum at a time of economic uncertainty 'would not be a responsible action for Her Majesty's Government to take'. It was also a wilful elevation of an internal party problem to the level of a national plebiscite. While I had long argued in favour of a referendum in the circumstances we had enshrined in law, I could not see the logic of asking millions of our fellow citizens a question just because a single political party, increasingly under pressure from UKIP, was unable to make its mind up for itself. It was a decision born of political weakness for which David Cameron would pay a heavy price – for ever remembered as the Prime Minister who presided over a collapse in Britain's standing in the world and possibly the break-up of the UK itself – and for which the country will endure a prolonged period of political and economic instability.

The Conservative Party has a deserved reputation as one of the most effective fighting machines in the democratic world, always ready to adapt its tune to suit the flavour of the times, ruthlessly sensitive to the public mood. Yet, on Europe, the Conservatives' feel for the public mood has always been faulty. Because of their internal splits on Europe, they have consistently confused their own fixation with the opinion of the public at large. In truth, once you excluded those who were passionately for and passionately against, the defining attitude of most people towards Europe has long been one of weary ennui.

Of course, there is a reason why the EU has become the focal point not only of internal dissent between Conservatives, but also of wider dissatisfaction amongst millions of voters across Europe: the distance between decisions taken by governments in Brussels and people's everyday concerns is, by its very nature, vast. There is a yawning gap between the technocratic deals made between officials, ministers and MEPs and the hardships and frustrations of everyday life. The lines of accountability between national parliaments and Brussels's decision-making elites are stretched thin. It is what academics call a 'democratic deficit'. This gap between the supranational reality of modern decision-making and the strength of national political loyal-ties creates a space in which a host of slights, grievances and suspicions can take root. The EU comes across, inevitably, as remote, obscure and unfamiliar – the perfect whipping boy for any populist with an axe to grind.

Many years ago, long before I decided to enter politics, I saw for myself how this arose. In 1991, I did a short stint as an intern in the European Commission (the executive body of the EU, Europe's Whitehall). Later I became a full-time employee working as a manager of EU development-aid projects in Central Asia, and later still as an adviser on international trade deals for Leon Brittan when he was Vice-President of the European Commission. During those years, the early Nineties, the Conservative Party was tearing itself apart, as Eurosceptics hounded John Major to within an inch of his political life. Westminster and Whitehall seemed paralysed by infighting. Furious, red-faced MPs harangued each other on the nightly

TV news, and the vitriol meted out to pro-Europeans in the tabloid press was shrill and nasty. To me as a young, idealistic internationalist it seemed a natural step to try and find my feet away from all this in the heart of the EU, in Brussels. Yet, much as I retained my admiration for the overarching objectives of the EU, any romantic illusions I had about the way decisions were taken in practice soon evaporated. It seemed perverse to me that as a youngster in my mid-twenties I had a virtually free hand in deciding how to spend large amounts of European taxpayers' money on development projects in the great expanses of Central Asia. It seemed even more perverse to me that – as an admittedly very small cog in the EU wheel – I had some say over the negotiations between China and the EU, governing the terms of China's entry into the World Trade Organisation. These were decisions that, I felt, should be taken by democratically accountable politicians, not young civil servants.

Above all, it quickly became obvious to me that the political debate – the battle for hearts and minds – surrounding Britain's fraught role within the EU was not going to be settled in the meeting rooms of Brussels, however important the decisions taken there were. For that, I needed to put my own neck on the line and enter directly into the political fray. In 1999 I stood for election to the European Parliament and was elected as the first Liberal parliamentarian in the East Midlands since the 1930s. Yet, once again, the way in which decisions were taken in the European Parliament soon struck me as falling well short of its lofty democratic ambitions: one of the first campaigns I was involved in, as a newly elected MEP, was to open up access to official parliamentary documents – restricted at the time to MEPs and the cottage industry of lobbyists in Brussels and Strasbourg – to the general public.

Furthermore, far from acting like a united European demos with a parliamentary identity of its own, the European Parliament felt at times like a reunion episode of *'Allo 'Allo!* With so many different nationalities represented, MEPs seemed to resort to the most hackneyed national stereotypes in order to

make themselves understood. The Italians were always immacu-
lately dressed and late. The French greeted every event with a
moody Gallic shrug. The Germans wore oddly coloured suits
and ended up running everything. It was as if, in order to com-
municate with each other, MEPs had to send themselves up.
British MEPs were often cartoonishly pompous and plummy. It
was the kind of environment that created characters like Daniel
Hannan, an engaging if zealous Conservative MEP who bore
the air of a minor character from *Brideshead Revisited*, happily
reciting Shakespearean sonnets to bemused MEPs from other
countries. Or Roger Helmer, a Tory-cum-UKIP MEP from my
patch in the East Midlands, replete with Colonel Blimp mous-
tache and a set of boorish saloon-bar assertions to match. In
Westminster, they would have been laughed out of court. In
the European Parliament, for some reason, they thrived.

More importantly, it soon became obvious that, whilst MEPs
did a crucial job in scrutinising draft legislation and the work
of European Commissioners, voters back home barely had the
slightest idea who their MEPs were or what they did. The role
of MEPs and MPs seemed to me to have become dangerously
inverted: MEPs were powerful legislators in their own right,
capable of blocking and amending laws on everything from
mobile-telephone standards to the quality of our drinking water,
yet they were largely invisible in the bear pit of domestic politics;
MPs, by contrast, could stand tall as recognised politicians in
their own constituencies and in Westminster but, unless they
were government ministers, generally had no say whatsoever
over the detail of the laws of the land. In other words, MEPs
were strong legislators but weak politicians, while MPs were
strong politicians but weak legislators. This struck me – and
still does today – as unhealthy for the quality of our democracy: decision-making power and public accountability should
go hand in hand rather than exist in separate parliamentary
silos. So, after one term as a MEP, I decided to move on once
again, this time to the epicentre of the British European debate
itself, the House of Commons.

Needless to say, my youthful meanderings betray a certain naivety when viewed with hindsight: excessively young officials brandishing excessive authority are hardly a problem of the European Commission alone. Years later, as Deputy Prime Minister, I would ask Sir Jeremy Heywood, the Cabinet Secretary, to do something about the rapid turnover of highly intelligent, ferociously ambitious and wholly inexperienced young British civil servants in crucial decision-making positions across Whitehall, especially in the Treasury. Far from fostering new thinking or innovation, this ensured that the brightest, youngest civil servants would have every reason to defend existing orthodoxy: it was hardly their fault – most of them were gifted, hard-working public servants – but they were being asked to take on significant responsibilities for insignificant amounts of time with insufficient experience. I should know, I did the same myself two decades earlier in Brussels.

Equally, many of the shortcomings of the European Parliament are hardly of its own making: given that MEPs represent every inch of a vast continent, the lines of accountability inevitably span huge distances. In population terms, the constituency I represented, the East Midlands, was four-fifths the size of Denmark. I spent much of my life either flying between Nottingham, my UK home at the time, and Brussels or Strasbourg, or racing up and down the M1 trying to make my presence felt across a huge region. It was a somewhat thankless task, not helped by the low turnout at European elections. On the day I was elected in 1999, I remember driving down the A43 near Silverstone to visit my parents in Oxfordshire, and working out in my head how few people had actually voted Liberal Democrat in order to get me elected: roughly 92,000 out of a total of more than three million eligible voters. It didn't feel like a great mandate.

Taken together, these experiences were indicative of the EU's 'democratic deficit': a noble undertaking to enable European governments to take decisions together, which is condemned to appear remote to Europe's citizens. Naturally, this is fertile ground for those who wish to blame the EU for every ill. It is all too easily characterised as some kind of malign spaceship hovering menacingly over our helpless, law-abiding islands, issuing edicts that we must dutifully obey and over which we have no control. But those shortcomings do not amount, in my view, to a case for removing ourselves from the EU altogether, because the need for some forum in which governments take decisions together at European level will still remain. Nor is it right to blame the 'democratic deficit' on the EU institutions themselves – the fault, such as it is, lies largely with national political elites who do not come clean with their own voters on the deals and decisions they enter into in Brussels. The national political classes have not been honest with people about the limits of their own powers. They perpetuate a myth of absolute authority, while much of the power they pretend to possess is in fact shared with other countries at a supranational level, invariably behind closed doors.

The truth, ironically, is that the apparent lack of accountability in the EU for its decisions is not because it is an authoritarian superstate, but rather because it is immersed in non-stop negotiation and haggling between its twenty-eight – soon to be twenty-seven – member countries. Decisions taken in the EU Council of Ministers are often impenetrable to the non-expert, not because of a secretive conspiracy, but because of their mind-numbing technicality.

When I first arrived in Brussels in 1994, there was a sense that, under the command and control of Jacques Delors, then President of the European Commission, and his highly effective enforcer, Pascal Lamy, the EU was on an onward march towards the manifest destiny of an 'ever-closer union'. Delors's great success was to persuade the UK and other member states that the next great step in European integration was the Single Market, itself the brainchild of a Brit, Lord Cockfield. This fuelled overexcited chatter among some arch-integrationists that the federal moment in European history had arrived. But those dreamers overlooked the residual loyalties of millions of voters to their own local and national democratic institutions, and underestimated the determination with which national political and bureaucratic elites would reassert their sway in EU decision-making. At the same time, the number of countries within the European Union kept increasing, each with their own traditions and sensitivities, leading to ever more complex haggling over the detail of every decision. Far from being a stepping stone towards a new federalist settlement, the era of Delors proved to be the high-watermark of *'grand projet'* integration. Ever since, decision-making in the EU has become more, not less, driven by national governments ferociously defending their interests.

We have struggled as an old democratic continent to transfer democracy and loyalty to something higher than the nation state. So the grand vision of a federal Europe – depicted so successfully by the Brexit campaign as a menace from which Britain must seek refuge – has in truth never come about and has never been a credible threat. The reality can hardly be described as a dangerous encroachment on national sovereignty – more often than not, it just leads to lethargic decision-making and gridlock. It took the EU almost thirty years, for instance, to decide on a chocolate directive (not least because of a raging disagreement between the British, in favour of chocolate made with vegetable fat, and the purists who considered cocoa the only base-ingredient worthy of the chocolate name). Any organisation that takes three decades to decide on a common definition of chocolate is unlikely to keep the children awake at night for fear of its overweening powers.

Essentially, then, the European Union has evolved into a confederal union of sovereign states – in which its central institutions act as a non-stop clearing house for negotiations between governments. In some ways, it could be claimed that this is a democratic arrangement because the buck stops with democratically elected governments. But it is also a fearfully opaque arrangement and one in which national administrative elites congregate and take decisions well beyond the reach of their domestic constituencies.

Part of the solution to all this may be mechanical – redesigning EU institutions, tweaking qualified majority voting arrangements, clarifying veto powers, reweighting each country's votes, expanding and contracting the number of EU Commissioners and MEPs, and so on. In fact, that is exactly what member states were doing pretty much non-stop for a decade and a half, between the mid-Nineties and the Lisbon Treaty in 2009. In that time, four Intergovernmental Conferences were held and three major new treaties were signed in Amsterdam, Nice and Lisbon. But this treaty-mania will only get the EU so far. If the problem could have been fixed with yet another new treaty, it would have been fixed by now.

In the end, political leadership and direction are more important to the future of the EU than further institutional tinkering. The progressive decline in British influence in Europe in the years preceding the fateful referendum was not because the legal provisions of the treaties were imperfect; it was because of a strategic loss of British leadership in European affairs. Part of this was, perhaps, inevitable as German economic dominance came to the fore. Part of it was because, rightly, the UK stood aside from the euro currency union, which created a hard core of countries at the heart of the EU. But far too much of Britain's loss of influence was self-inflicted.

On my first day in the European Parliament in 1999, an amiable veteran Belgian MEP, Willy de Clercq, observed to me that the problem with the European Union was that it had become too British. He said we had won all the big debates. The Single Market, a British idea pushed hard by Margaret Thatcher, had entrenched the Anglo-Saxon idea that the market is supreme. Continental *dirigistes*, who favoured greater state control of the economy, had been vanquished. A succession of international trade agreements, not least the agreement to establish the World Trade Organisation itself, had thwarted the protectionists for good. And the dramatic enlargement of the European Union into Central and Eastern Europe, long a cherished diplomatic objective in London, had loosened the grip of the Franco-German duo. De Clercq saw it very clearly. On the big, big things, Britain had won – and won comprehensively.

Yet, at the very same time, Westminster was immersed in internecine warfare about Britain's place in Europe, oblivious to the achievements of British statecraft. We refused to accept the evidence of our own successes. And we have continued to squander our natural advantages ever since. When I first arrived in Brussels, Britain was lauded by the countries of Central and Eastern Europe because of our help in bringing them into the EU fold. Having cast off the mantle of top-down communism, they were natural allies in our desire to see a more flexible, less centralised EU. They looked to Britain for leadership. Yet today, barely a decade later, the UK is vacating the EU altogether and Poland will fulfil its long-held strategic objective of displacing us as one of Europe's leading powers. This would have been unthinkable even a few years ago. In 2014, an expletive-ridden rant by the Polish Foreign Minister, Radosław Sikorski, was caught on tape, in which he accused our Prime Minister, in colourful terms, of incompetence over the government's handling of Europe. Sikorski is a zealous Anglophile, a former member of the Bullingdon Club, complete with three-piece suits and impeccable clipped BBC English. I spoke to him in the margins of the Nato summit in Cardiff that same year and he told me how much he despaired at our demise. He was right: it's a long way to fall.

Perhaps the most poignant recent moment highlighting Britain's declining leadership came during the Ukraine crisis in early 2015. Angela Merkel and François Hollande travelled to Russia and Ukraine together to meet first the Russian President, Vladimir Putin, and then Petro Poroshenko, the Ukrainian President, to agree an emergency summit that all four would attend a few days later in Minsk. They didn't even bother to inform Whitehall. The Foreign Office and Number 10 were initially shell-shocked. Then, desperate to cover up the indignity of the whole episode, it was soon put about that it was, after all, a jolly good thing we were not there, because the French and the Germans were bound to mess things up. At least we could provide a useful double-act with the Americans, when it was time for the grown-ups to get involved. It was a ludicrously patronising, self-serving response. I have heard Angela Merkel speak about Ukraine in public and private on a number of occasions. Her forensic knowledge of every single oligarch, region, industrial interest and political player in the unfolding tragedy in Ukraine – not to mention her complex relationship with Vladimir Putin, forged in fluent Russian – was greater than could be mustered across the whole of Whitehall.

The real tragedy of this progressive loss – and now entire absence – of British leadership in Europe is this: other countries were crying out for us to step up to the plate. American support for British leadership in Europe has been a constant lodestar of their foreign policy in the whole post-war period. Central and Eastern European countries have always been anxious, not least because of their fraught histories, to avoid being dictated to by the Franco-German duo. Germany itself, unsurprisingly, has always been a somewhat reluctant hegemon, keen to avoid overstepping its natural advantages as the biggest economic power in Europe. Even France, always the most ambivalent in its attitudes towards its old cross-Channel foe, has been keen to promote greater British activism in defence and foreign policy. Britain and France are the only meaningful military powers in Europe, yet we have consistently failed to exploit the natural leadership we could have exercised together.

And British leadership could have been deployed to great effect right now, because Europe is facing existential challenges on several fronts: the imbalances in the eurozone require, among other things, a consistent focus on improved competitiveness and economic reform; the mass migration of hundreds of thousands of refugees from war-torn Syria, Iraq, Afghanistan and East Africa into the EU requires both foreign-policy leadership beyond the EU's borders and a complete overhaul of the EU's external borders themselves; the horrors of Isis extremism and terrorist violence on the streets of European cities demand a step-change in cooperation between Europe's police, judicial and security services; the economic, social and political instability across the Mediterranean basin requires collective intervention on the scale of the USA's rebuilding of Europe after the Second World War – a 'Marshall Plan for the Med' – or of the support given by the EU and the rest of the world to the ex-Soviet states of Central and Eastern Europe after the collapse of the Berlin Wall. In all these areas, Britain possesses unrivalled leadership qualities, which could have helped to build a more prosperous and safe European continent. Instead, Westminster and Whitehall will turn in on themselves as the British establishment attempts to digest the enormity, legal complexity and commercial uncertainty of the momentous decision we have taken. Never in modern history has a country's interests been so gravely betrayed by the arrogance and casual incompetence of its leaders.

So what will Brexit actually look like? What kind of relationship can we expect to enter into with the EU's remaining twenty-seven member states? Whilst it is difficult to pick a clear route through the innumerable uncertainties that will abound in the years ahead, the following seems incontrovertible: first, there is an obvious new deal to be done between the UK and the EU. The EU could adopt tailor-made restrictions to the principle of freedom of movement of EU citizens – either just for the UK or, more palatably, for the EU as a whole – such that, for example, the entitlement would be more strictly focused on the right to work, and/or there would be an emergency 'brake' on the number of EU citizens moving into a member state above a certain level. In return, the UK could agree to a status similar to Norway's and that of other members of the European Economic Area, in which British exporters enjoy unhindered access to the Single Market on the condition that the British Government continues to adhere to the rules – and rulings – of the EU Single Market and to make a contribution to the EU budget. This deal – restricted EU immigration and extensive market access, in return for the supremacy of Single

Market rules and money – would go some considerable way to answering the political concerns about EU immigration that loomed so large in the referendum campaign (even if, as I will explain later, it would do little to address the underlying social and economic insecurities that drove many people to vote for Brexit), whilst mitigating the profound damage that otherwise awaits our economy.

But while it may seem logical on paper, and is surely our best option in the absence of better alternatives, it faces huge obstacles in practice. For a start, it is difficult to exaggerate the resentment that has accumulated in many European capitals towards the UK, even in Anglophile circles. The EU referendum result may have caused economic uncertainty in the UK, but it has in many ways provoked even greater instability in the fragile markets of the eurozone. Understandably, the leaders of eurozone countries want to cut their losses and are in no mood to strike a sweetheart deal with a Brexit government that has caused such needless harm to their own, vulnerable economies and has spurned the long list of concessions granted by the EU to the UK in the past. Why should, for instance, France or Germany or the Netherlands – all keen to attract financial-services businesses to their own territories – now grant the UK financial-services sector the 'passporting' rights it would require to continue to trade effortlessly on behalf of clients and in markets across the whole EU? Of course, assuming Britain were to place equivalent restrictions on EU businesses in return, it would do some damage to French or German or Dutch exporters who depend on ready access to the UK market. But assuming (for reasons we are about to come to) that the UK refuses to play by the basic Single Market rules of the EU game, it will be nigh-impossible for EU governments to do anything else: they would surely be forced to treat the UK like any other non-EU country, none of which enjoy such 'passported' privileges. As Theresa May said when she launched her leadership bid for the Conservative Party, 'Brexit is Brexit.'

Which brings me to the other reason why it is, unfortunately, unlikely that an optimal deal will be struck between the UK and the EU: the deep contradiction in the stance taken by the Conservative Party and other Brexiteers, who boxed themselves into a corner during the referendum campaign from which it will now be politically very difficult to escape. Michael Gove's own words best illustrate the problem: 'We should be outside the Single Market, we should have access to the Single Market but we should not be governed by the rules.' Yet the plain fact is that you can't have untrammelled access to the Single Market without abiding by the rules of the Single Market, so either Michael Gove and other Brexiteers will have to eat their words – conceding what they appear not to understand – and thereby admit that they campaigned in the referendum on a false prospectus; or they will need to explain to large swathes of the British business community, most especially the services sector, which makes up nearly 80 per cent of the nation's GDP and whose future success depends in part on the UK's leading role within the EU Single Market, that such access to the Single Market will not be forthcoming after all.

Assuming they decide the latter option is too unpalatable, Theresa May as the new Conservative Prime Minister faces the unenviable task of persuading the nation that, having voted to 'take back control', it must now accept that the only economically sensible alternative to EU membership involves a catastrophic loss of sovereignty: one in which Britain, like Norway and other non-EU countries dependent on the Single Market, will nonetheless have to abide by rules set by the EU, either directly by transposing EU laws into domestic legislation or indirectly by passing 'equivalent' rules and regulations of our own, having thrown away any say we once had in the formation of those rules. Even though Theresa May herself supported our continued membership of the EU – if with invisible effort or enthusiasm – she is now trapped by the remorseless logic of her party's Brexit instincts and by the false expectations raised during the referendum campaign itself. She is condemned to claim that there is an economic utopia outside the EU, notwithstanding her own doubts. In other words, it is difficult to see how the Conservative Party can escape the fundamental dishonesty of its own position: it turns out that in the EU, as in all other walks of life, you can't have your cake and eat it after all.

Second, regardless of the Prime Minister's personal preferences, it is economic circumstances that will drive the politics of what happens next. If the Brexit vote leads to another downward spiral within the eurozone – perhaps a banking crisis in Italy or even Germany, a loss of confidence in France's half-baked economic reforms, another bout of budgetary crises in Greece – sentiment in EU capitals will shift sharply. It may, finally, compel eurozone leaders to agree to a more durable solution to the imbalances of the eurozone, not least because they will not be able to rely on the European Central Bank to ride to the rescue of the eurozone again, given that it is running out of monetary responses. The better solution would include a proper fiscal union, in which fiscal liabilities are shared between debtor and creditor countries and stricter budgetary discipline and economic reforms are enforced in the weaker eurozone countries. If the eurozone emerges, in the end, stronger from those long-overdue reforms, sentiment towards Britain will harden, as the eurozone negotiates from a position of increasing strength rather than comparative economic weakness.

At the same time, if the economic consequences of the Brexit vote in the UK are demonstrably negative, the UK will increasingly lose leverage in its discussions with the other twenty-seven EU states. Immediate market reactions to the referendum result – initial panic followed by a period of disbelief – are no guide at all to the long-term economic consequences for the UK. But as the reality dawns that Brexit is for real, that there is no effortless second-best alternative available to the UK, and as the dramatic drop in investment decisions becomes clear, further upheaval in the markets is likely. This pattern – panic, denial, upheaval – will soon coincide with growing evidence of damage to the real economy for ordinary families, from higher petrol and holiday prices to job losses in the financial-services sector and a wider chill in business activity. Those conditions may well then feed off each other, creating a downward spiral of confidence in the UK economy as a whole. Given that we have the largest current-account deficit since records began – in other words, an overall deficit across all of our international transactions, including trade – and so rely on investors abroad putting money into UK assets (or, as Mark Carney has put it, the 'kindness of strangers'), the possibility cannot be discounted that these conditions will lead to a wider collapse of confidence in the UK's ability to pay its way in the world. If that were to happen, the political consequences would be brutal. The millions of British voters who were lured by Boris Johnson, Michael Gove and others to vote for a sunny Brexit future will be enraged that their personal economic well-being has been damaged, and will demand different leadership in Westminster and possibly even a rethink of the decision to quit the EU in the first place.

Of course, it may be that none of these economic scenarios materialises. Perhaps the eurozone will muddle along without much disruption or reform for years to come. Perhaps the UK economy will quickly find a new equilibrium, experiencing no more than a temporary and shallow recession. If that were to be the case, then clearly the UK will be able to negotiate with the rest of the EU from a position of greater strength and will not be fearful of allowing the talks to drag on to the wire. There is also a barely disguised hope, on the part of many senior Brexiteers, that the eurozone and then the EU itself will collapse altogether under the hammer-blow of Brexit. This apocalyptic approach – actively seeking wholesale economic and political instability across the European continent – is so breathtakingly malign and self-harming that it is hard to engage with it seriously. In my view, we would be well advised not to bet on such complacent or destructive predictions.

What is certain, though, is that there will be several moments in the coming years when the British people, and their MPs, will be called upon to make further judgements about the terms of the Brexit package that the government will seek to negotiate. The referendum outcome was a mandate to pull the UK out of the EU; it was not, however, a mandate on how to do so, given the refusal of Brexit campaigners to spell out what the future relationship with the EU should be. Just as democratic legitimacy was conferred by the referendum on the decision to leave, so democratic legitimacy must now be conferred on the process by which we depart and define our new status outside the EU. For a start, there should be an early general election, once Theresa May has published a full, detailed plan for the Brexit negotiations, so that voters are given an opportunity to express their approval, or otherwise, of what life outside the EU may actually look like. If the British people decide that they do not wish to grant the Conservative Party a majority in that election, it will be up to other parties to try to form a government – possibly a Government of National Unity – whose sole purpose will be to steer the country through this unprecedented period of constitutional and economic turmoil by striking a better deal for Britain with the EU.

MPs in Parliament will need to play a role, too, in scrutinising the legality and workability of the government's Brexit negotiations and will need to provide their consent to the opening and conclusion of the so-called 'Article 50' process by which the UK will settle the terms of its exit from the EU over a two-year period. This crucial role for MPs will draw on the precedent that was set during the coalition when we secured a vote of support from MPs both to open and conclude negotiations with the rest of the EU on Britain's 'opt-out' of certain police and judicial cooperation measures. And there is a strong case for a further referendum when the completed agreement between the UK and the EU is finally thrashed out, so that voters can choose to adopt or reject the specific new status on offer for the UK outside the EU.

During the referendum campaign it became fashionable to claim that, whatever the outcome, Britain would no doubt keep calm and carry on, in time-honoured fashion. As the *Financial Times*'s political commentator Janan Ganesh wrote in 2015: 'If we vote to leave, we will not really leave. A bargain will be brokered that preserves some British access to the European market in exchange for some duty to observe European laws . . . And if we vote to stay, we will never become a truly European nation anyway.' In one narrow sense, this was correct: our relationship with the European Union would have been messy and imperfect, regardless of the outcome of the referendum. In another sense, however, such insouciance dramatically under-states the significance of the referendum outcome. Because, in the end, the referendum was not so much a debate about Europe, Brussels or whether Britain could or could not stitch together an alternative working arrangement with the EU. It was really about us. About who we are and what country we want to become. Open or closed. Engaged or disengaged. Leading others or detached from our neighbours.

Above all, it was a debate that pitted the politics of reason, imperfection and compromise against the politics of anger, utopianism and grievance. That the latter triumphed in the referendum makes the challenge for the politics of reason all the more difficult in the years ahead. But it also makes it all the more urgent that we identify a route forward for moderation and internationalism around which the millions of people who worry about the direction of our country can congregate.

CHAPTER 9

Between the Extremes: The Return of Liberalism in an Age of Unreason

In February 2013 the Liberal Democrat MP and former Cabinet Minister Chris Huhne pleaded guilty to the charge of perverting the course of justice, after admitting that his wife had claimed responsibility for a speeding violation that in fact he had committed, and resigned from his seat in Eastleigh, Hampshire, triggering a by-election.

Despite widespread predictions that the Lib Dems would lose the seat, our candidate Mike Thornton held on to it by a slim margin. Our huge relief at the result was tempered, though, by a massive surge in votes for UKIP in the constituency, knocking the Conservatives into third place. In order to understand what was going on, researchers from Liberal Democrat Headquarters held a 'focus group' shortly after the by-election of around a dozen voters who had been identified as previous Lib Dem supporters, but who had switched to UKIP in the by-election itself.

The discussion in the focus group was revealing: person after person spoke up about their unease with various aspects of modern Britain, ranging from the programmes on TV to impolite car drivers in Eastleigh, from the behaviour of teenagers to the loud music in supermarkets. Interestingly, whilst immigration was mentioned, it was a wider malaise with the pace and nature of change that seemed to unsettle people the most.

Towards the end of the session one of the somewhat exasperated Lib Dem researchers asked the group: 'Can anyone perhaps tell me of one thing they actually like in modern Britain?'

A long silence ensued. And then a man raised his hand and said: 'Yes, I know. The past.'

Whether that gentleman knew it or not, he spoke for many people outside the room. Perhaps it has always been a tendency of every older generation to believe that the values and certainties of the past are being frittered away by the impatience and naivety of youth. But as change has accelerated, as the boom–bust insecurity of our economy continues, as globalisation overwhelms the habits of nations, this longing for a more restful past has grown in force. Many of us are unsettled by technology we don't understand, by the rise of extremist violence, or by mass migration from conflicts in distant parts of the world. No wonder the idea of reverting to a more secure, familiar past is a seductive one. At that time, at least, the man-down-the-pub populism of Nigel Farage appealed to that hankering to turn back the clock.

Britons are not the only people to feel this way. Marine Le Pen's Front National in France, Golden Dawn in Greece, the Danish People's Party, Geert Wilders's Party for Freedom in the Netherlands, Jobbik in Hungary, the Swiss People's Party (one of whose campaign advertisements depicted an Islamist terrorist with an EU armband, about to decapitate a beautiful blonde Swiss woman), Sarah Palin and Donald Trump in the US, the Freedom Party in Austria ... All these parties, to a greater or lesser extent, claim that our fears can be allayed by rejecting multiculturalism, condemning Islam, stopping immigration, limiting minority rights, withdrawing from the EU, ignoring judges, scrapping human rights, stringing up bankers, vilifying liberal media elites and restoring past traditions. These parties are no longer fringe movements with little influence on the political mainstream – in many cases, they already dominate it. In Poland and Hungary, they are in government, busily neutering the judiciary, the independent press and any meaningful political opposition in their parliaments. In Switzerland, Finland and Denmark, they are in governing coalitions. They top the polls in France and the Netherlands. In Britain, they won the Euro elections in 2014 and ushered in the vote for Brexit. Their support is at record levels even in Sweden.

In 1993, I spent several months in Budapest, having won a writing prize from the *Financial Times*, examining the mass privatisation schemes that were taking place across Central and Eastern Europe. Back then, Viktor Orbán was the leader of a fizzingly liberal, youthful party, Fidesz. Indeed, its commitment to the virtues of youth was such that it introduced a ban on any Fidesz party member being aged over forty. The contrast with the Orbán of today – Vladimir Putin's chief cheerleader in Central and Eastern Europe – speaks volumes about the dramatic lurch towards insularity and nationalism in European politics since the collapse of the Berlin Wall. If the politics of reason is to survive, if extremism and populism are to be defeated, we need to understand why this abrupt change has come about.

I have experienced abrupt political changes myself – lauded as an outsider before the 2010 general election, criticised as an insider since – and have witnessed up close the steady erosion of the liberal, centre ground not only in British politics, but across Europe and the USA, too. In my case, much of that may be due to a combination of my misjudgements and others' unrealistic expectations. But clearly something bigger has gone awry, too.

There are many reasons for the astonishing rise in right-wing populism. An increasing terrorist threat, combined with the huge movement of refugees into Europe fleeing destitution and conflict, has highlighted the impotence (and incompetence) of governments across Europe. In the aftermath of the terrible attacks on young concert-goers in Paris in November 2015, on commuters in the airport and a metro station in Brussels in March 2016, and on people celebrating Bastille Day in Nice in the same year, a toxic combination of concerns has taken root in the public imagination: will we ever be safe if the terrorists want to target such innocent, carefree activities as a music concert, an evening drink with friends, the daily commute to work, or simply taking an evening stroll on a beachside promenade? Why are people coming into Europe from the bloodbath of Syria unchecked and uncontrolled? And why on earth could the security services in adjacent EU countries not exchange information better, to keep an eye on the extremists? A feeling that our values are under attack, our borders overwhelmed and our security authorities unprepared fosters intense fear in already-fearful societies.

More profoundly, since the collapse of the Berlin Wall, far from the unalloyed triumph of the 'West' or the 'end of history', as was predicted at the time, subsequent years have witnessed a notable decline in self-confidence in liberal democracies and market economies. The 2008 crash illustrated the hubristic dangers of poorly regulated private-sector greed, just as a new form of authoritarian capitalism – most especially in China – rose up to challenge the 'West' on the world stage. Instead of standing up for our own values in this changing world, too many of our politicians have rushed to embrace authoritarian capitalism: George Osborne's gratuitous pandering to China's rulers in Beijing in pursuit of commercial advantage springs to mind.

One of the signature tunes of Trump-style populism in the USA is precisely the accusation that President Obama and the Washington establishment have been too soft, too indecisive, too reluctant to act in a world in which authoritarians everywhere seem to be strutting their stuff without any meaningful challenge. The manner in which Vladimir Putin unilaterally bombed Western-backed rebel groups within Syria – whilst failing to abide by any of the agreements in the frozen conflict in Ukraine – was the clearest demonstration yet that authoritarian regimes around the world are now able to act with a degree of impunity that would have been unimaginable even a few years ago. No wonder Sarah Palin received a thunderous reception in her endorsement speech for Donald Trump when she shrieked that 'We kowtow and apologize and then bend over and say "thank you, enemy"', when what America should do instead is 'let our warriors do their job and go kick Isis's ass'.

If Western governments are apparently unable to stand up for their own values, at the same time as failing to control their borders or regulate the banking system or stop terrorists from attacking youngsters at a rock concert, then it is little wonder that populists on the right who wish to turn away from the outside world get a sympathetic hearing from millions of voters. But the rise in extremism is by no means limited to the right, nor is it caused solely by fear of the outside world.

It would be hard to exaggerate the impact of the financial crisis of 2008. National incomes and living standards in many countries are 10 per cent or more below what they would have been if the crash had not happened. The percentage of the US population that is employed fell to a thirty-five-year low; in Spain, unemployment ballooned to a staggering 26 per cent; and in the UK, whilst mass unemployment was avoided, real wages fell by 5 per cent – more than in any other leading industrialised nation – and per capita income remains below its 2007 peak. Not only are millions of people furious at the failure of governments and regulators to protect them from an overstretched and irresponsible banking system, but they are now subject to a profound sense of insecurity in their everyday economic fortunes. The fear that the ground beneath your feet may give way at any moment – due to actions entirely beyond your control – is a new reality for millions of people.

Within one generation, many workers have shifted from a culture of lifelong employment in one or two jobs to a labour market as changeable as quicksand. In Britain, even though there has been an impressive growth in 'high skill' and full-time employment through the recent downturn, for a significant minority of workers, job insecurity has indeed deepened considerably. The allegation I heard from Labour MPs throughout the last parliament that all new jobs were poor-quality, zero-hours contracts may have been untrue – zero-hours contracts are a matter for serious debate, yet only 2.5 per cent of the total workforce are on such contracts – but it is undoubtedly the case that many men, and especially young people, have experienced sharply rising insecurity. (By contrast, older people and women have become relatively more secure in their jobs, according to the Resolution Foundation.) Insecure jobs, by definition, are temporary, part-time ones on relatively low pay, in which the employee has not been in position long enough to qualify for various employment rights. By this measure, of all eighteen- to twenty-nine-year-olds in work, 66 per cent were categorised as insecure in 2014, up from 55 per cent in 1994. Crucially, this sharp increase in insecurity for parts of the labour force appears to have been accompanied by a decline in job mobility, exacerbating feelings of powerlessness to get on in life.

In the past, immigration has been portrayed by those on the right as the primary threat to job security. But a young graduate stuck in an insecure job with very few prospects might just as plausibly be drawn to the left-wing politics of Podemos in Spain, Syriza in Greece or Jeremy Corbyn's Labour Party in the UK. End austerity! Smash the bankers! Down with globalisation! All of these make sense, if you're in a dead-end job at just the point in your life when you should be most optimistic about the future.

Furthermore, fuelling dissatisfaction at both ends of the political spectrum is a now semi-permanent cynicism about politics itself. Many of the middle-class, idealistic youngsters who flocked to support Jeremy Corbyn as he rose to become leader of the Labour Party were open in their contempt for 'conventional' politics. For them, its messy, imperfect compromise between idealism and power is inherently unsatisfactory. And this is where the bridge between the populism of the right and the populism of the left exists. Supporters of Podemos in

Spain would be aghast that there may be any link with the supporters of Donald Trump in the USA. Supporters of Syriza in Greece would be outraged at the notion that they have anything in common with the supporters of the Freedom Party in Austria. And an earnest idealist from Islington who pledged undying loyalty to Jeremy Corbyn would be incensed at the suggestion that she shares any link with an activist in the Danish People's Party. But – if from entirely opposed ideological starting points – all these parties and movements express visceral disgust at the 'establishment', at the mainstream media and at political and commercial elites.

Much of this is of course the self-inflicted fault of the establishment: MPs brought the expenses scandals upon themselves. Bankers were irresponsible and greedy. There have been notable instances of corruption and incompetence in the police. Lawyers and QCs can be as pompous as they are overpaid. The House of Lords can be farcically self-regarding. Journalists should not hack phones. The vile behaviour of Jimmy Savile should have been spotted and stopped by the BBC and the NHS. Some junior members of the Royal Family haven't exactly covered themselves in glory. And so on.

But there is also an unconstrained cynicism about anyone in a position of authority, which is as relentless as it is breathless. In an increasingly congested newspaper market with a shrinking readership, it is perhaps no surprise that the press has developed an insatiable appetite to cast MPs, GPs, judges, corporate bosses, local authorities, minor royals, peers, BBC executives, regulators, accountants, lawyers, police officers – basically, anyone in a position of authority, with the exception of the Queen herself (and, of course, newspaper editors and proprietors themselves) – in the worst possible light. Naturally, nothing can or should be done to change this, because nothing can or should be done to tell the press how to do their job. Besides, the distinction between rightful scrutiny, mockery and criticism on the one hand, and the wholesale denigration of the motives of anyone in public life on the other, is a fine one. I would prefer to live in a society in which the rich and powerful are ruthlessly mocked rather than treated with misplaced deference. But it is undoubtedly true that in a climate of rampant press cynicism, it is considerably easier for populists to claim that mainstream institutions and politics are irretrievably rotten.

There is another – less obvious – reason why populism is receiving such a ready hearing these days: what David Brooks, the American commentator, calls 'expressive individualism'. In a world in which the old ideological battle lines have blurred; in which individual consumers are empowered as never before to make choices tailored to every aspect of their lives; in which people no longer feel obliged to vote the way their parents or grandparents did; in which the digital revolution and social media give people access to boundless information and to limitless avenues of self-expression; in which class-based tribalism has declined in politics, and in which cynicism about the capacity of governments to effect change is at an all-time high – in such a world, an increasing number of voters, especially younger voters, turn to politics not to make a balanced judgement about what is best for them, their family or their country, but as an expression of their own individual identity. As Brooks puts it, 'Sarah Palin was a pioneer in seeing politics not as a path to governance but as an expression of her followers' id.'

The legions of middle-class, idealistic youngsters who have flocked to support Podemos or Jeremy Corbyn are open in their contempt for mainstream politics. What they sought – and still seek – is individual authenticity as the supreme value. They're more interested in self-expression than in government. For them, politics is an expression of uncompromised values *opposed* to conventional politics as the art of compromise. Unsurprisingly, it is precisely these voters who were most disappointed by the give-and-take of the coalition government. The danger, however, is that politics as 'expressive individualism' becomes a shifting mosaic of fads, fashions and political cults in which wildly improbable hopes are invested in leaders, followed, invariably, by disappointment. As Brooks puts it more sharply, politics will simply decay 'in a country in which people would rather live in solipsistic bubbles than build relationships across differences'.

Joshua Mitchell, another American commentator and academic, adds a slightly apocalyptic twist to the same phenomenon in describing it as 'the Age of Exhaustion' – a time when people have lost all confidence in established institutions, parties and politics, and retreat instead into a world of digital individualism, online self-exploration, in which the 'ever-changing external world gives way to the celebration of a self-satisfied inner world. "Finding ourselves" becomes more important than building a world.'

Hints of this kind of outlook can be seen in the purism that has characterised recent arguments about free speech on British university campuses. When the unsullied sentiments of students have become so sacrosanct that even Germaine Greer is threatened with exclusion from a university platform, then clearly something is afoot. And if Germaine Greer's views on transgender rights are considered so intolerable that they should not even be heard, then it is little wonder that – for some voters at least – the very premise of politics as a messy, imperfect way of reconciling differences seems unappealing. To them, the ferocious purism of a populist – from the left as much as from the right – is far more likely to offer the kind of unbending politics they seek.

This is why I call the rise of this kind of politics – populist politics from both left and right – an 'Age of Unreason'. Not because the individuals who support these parties are necessarily irrational, but because reason is underpinned by doubt and open enquiry – both of which are shunned by populist politics. The politics of reason rests on a belief in the value of scrutiny and debate. It therefore requires an open state of mind, not a closed mantra of certainties. More than this, it requires a continuous acceptance of the possibility that one's opinion could be wrong. It is the means by which an imperfect world is navigated, even improved, but never made perfect. It is restless because it knows that the search for progress never really ends – it leaves the dreams of perfection to religion. None of these things are acceptable to the politics of unreason. Donald Trump can no more readily accept that he might – just might – be wrong than can the academic purists who lead Podemos or those who argued that a utopia awaits Britain outside the EU. They inhabit a world of raging certainties, not reasoned assumptions. They paint in bright, bold strokes. The brush-strokes of reason are always more tentative.

And reason lies at the core of liberalism. Modern liberalism stems from the enlightenment, from the power of science, from the Reformation and the rejection of divine rule. At its heart is a belief that the individual – not the tribe, the community, the nation or the divine monarch – is sovereign and that, by way of reason, the liberty of the individual can be enhanced and protected. Superstition, convention and myth are the tools of unreason by which individuals are kept in their place. Reason is subversive because it has no respect for tradition, or custom or hierarchy. This is why, even today when so much of society is more liberal than ever before, liberals spring to the defence of individual privacy in the face of new surveillance powers, when others might think it an arcane concern. It's why education is often at the top of a liberal's priorities, because education is the great liberator of an individual's potential, regardless of the circumstances of their birth. Similarly, liberals abhor the secrecy and centralisation of the modern state because the more that power is concentrated, the less empowered the individual becomes. Hence, also, their belief in the inherent value and dignity of work, because it gives people autonomy. It is no coincidence that liberals were the first to argue for gay rights, equal marriage and transgender equality, because these rights are essential if all individuals are to be free regardless of their sexuality or gender.

Above all, liberalism is an optimistic creed because it believes that individuals, left to their own devices and empowered to take decisions for themselves, will generally make good decisions. A Conservative takes a more pessimistic – no doubt they would say realistic – view of human nature, in which the pecking order is broadly conserved, traditions upheld, hierarchy applauded and claims about progress regarded with scepticism. A socialist believes that the state is the battering ram for progress, that society is composed of interests, groups and classes to which the individual is subservient. A socialist government enhances society by tackling the groups and vested interests that stand in the way of the needs of the disadvantaged. A laudable aim, of course, but one that elevates class above the individual.

The problem for liberalism is that optimism, reason and compromise don't fare well in a climate of fear. No one fearful of a terrorist attack wants to be told there should be limits to what the state can do to keep us safe. If we fear mass immigration, it's no comfort to be told that we can't just seal our borders. Telling someone who feels their very identity is under threat because of the EU that they must learn to rub along with others hardly displays an understanding of what it is they face. It is clear, with hindsight, that much of the liberal political and media class in Britain was slow to recognise people's growing fears about immigration over the last decade, and the impact it has been having on how people feel about their own identity. Equally, there is little point in liberals simply telling people that our imperfect international institutions – from the EU to the IMF – are our best bet at a time of globalisation when so many people have become deeply disenchanted by the way those institutions function. Fear grips the heart – there is little point in liberals answering with an analytical response of the head.

Of course, populism, intolerance and extremism have held sway in Europe many times in the past, before waning or being defeated. We have been here before, some might say; it will pass. Indeed, many populists today draw on the traditions of previous generations: the Front National harks back to the anti-Dreyfusards of the early twentieth century (supporters of one of the most notorious anti-Semitic witch-hunts of the modern era), General Boulanger in the 1880s (the hugely popular political leader who called for vengeance after the defeat of the Franco-Prussian War) and even Napoleon's *coup d'état*, which supplanted the Second Republic in 1851 with a form of dictatorship. Jobbik's polemic in Hungary echoes that country's fascism between the wars under its regent, Admiral Miklós Horthy. Right-wing Italian populists appeal to the same mood that brought Mussolini to power in the 1920s. The present populist storm, some might be tempted to conclude, will simply blow itself out once again. Down the ages, Europe has produced thinkers – Marx, Nietzsche, Heidegger and many others – who in very different ways have challenged the supremacy of liberty, reason and the individual, yet each time liberalism has survived intact.

As Steven Pinker has powerfully argued, '[t]he world is not falling apart'. The kinds of violence to which most people are vulnerable – homicide, rape, battering, child abuse – have been in steady decline in most of the world. Autocracy is giving way to democracy. Wars between states (by far the most destructive of all conflicts) are all but obsolete.

Pinker believes that the Internet and the surfeit of news and information exacerbate gloom and obscure the gradual shift towards a less violent, more democratic world. Given that so much of our current insecurity derives from the economic distress caused by the financial crash of 2008, perhaps – as the economies of Europe and the USA slowly find their feet – voters will rediscover greater optimism about the future, too. Recessions come and go, some will say; sunnier times lie ahead.

Closer to home, it is incontestable that British society – in keeping with most countries across the developed world – is far more liberal in outlook than ever before: race, gender and sexual equality; free lifestyle choices; equality before the law; the value of education; compassion for the poorest; the importance of science; respect for other faiths. All these quintessentially liberal priorities are now, broadly speaking, hard-wired into society at large. So perhaps concern about modern populism and the rise of identity politics is overdone. Liberalism has won, has it not? The present squall of angry populism will fade. Maybe liberals are just running out of new foes.

There is much that I agree with in all these assumptions. Political fads will pass. Breathless media headlines tend to make the world look like a darker place than it really is. The violence in North Africa and the Middle East will end, one day. Isis will be defeated. Marine Le Pen and Donald Trump will come unstuck. Nationalism never works, in the end. The UK and the EU will find a new settlement, one day. All that is true. Yet it would be a huge mistake to believe that all we need to do is keep our heads down, let the storm rage overhead, and then re-emerge when sunnier climes return.

Beyond all else, such complacency fails to recognise the growing threat that illiberal, extremist ideas can – when taken up by individuals with disturbed minds – provide the impetus for extreme political violence. The slaying of forty-nine people in a gay nightclub in Orlando, Florida, on 12 June 2016 and the murder of Labour MP Jo Cox in her Yorkshire constituency four days later were two acts of brutal violence in two separate continents that shocked the world. But they were united by one thing: they were acts of violence deliberately targeted at the tolerant, liberal values epitomised by the LGBT community and by an MP renowned for her fearless campaigns on behalf of refugees. The lesson is clear: when populists use dog whistles, some mad dogs will bark.

So, the politics of reason must fight back, and not just assume that the pendulum will swing back.

For that to happen, mainstream politics must rediscover the ability to grapple meaningfully with the big imbalances and failings of society – with the sources of populism. Until it can provide people with answers to these wider problems, their anger and disillusionment will inevitably continue.

So how can that be done?

In a democracy, it is the job of politicians not just to tell people what they want to hear, not just to duck and weave through the ebb and flow of daily politics, but also to shape and lead debates on the future direction of our country. Democracy is not just a race to scrape together the necessary number of votes; it should also be a means by which we collectively resolve how to keep our country safe, strong and prosperous in the future. All too often, recent elections have been reduced to the tyranny of small differences between the mainstream parties, rather than a meaningful debate about their competing visions for the future. The miserably cynical election campaign conducted by the Conservative Party in the 2016 London Mayoral contest is only the latest, if clearest, example of what happens when elections are gutted of all substantive meaning. Desperate to eke out a few thousand extra votes from carefully targeted ethnic and religious communities in London, the Conservatives ran a remorseless – and eventually unsuccessful – campaign to conflate Sadiq Khan's Muslim faith with wider fears of extremism. Instead of victory, they reaped contempt.

But if there is one thing that modern, rational politics can offer, which the politics of identity – of 'us vs them', of nationalism and populism – cannot, it is an ability to talk about and provide a vision for what lies ahead. All the new populist forces in politics hanker in one way or another for a mythical past: so the challenge for mainstream politics is to understand, explain and shape the future.

There are of course a multitude of dilemmas that our country, in common with most developed market economies, now faces: climate change, an ageing population, extremism, clapped-out political institutions . . . the list goes on. But I believe there are three particular challenges in our near future that stand head-and-shoulders above the others, and which should serve as the focus for the politics of reform and reason.

The first of them is economic. There are worrying signs that the kind of growth rates we were used to in the post-war period may fail to return for the foreseeable future. And if that is true, the implications for progressive politics are profound. Without stronger growth, their central purpose – spreading opportunity – will become considerably harder to enact.

The rebound in economic growth traditionally expected after a sharp downturn simply hasn't happened, undermining basic assumptions about the modern capitalist economy. The remarkably anaemic recovery of the American economy, despite rock-bottom interest rates, has led Larry Summers, one of the world's most renowned economists, to warn of the dangers of 'secular stagnation'. Robert J. Gordon, another American economist, has gone even further, arguing that long-term growth will remain low for the foreseeable future across the developed world, as the productivity benefits of industrial and technological innovation diminish. Chillingly, he predicts that the future growth in consumption for the vast bulk of society – with only the richest exempt – could fall below 0.5 per cent per year, for an extended period of decades. His analysis is in part based on his scepticism about the benefits of the latest wave of digital innovation. Gordon argues – persuasively, to my mind – that these innovations are not nearly as significant for the productivity of the economy when compared to the inventions of previous technological revolutions, such as electricity, the internal combustion engine or even indoor toilets.

Adair Turner, meanwhile, who was chairman of the Financial Services Authority in the five years that followed the financial collapse, has recently argued that the success of governments and regulators in rescuing the banking system – at the cost of billions of pounds of taxpayer-funded bail-outs – masks a deeper problem: the banking system is still creating credit and money that increase consumption and inflate house prices, without necessarily supporting new business investment or growing the economy. 'Self-reinforcing credit and asset price cycles of boom and bust are the inevitable result', accompanied by ballooning and unsustainable levels of public and private debt. As Deputy Prime Minister in the government that was on the front line dealing with the fallout of the 2008 banking crisis, I would agree. The banking system has long departed from its original purpose. It no longer serves as a kind of utility in the economy to keep people's money safe on deposit and lend prudently to borrowers. Its purpose is instead to generate purchasing power that previously did not exist. Such a system of credit creation on steroids – chasing returns on assets that are in short supply, such as urban housing, and reliant on consumers on low incomes who are unable to keep up without continued household borrowing – is a recipe for instability and low growth.

Given all this, it is conceivable that the UK and other developed economies are 'turning Japanese'. Just over a quarter of a century after the market crash in Tokyo, the average Japanese salary is lower than it was then, the Nikkei Share Index stands at less than half its peak value, average shop prices are roughly where they were twenty years ago and house prices have declined by more than 40 per cent. Nonetheless, in one important respect, Japanese workers are actually better off than their British counterparts: deflation in Japan has meant that real wages have been flat, compared to the real-terms drop in wages in Britain. It is a cruel irony that just at the point when wage increases were starting, finally, to outstrip price increases in the UK after years of real-terms reductions, it is very likely that Brexit will lead to higher prices once again, squeezing the take-home pay of millions of working people.

It is now evident that the patch-and-mend job to our banking system and our public finances after the 2008 crash was not enough, on its own, to create balanced, sustainable growth. In the UK, consumer spending is once again being relied upon to act as the locomotive of growth. Private and public-sector debt is stubbornly high. The services sector dominates, as construction and manufacturing splutter. And the marked inequalities in society are not abating. All these imbalances will now be exacerbated by the knock-on effects – market and currency turbulence, investor caution, uncertainty about future market access – of the referendum. Despite this, the Conservative Government has displayed little new thinking on how to rewire and rebalance the economy, while the Labour Party's response has so far been to embark on a nostalgic rerun of the economic policies of the 1970s. There is a pressing need for a new approach that seeks to address the entrenched deficiencies of the economy.

It is now broadly accepted, for example, that capital investment in the UK – private and public – has generally been insufficient and erratic. The considerable economic gains to be had from an ambitious renewal of Britain's road, rail, energy, housing and telecoms infrastructure have been stymied by the government's policy flip-flops (especially in the energy sector where incentives for investment in low-carbon energy have been abruptly altered), which have frightened off private investors, and by a stubborn refusal to borrow for long-term investment. Whilst a nervousness about borrowing for capital investment was perhaps understandable in the fiscal firestorm immediately after 2008, to retain that caution now, when it is obvious that borrowing costs are going to remain very low for some time to come, is self-defeating. The public understands the difference between frittering away borrowed money on day-to-day government expenditure, and the need to borrow for the long-term growth of the economy. In housing, in particular, the public mood has changed dramatically. I believe an aggressive, publicly funded and publicly directed house-building programme – including the construction of a belt of new Garden Cities in the South-East – would now be acceptable to the vast majority of people. The barrage of government enticements to private-sector developers and first-time buyers will not come anywhere near what is needed to meet the huge shortfall in new, affordable housing. There is now a once-in-a-generation opportunity for a liberal housing crusade led by government-directed schemes, funded affordably and cheaply from public borrowing at historically low interest rates.

Again, the outcome of the EU referendum has only made the dismal state of the British housing market even more acute: the share prices of private house-builders took a nosedive in the immediate aftermath of the referendum, as did the value of the banks that provide cash to those house-builders. Even if their share prices recover over time, it seems obvious that a reliance on the private sector – house-builders and banks – to build the hundreds of thousands of new homes required each year is now misplaced. The state must step in instead.

The social and political imperative to do so has also been underlined by the referendum: a shortage of affordable housing in deprived areas is one of the most powerful catalysts for the anger and frustration that drove so many lower-income voters to back Brexit in the first place. They simply do not feel they get a fair share of the public cake – housing, good schools and hospitals, good-quality social care – and blame outside forces like the EU, Westminster or immigration for their woes, even in areas where immigration is in fact low. Indeed, this is the principal reason why I do not believe that a statistical immigration target or cap – which became the totemic rallying cry for anti-EU opinion in the referendum – is a proper answer to people's sense of disenchantment. A recent report from the London School of Economics showed that there is no overall correlation between EU immigration and the jobs and pay available to UK workers, except for a small effect in a few very specific low-paid roles. The recent pressure on wages has largely been driven by the 2008 crash and the subsequent recession, not by an influx of EU workers (in fact, between 2007 and 2010 the number of people coming into the UK from the rest of the EU roughly halved). It is also well established that all immigrants, both from the EU and beyond, make a significant net fiscal contribution to help fund public services – services in which they also work in large numbers. Most strikingly, the areas in which concerns about immigration are most widely cited by voters among their reasons for backing Brexit are generally speaking the areas that have experienced the lowest levels of immigration, and vice versa. There are some exceptions, such as those parts of Lincolnshire and the east of England where there has been a significant change in the local population, but in large swathes of the North and the Midlands it is more typical to find places such as Redcar and Cleveland, where only 2 per cent of the local population were born outside the UK, yet the vote to leave the EU was 66.2 per cent; by contrast, 36 per cent of the population of London was born elsewhere, yet 60 per cent of London's voters voted to remain in the EU.

It is also the case that in areas which have experienced community tensions in recent years, especially in the Midlands and the North-West, a reduction in immigration from the EU is largely irrelevant to the issues at stake. The problems, for instance, of a lack of economic, linguistic and cultural integration between Pakistani Muslim communities, especially older women, and the wider community in parts of the North-West will not be affected in any way by our exit from the EU, as all the people concerned hold British passports.

In other words, a huge effort to slash or cap net immigration – which is likely to decline anyway, as a post-Brexit economic downturn makes the UK a less attractive destination – may damage places like London where immigration is broadly accepted, yet it will make little practical difference in the areas where immigration and/or cultural segregation is hugely controversial. A truly ambitious undertaking to resolve Britain's housing crisis would, instead, be a far more effective way to address the sense of grievance felt by so many voters in deprived areas: it would alleviate huge social-housing waiting lists (where the presence of immigrant families also queuing for a scarce public resource can lead to tensions), and it would instil a sense of opportunity and aspiration for younger people in deprived communities, who presently have no chance of getting their feet on the first rung of the property ladder. If there is to be a durable new settlement between the EU and the UK in the coming years, it seems politically unavoidable that it must involve some kind of amendment or backstop limit to immigration from the EU, but in the end there is no short-cut alternative to providing better jobs, housing and public services to those who feel left behind. Until that happens, concerns about immigration will continue to act as a symptom, as much as a cause, of underlying economic and social distress.

There is also an urgent need to revisit the way in which our financial system works. Whilst the banking system has been stabilised, and the worst excesses of the big-bonus culture and risk-taking have been addressed, the fundamental dilemma of turbocharged credit creation remains. This is not a new problem. In 1933 a group of eminent economists proposed the 'Chicago Plan' to President Roosevelt, which would have required all banks to operate with 100 per cent reserves and would have meant that banks could hold people's money on deposit and make payments between accounts, but would have had no other economic function. Such was the fear at that time of the effect of unconstrained private money creation by the banks. Of course, such a plan would be unworkable in today's world. But, as Adair Turner persuasively argues in his recent book, *Between Debt and The Devil,* something radical nonetheless needs to be done, if we are to escape the cycle of unlimited private credit creation, excessive household borrowing, house-price bubbles, low growth and persistently high levels of public debt. Turner proposes much higher bank capital requirements, new limits on mortgage lending, tight mortgage underwriting standards and limits on the advertising of very high interest credit. As he puts it 'We have to constrain and manage the quantity and mix of credit that the banking or shadow banking systems create.'

More radically still, Turner suggests that just as we should be more cautious about the risks of unlimited private credit creation, we should be more permissive of public money creation, which could, in carefully limited conditions, do more to spur growth and erode unsustainable public levels of debt. As he points out, because of the near prohibition on governments 'printing money', we have embarked on a variety of surrogate measures to support the economy, notably Quantitative Easing, by which the Bank of England buys bonds and other financial assets from pension funds, insurance companies, banks and other private institutions, in an attempt to release money otherwise tied up in those assets into the real economy. But such a roundabout way of trying to get more money into the economy can have an uneven effect. In the UK, the Bank of England has conducted Quantitative Easing purchases of around £375bn, which have helped to push down long-term interest rates and increase bond, equity and property prices, but it is debatable whether it was the most effective way to get the wheels of the economy moving. If even a fraction of that money had been used instead to cut taxes for people on low and middle incomes or increase public investment, it would probably have provided a greater boost to the real economy. In other words, the established orthodoxy that treats 'free market private credit creation as by definition optimal and fiat [public] money creation as in all circumstances dangerous' may have run its course.

I remain wary of the implications of allowing governments and Central Banks off the leash when it comes to printing money. As John Maynard Keynes said, 'There is no subtler, no surer means of overturning the existing basis of society than to debauch the currency.' The spectre of runaway inflation in places as different as pre-war Germany and Mugabe's Zimbabwe is warning enough of what can go wrong. But Turner is surely right to assert that the over-reliance on private credit and unsustainable private debt is no way forward, either. Liberals are ideally placed – neither enthralled by the market nor enamoured by the state – to lead the debate towards a new equilibrium.

The second major challenge we face is inequality. Traditionally, the debate about inequality has largely been between those who think it's unfair and should be reduced as a matter of principle, and those who believe inequality is an inevitable feature of a free-enterprise economy and should be accepted as part of the natural order of things. More recently, however, as the unstable imbalances in developed economies have persisted, a new set of concerns about the effects of inequality has emerged, which relates directly to the rise of populism. It has, for instance, become increasingly evident that there is a link between inequality and boom–bust credit cycles. In essence, as argued by Raghuram Rajan, the Reserve Bank governor in India, and others, as the rich have got richer and invested more of their money in savings and in assets, notably property, the stagnant wages of the poor are supplemented by ever-higher levels of borrowing. This cycle of asset-rich gains at the top and growing indebtedness at the bottom of society keeps the merry-go-round of demand and growth going for a while, but inevitably hits the buffers when borrowing becomes unsustainable, property bubbles burst and banking crises ensue. When that happens, it is the poor who suffer again, as their jobs and livelihoods are hit a lot harder than those with more significant incomes, savings and assets to fall back on. In other words, in addition to the long-standing moral concern about excessive levels of inequality, there is increasing acceptance of the idea that inequality itself is a significant cause of the very boom and bust that makes the rich richer, the poor poorer, and creates the kind of insecurity upon which populism thrives.

Given this, it is little wonder that millions of people on low and stagnant wages, bombarded by blandishments to borrow money at outlandish interest rates from payday lenders and the like, feel helplessly trapped by a system that seems programmed to reward those at the very top. The present UK Government's decision, for instance, to give a huge Capital Gains Tax cut to the wealthy – opening up another incentive for people to avoid income tax – seems designed to make a bad situation worse. As the Bank of England has recently pointed out, rising capital income is a much-overlooked feature of rising inequality. A political system that appears to trap millions of its citizens in a cycle of stagnant wages, rising consumer debt and unjust taxation only has itself to blame when those same people turn to the politics of anger and nationalism for a better answer.

The dividing lines created by inequality separate not just the rich and the poor, but the young and the old. The symptoms of this imbalance are rife: relative incomes have fallen for younger people as the precariousness of their employment has increased, while the incomes of British pensioners have risen faster than for any other age group in the last thirty years; the over-sixties are the only age group to have become better off since the banking crash of 2007/8; the level of pensioner poverty is currently below that of working-age people without children (and far below those with them). It doesn't help that only 43 per cent of eighteen- to twenty-four-year-olds voted in the general election in 2015, compared to 78 per cent of over-sixty-fives; nor that the proportion of the UK population aged sixty-five and over is forecast to jump from 17.6 per cent in 2014 to 27.1 per cent in 2064. As well as being socially and ethically unjust, this situation is also economically unsustainable: the number of workers relative to dependants is going to fall substantially, meaning that the tax burden on the working-age population will have to increase significantly to finance the same provision of services and pensions for the elderly. I am aware that some believe the increase in tuition fees to be the source of much of this intergenerational inequality. Leaving aside the fact that tuition fees are repayable only according to income, are written off if repayments cannot be made, and are not paid by the many young people who don't go to university, these intergenerational tensions in truth extend far deeper and wider into society.

A new grand bargain between the generations is needed if we are to avoid an increasingly acrimonious tug of war between the young and old, for limited public subsidies at a time of low or stagnant growth. The writing is on the wall: either mainstream politicians start to lead the debate towards a more sustainable settlement between the generations; or populist politicians will prey on the fears of older voters to secure electoral advantage, at the cost of an increasingly fractured society. The stark difference between the generations in the EU referendum – which left many young people who wished to remain in the EU feeling angry and disenfranchised as their preference was overturned by older voters – demonstrated how inflamed those intergenerational tensions have become.

Some of the most straightforward reforms are easy to identify: the skewing of welfare benefits towards the elderly is now glaringly unfair. The Resolution Foundation estimates that by 2020, compared with pre-crisis levels, working-age benefits will be 9 per cent lower per person, child benefits 15 per cent lower, and pensioner benefits 13 per cent higher per pensioner. Age-related welfare perks persist: the winter fuel allowance, free bus travel, free TV licences and the newly introduced pensioner bonds (subsidised savings exclusively for the over-sixty-fives). It should be a source of enduring shame that in the face of such lopsided perks, David Cameron and George Osborne never had the courage to reform these universal pensioner benefits, despite repeated pressure from me, and even from within their own ranks.

People build up two main assets during their lifetime: a home and a pension. It is in these two areas that the greatest and most controversial reforms are needed. The chronic lack of housing means that home ownership is increasingly beyond the grasp of younger generations. In 1991 the proportion of owners among sixteen- to twenty-four-year-olds was 36 per cent, and among twenty-five to thirty-four-year-olds it was 67 per cent. By 2011 this had dropped to 12 and 47 per cent respectively. Meanwhile, over the same twenty-year period, amongst those aged sixty-five to seventy-four, it rose from 62 to 76 per cent. For those aged seventy-five and above, it rose from 53 to 75 per cent. Today, the under-fifties own only 18 per cent of the UK's property wealth. Just as our economic future demands it, so too do our young: a large-scale, publicly directed and underwritten house-building programme sustained across the country over many years. The present government's blizzard of small-scale schemes and incentives are either too small to make a substantial difference or – as in the case of the sell-off of affordable local housing under the Right to Buy policy – calculated to make the situation even worse. More aggressive incentives, such as removing Stamp Duty on smaller homes bought by older buyers, should be considered to encourage the asset-rich (if income-poor) elderly owners of large properties to downsize into smaller homes, thus freeing up more of the existing housing stock for younger families. There are an estimated twenty-five million bedrooms empty in the UK, largely because older people are under-occupying.

At the same time, there are major question marks about the sustainability or fairness of the pension system. During the co-alition government, Steve Webb's five-year stint as Pensions Minister heralded an unprecedented burst of reform: raising the retirement age; the establishment of a new state pension; auto-enrolment of millions of workers into pension schemes; and the introduction of the 'triple lock' by which the state pension increases automatically by prices, wages or 2.5 per cent, whichever is highest. This last innovation – pioneered and put into place by Liberal Democrats – was needed to counter-act the long diminution of the value of the state pension ever since Margaret Thatcher severed the link with earnings in 1980. But this process is now arguably complete and the long-term sustainability of a minimum 2.5 per cent annual increase in pensions, in a world of slow growth and low inflation, is in question: it means that pensioners continue to receive an ever-increasing disposable income, irrespective of economic conditions. It means that the full force of any future economic shocks are borne by the working-age popula-tion alone. It implies that there is no sharing of risk between the generations.

Of course it is right that as a society we support those who have worked hard all their lives and are vulnerable in old age. The generational tensions are also far more nuanced than are often portrayed: after all, the working population will themselves be a generation of pensioners one day; equally, most pensioners are also parents and grandparents, so they have a heartfelt interest in the young. For these reasons, it may be easier than we think to make an appeal to generational altruism. The Conservative Party, in particular, must rediscover a willingness to govern for all generations, and not simply treat older voters as a political client group who must be cosseted at any price. It should, for instance, be possible to persuade older and younger voters to reduce the automatic 2.5 per cent minimum pensions increase to a more affordable level at a time of persistent low growth. Continuing to increase the pension age itself, in line with longer life expectancy, is also a legitimate way to spread the costs of pensions more fairly between the generations. And for those on private pensions, it might be more sensible to introduce 'auto-escalation' of pension contributions every time workers receive a pay increase, as suggested by Steve Webb. That way, pension pots will grow faster, but without placing unsustainable fiscal burdens on the next generation.

The third great challenge that the politics of reason must meet is part cultural, part psychological: the need to create a shared sense of belonging, of modern patriotism, especially in the wake of the gaping divisions in society that were exposed by the EU referendum. One of the most powerful attractions of populist parties is that, unlike the threatening outside world or a distant patronising elite, they proudly, unashamedly speak the common language of their supporters' tribe. Patriotism, especially angry patriotism, comes naturally to the modern populist. Progressive political parties have always had a bit of a problem with this.

As George Orwell famously observed, 'England is perhaps the only great country whose intellectuals are ashamed of their own nationality.' He complained of the way left-wing thinkers believe ' . . . it is a duty to snigger at every English institution, from horse racing to suet puddings.' But coming together in a shared sense of belonging is the most powerful, and comforting, response to a world of uncertainty. Liberals, then, must find a way to provide this – a sense of belonging – even if that means learning to love suet pudding. And they need to do so in such a way that it breaks the link between liberalism and elitism.

Because it is the feeling that people no longer quite understand, or belong to, the country they inhabit that fuels the support for populist parties. The SNP has skilfully positioned itself as the party that 'belongs' to Scotland, and that authentic Scottishness 'belongs' to it. UKIP and the Conservatives compete to demonstrate that they alone understand what it means to 'belong' to England. In truth, of course, there is nothing authentic – and a great deal that is false – about these appeals to patriotism. It is insulting to the 50 per cent of Scots who did not support the SNP to insinuate that their Scottishness is any less wholehearted because they do not sign up to a separatist agenda. It is equally insulting to the millions of English and Welsh voters who don't subscribe to the world view of the Conservatives or UKIP to suggest that their love and pride of country are any the less for it.

At the same time, patriotism has all too often come to imply a defence of the status quo – as if pride in one's country goes hand in hand with defence of tradition, hierarchy and custom. And yet one of the things that makes me immensely proud to be British is our culture of ingenuity and peaceful, progressive reform. Like many people whose parents and grandparents have come from elsewhere to make a home in Britain, it is the combination of the rule of law, tolerance and innovation that has fostered in me a profound sense of belonging to this country. During the long years I fought to promote constitutional reform, I was struck by how its opponents successfully cast any change to the status quo as an assault on Britishness. In fact, the liberal tradition of political reform is a quintessentially

British one. A first step would be to present it as such. It is patently absurd that the specious arguments in favour of, say, an unelected legislature should be paraded as defending British values. Liberals should be more outspoken in condemning the vested interests that block change, as working against the democratic values of our country. It is time we exposed false patriotism.

The clearest display in recent times of modern, inclusive patriotism was the pride, pomp and ceremony of the London Olympic Games in summer 2012. From the slightly mawkish celebration of the NHS to the steel-bashing genius of Isambard Kingdom Brunel, from the humorous encounter between James Bond and the Queen to the swagger of a succession of British pop and rock stars, the self-confidence of Britain and Britishness shone through. Past and present, tradition and ingenuity, public services and individual endeavour, the Industrial Revolution and the arts, pride in nation and leadership in the world – all jostled together that summer to create a hazy, yet powerfully felt sense of collective belonging to a country we all call home. There was nothing angry about that summer's patriotism – it fostered a feeling of immense generosity and common purpose. The fact that it coincided with a period of great economic anxiety for many people across the UK may, if anything, have sharpened its appeal. This is the kind of contemporary patriotism liberals should aspire to foster.

Of course, there *is* a tension between the liberal emphasis on the primacy of the individual and the role of community and neighbourliness in drawing us together as a society. Liberals have tended to be wary of patriotism not so much because of an aversion to suet pudding, but because of a certain unease at the collective, tribal affiliation upon which patriotism relies, whereas liberalism rightly seeks to emancipate individuals to follow their own path. But rampant consumerism, globalisation and the decline of many of the institutions and fixed points in society have given rise to the opposite problem: isolated individuals occupying increasingly atomised existences. So liberalism's answer must be to help people to create communities of their own. There is an umbilical link between the devolution of the British state and the rediscovery of a modern, positive patriotism. Excessive centralisation disempowers the communities that make up Britain's modern, plural identity. Radical decentralisation is not just an answer to the failings of Westminster and Whitehall, it is an essential prerequisite for flourishing communities, which are key to satisfying our human need for belonging.

British politics is crying out for wholesale renewal. Our unwritten constitution is creaking at the seams. Public distrust of politics is at an all-time high – confidence in political, media and commercial elites at an all-time low. Our Parliament is a warped representation of the true sentiments of voters. Whitehall remains unduly centralised and secretive. Political and media elites congeal unhealthily in the capital, divorced from the rest of the country; resentment against the economic and political power of London and the South-East grows accordingly. We are all empowered as consumers like never before – yet infantilised as citizens in a top-down political system. Reformists in all parties should resolve to work together to renew our politics. If they do, they will be taking the most important step towards wresting from the populists their claim on our emotions. There are signs that this is starting to happen. A group of Labour MPs have begun a campaign to establish an English anthem. Stephen Kinnock and others are supporting calls for more citizenship education in schools and a full-scale Constitutional Convention. The outlines of a powerful link between patriotism and reform are starting to take shape.

Above all, what liberalism can offer, which no one else can, is an accommodation with plurality: the idea that you can be any number of different things, identify with any number of different groups, and *also* be a patriotic liberal; that you can hail from different communities, faiths and viewpoints and yet share a patriotic, bedrock belief in tolerance, human rights and open discourse. Liberalism's genius is not just in the values it seeks to enshrine – liberty, tolerance, equality before the law, compassion, internationalism – but in the method, the manner in which liberal politics is conducted: debate not diatribe; evidence not prejudice; enquiry not dogma. Michael Gove's infamous declaration during the EU referendum campaign that people 'have had enough of experts' is the antithesis of the liberal method. It leads to the kind of bizarre, intolerant populism that prompted him to make a comparison a short while later between economic experts who support the UK's membership of the EU and Nazi stooges who denounced Albert Einstein in the 1930s. Perhaps the most precious quality of liberalism, then, is that which is most readily taken for granted: the toing and froing of open, democratic debate itself.

For it is precisely that democratic, open-minded method that is now under threat across the democratic world. The new, nationalist government in Poland is seeking to force a museum in Gdansk dedicated to the Polish resistance against the Nazis to delete all unflattering references to Poland's past; Ken Livingstone, a hard-left former Mayor of London, has sought to rewrite history by claiming that Hitler was a Zionist; Donald Trump and the Republican right have questioned the birthright of Barack Obama and wish to ban all Muslims from entering America; President Erdogan of Turkey muzzles a free press in the name of Turkish security and nationhood. All these examples and so many more reveal a steady drift towards conformity, discrimination and intellectual intolerance across the democratic world.

It is one of the tragedies of our age that just as globalisation poses unparalleled threats and opportunities to nations, the gravitational pull of domestic politics is to withdraw from the world. Just as our world expands, so we need a kind of politics that can accommodate that expansion. When Tip O'Neill, the legendary Speaker of the US House of Representatives, famously declared that 'all politics is local', he probably couldn't have anticipated that this should become more, not less, true as time has passed. But it makes perfect sense: if you believe that much of what happens in the world is beyond your control or that of the people you've elected, then you might as well get them to do something useful and sort out that irritating speed-bump at the end of your road.

Nationalism and parochialism are yoked together as logical responses to the same perceived problem: a runaway world governed by incompetent elites. A reassertion of country and of identity is the lifeblood of the new politics of grievance. If mainstream politicians fail to address this groundswell of despair by reasserting their own patriotism, their own sense of community, it may well become impossible for governments to act coherently together at all. The cruel irony is that the longer the politics of unreason goes unanswered, the harder it will be for nations to cooperate to provide the security and stability that voters so desperately crave.

In the wake of the EU referendum in the UK, we may well be approaching a tipping point in Europe where either the patriotic case for internationalism is going to be successfully remade, or a retreat to beggar-thy-neighbour politics is going to disfigure our continent once again. International cooperation has always come about in response to crisis, and the ongoing migration crisis in Europe is a textbook example. National governments are responding to the understandable alarm of their citizens by taking unilateral actions that will only make the problem worse. I suspect many ordinary European voters know in their hearts that as hundreds of thousands of desperate men, women and children flee the bloodshed of Syria and other conflicts, the only solution is a European one, not this inhumane game of pass-the-parcel at Europe's threadbare borders. The failure of the British and other EU governments to participate in an equitable sharing of this burden – the refugees, whilst large in number, constitute a fraction of 1 per cent of the EU's total population – is an example of the worst kind of short-term, short-sighted politics.

But all is not lost.

Just at the point when liberal internationalism seems to be being buried by fear and recrimination, there are some startling examples of successful internationalism, too: the painstakingly negotiated agreement between the UN, EU and Iran regarding its nuclear programme and the unexpected breakthrough in Paris at the UN Climate Change talks in late 2015 show that, with will and persistence, internationalism can still prevail.

It remains to be seen whether this latest, Brexit-induced crisis in Europe – coming so soon after the 2008 banking crash and the tensions within the eurozone – will be the catalyst for a downward spiral of disjointed responses or the spur for a coherent internationalist solution. But I believe, in the end and after several false starts, national governments will peer over the precipice and realise that they are condemned to work more closely together for their own sakes, even if they will now do so without Britain. A collective response may well come later than it should have done, and will no doubt be imperfect, but come it will, in some shape or form. The alternative – a continent riven by angry populism, gaping economic imbalances between the northern and southern countries of the eurozone, and roving bands of sick, hungry and frightened immigrants – is no alternative at all.

For a continent torn apart by fascism and drenched in blood for so much of the twentieth century, it is simply unimaginable that we could retreat once again to the politics of hatred and nationalism in the early part of the twenty-first century. But it is not impossible. This makes the rebirth of political liberalism across Europe such an urgent task. Because it is impossible to imagine a resolution to any of the major dilemmas of the future – an ageing population, climate change, violent sectarianism, extreme inequality – without the tools of open debate, evidence and compromise, which only liberalism can bring to bear. There is no other viable option in a world that is struggling to bridge differences, unite diversity and heal segregation. It will now be immensely harder for liberalism to reassert itself in Britain, as Westminster and Whitehall plunge into years of introspection in the wake of the Brexit vote, but it must nonetheless be attempted. The referendum outcome may have killed the dream of British leadership in the EU, but it cannot be allowed to strangle that long, proud tradition of liberal internationalism in Britain.

As we face this period of immense volatility, the five years of the Liberal Democrat–Conservative coalition government should offer some hope. It was a remarkably stable, centre-ground government at a time when politics elsewhere in Europe and America was being pulled to the extremes. The pressures to depart from the centre ground were immense, given the public rage at the banks, anger at the fiscal savings, anxiety about immigration and extremism, the panic amongst Conservatives about the rise of UKIP and the ascendancy of Scottish nationalism.

The Liberal Democrats played a thankless role, harangued non-stop from right and left, in ensuring that the government remained a moderate one. From the point of view of the party itself, the timing could not have been worse: finally making the transition from perpetual opposition into government at just the point when the whole of Europe was pitched into a prolonged bout of austerity, and when extremism and identity became growing preoccupations for so many people across Britain and elsewhere. We had to prove that coalition government could work, and prove that Liberal Democrats could govern in the unforgiving Petri dish of a Westminster system unaccustomed to multi-party governments, an electoral system resistant to change, implacable hostility from powerful vested interests in the press, and in the middle of a grim rescue mission for a battered and bruised economy. In other words, the coalition showed that the politics of reason, of balance and of compromise is possible (if unforgiving for the smaller party) even in the most unfavourable conditions. And that matters because it is a style of politics – and a method of government – that will return.

It is inconceivable that single-party governments in Britain will continue to be given such untrammelled authority on such a slender mandate from the people. The fragmentation of politics that has emerged in recent times will not suddenly revert to the duopoly of the past. Indeed, cross-party collaboration, perhaps even a Government of National Unity, may well be required to rescue the country from the spiralling uncertainties we now face. Voters, like consumers, are both more cynical and more choosy than before. Whether we like it or not, the individual is now supreme – allegiances of class, family and habit have given way to more changeable voter behaviour.

True, things may well get worse before they get better. It will take time for the raging certainties of populism and identity politics to be exposed for what they are. The profound economic imbalances within the British and global economy will deliver further ructions and recessions. Violent extremism is unlikely to subside any time soon. The UK and the European Union will need time to settle upon a new relationship. The vested interests – commercial, media, political – that sustain the current hegemony of the Conservative Party won't give up without a fight. The Labour Party has to find its long way back to electability. The Liberal Democrats are on a long recovery march of their own. The SNP have a long way to fall. And the hankering for a simpler yesterday, which sustains UKIP, will not simply fade away.

But – at some point – political parties that believe in reason over populism, in moderation over the politics of grievance, in compromise over factionalism, will be called upon once again to put the national interest first.

This will only happen, however, if mainstream politicians rediscover their self-confidence and demonstrate an ability to grapple with the big, looming challenges of the future: a rewired economy that can grow again; a new approach to inequality, including a new deal between the young and old; and a reassertion of liberal patriotism at a time of globalisation. These are all essential steps in the rehabilitation of the politics of reason.

Open, moderate debate is a sign of strength, not weakness. Give-and-take is a sign of maturity, not feebleness. A faith in evidence in policy is a sign of rigour, not indecision. And a willingness to address deep-seated problems about the future is, in the end, far more persuasive than the tactical gamesmanship that disfigures modern elections.

So it can be done.

Reason, in the end, will win against unreason.

Afterword

This is a time when things are coming to an end – but we can't tell what comes next.

Britain's decision to pull out of the EU, the election of President Trump and the rise of populism across the democratic world signify the end of the post-war consensus that supported multilateralism and liberal democracies. The multilateral rule of law, liberal economics and pluralist politics, and the supremacy of American military might – the three pillars on which the post-war settlement was built – have not disappeared entirely, but the consensus across the developed world that sustained them has come to a juddering halt. Protectionism, nationalism, Putin-style strongman politics and the steady rise of Asia are rushing to fill the breach.

Yet it is unclear what kind of ideological plan the populists have in mind for the future, or whether they have a plan at all. This heady brew – of protectionism, nationalism and authoritarianism – embraced by populists from Farage to Trump, from Orbán to Le Pen, is a coherent platform from which to appeal to angry voters and point the finger of blame at others, but as a programme for government it is ideologically all over the place. That is why it is so much easier to lament what is passing rather than understand what is to come. The political trends that I have examined in this book – fragmentation, grievance, identity – are accelerating in a highly unpredictable fashion. We are embarking on a new journey without really knowing where we're headed.

For anyone interested in defending rational, moderate liberalism, it is all the more important to understand the strengths and weaknesses of populism, which have become a little clearer since this book was first published.

For a start, populist leaders have been successful in depicting themselves as mouthpieces for an indivisible, homogenous *volk*, who are disgusted en masse by the establishment/experts/technocrats/Islam/immigrants. Populists assert that there is something pure and unsullied about the collective will of the people, which is threatened by the questionable ethics of the establishment, of foreigners and of foreign institutions. So for Nigel Farage the Brexit vote was a 'victory for real people' – making 48 per cent of the voting public 'unreal', presumably – whilst Donald Trump asserted that 'the only important thing is the unification of the people – because the other people don't mean anything'.

This celebration of the wisdom and purity of 'real people' can only be sustained if anyone and anything that opposes populism is disparaged and demonised. Hence the relentless assertion in the anti-European press that the referendum delivered an 'overwhelming' vote in favour of Brexit, when it did nothing of the sort (only 37.4 per cent of all eligible voters backed Brexit in the end). Hence, too, the attacks on the Governor of the Bank of England, the CBI and the Supreme Court judges who ruled that the government must hold a parliamentary vote before it can trigger Article 50 (famously vilified as 'enemies of the people' by the *Daily Mail*, in a direct echo from 1930s Germany), and the false claims that the Queen – the embodiment of the British *volk* – 'let rip' at me over lunch, in favour of Brexit.

All these myths and fabrications are essential ingredients in the populist narrative of a spontaneous, authentic, grass-roots uprising against a clapped-out, remote and dysfunctional ruling political elite. In truth, of course, there is nothing remotely grass-roots about the powerful vested interests that lined up to back Brexit. Whilst they may be commercial competitors, it was nonetheless striking that a small clique of elderly wealthy men, some of whom neither live nor pay conventional taxes in the UK, emerged as the powers behind the Brexit movement: the Barclay Brothers, the owners of the *Telegraph* media group; Rupert Murdoch, the owner of the *Sun*; and Paul Dacre, the secretive multimillionaire editor of the *Daily Mail*. It would be wrong to suggest that the Brexit-supporting press foisted their anti-European prejudices on their readers – they were reflecting existing sentiment as much as shaping it – but it would be equally wrong to believe that the referendum could have been won by the Brexit campaign without the vital support of this moneyed media elite.

In that sense, the rejection of the establishment in the Brexit referendum is quite different from the populism of Marine Le Pen in France, Podemos in Spain or Geert Wilders in the Netherlands, none of whom enjoy the backing of such rich and unaccountable vested interests. They are, curiously, far more authentically 'anti-establishment' than the mix of fund managers, newspaper proprietors and editors and Conservative MPs who orchestrated the Brexit campaign. In a way perhaps typical of Britain's political idiosyncrasies, the Brexit revolution was engineered by one part of the establishment against another.

What all populism has in common, though, is a wholesale rejection of pluralism, the principle that, in an open society, competing beliefs and values should be expressed and, as much as possible, accommodated. Pluralism and liberalism are indivisible, as I have sought to explain in this book: their essence is the non-stop toing and froing of competing ideas, leading to a compromise or even a synthesis of rival views. Governments of the centre-left have long sought to steal some of the good ideas of the centre-right, and vice versa. From one election to the next, the pendulum of opinion swings one way, then another, as different parties replace each other in power. In other words, the pluralism of a mature democracy gives everyone hope that their views will be listened to and acted upon at some point.

Populism abhors this idea of compromise, of accommodation. This is exacerbated, of course, by the polarising effect of a yes/no referendum: a binary choice is not conducive to a reconciliation between the losing and winning sides. Rather, it lends itself to an irreversible, winner-takes-all outcome.

The dangers of such an approach are obvious: close to half the voting public in Britain have in effect been disenfranchised, their hopes and aspirations brushed under the carpet. Theresa May's infamous declaration that people who feel an affinity not just with their locality but with places and people abroad are 'citizens of nowhere' revealed the extent to which she subscribed to the populist, rather than pluralist, interpretation of the referendum outcome.

If she had chosen to, Theresa May could have stated shortly after becoming PM that whilst she would deliver Brexit, she could not in all conscience disregard the aspirations of millions of Remain voters. She could have announced that she would seek an accommodation between the two sides by, for example, joining the European Free Trade Association and the European Economic Area (in which the UK would have remained in the Single Market, even as it leaves the EU). In doing so, she could have shown that she understands that to govern a deeply divided country – divided by region, by age, by class, by education – compromise is a necessity, not a choice.

Instead, Theresa May's government is pursuing a distinctly 'hard' and uncompromising approach to Brexit. And no wonder: they are imprisoned by the populist logic that requires them to disregard the losing side, as well as being beholden to the Brexit press for their own political survival.

So what comes next for British politics? And can liberalism make a comeback?

I do not intend to add to the growing mountain of speculation about the precise outcome of the Brexit negotiations, other than to observe that the uncompromising stance taken by the British Government will, inevitably, encounter an equally uncompromising determination among the other twenty-seven member states to safeguard the integrity of what is left of the EU. They can hardly be expected to do otherwise. There is, in my view, a relatively straightforward way to reconcile the political focus on EU immigration in Britain with the wider anxieties about mass migration in the rest of the EU – if only the British Government were prepared to tackle the issue of immigration on a Europe-wide basis rather than unilaterally. That would open the possibility not only for a new EU-wide immigration policy, including safeguards applied to immigration within the EU, but also for continued trade integration between the UK and the EU within a shared Single Market. Any hope of such an outcome now seems remote, but it may well re-emerge as the only sensible settlement towards the end of lengthy and possibly acrimonious negotiations.

More broadly, what happens next will in large part depend on the EU itself: whether it strengthens itself through reform or limps from one crisis to the next with the possibility of breaking up altogether. The latter fate may have been unthinkable until recently, but under the pressure of Brexit, growing populism, authoritarian governments in Central and Eastern Europe, terrorist violence, porous external borders and economic distress within parts of the eurozone, it is now a real possibility. The founding motives of European integration – peace, reconciliation, economic integration – have given way to beggar-thy-neighbour politics in which collective decisions are stymied by national rivalries.

Germany, the undisputed political and economic hegemon of Europe, continues to impose its authority on the rest of the EU whilst simultaneously arresting its development. Berlin's refusal to countenance any form of fiscal union within the eurozone (for fear it will let feckless governments off the hook and impose new burdens on German taxpayers) remains, in my view, one of the greatest mistakes in contemporary European politics, because a lopsided eurozone not only jeopardises the

EU itself, but its collapse would impose huge costs on Germany, too. Any sign in the coming years that Germany is – perhaps under pressure from a new French President – finally prepared to countenance measures, such as mutualising debt, that are needed to stabilise the eurozone will be a hugely positive step for the future of the EU. A failure to do so will ensure that the EU remains more fragile than it needs to be – and its collapse would, of course, only embolden populism everywhere and vindicate the staunchest Brexiteers.

Among the many wider factors that will also play a role, Donald Trump's attitude towards the EU will be significant. My hunch is that if he tries to collude with British Brexiteers and Vladimir Putin to undermine the EU – and the principle of multilateralism more generally – then he may provide just the spur the EU needs to get its act together. In any event, European governments will need to radically strengthen their contributions to the continent's security within the umbrella of Nato. Again, Germany's stance – traditionally diffident on military matters, for obvious historical reasons – will be crucial. The announcement in 2016 of a 60 per cent increase in paltry German defence expenditure and the deployment of a significant German military presence in the Baltics to fend off Russian threats are important early signs that change is afoot.

As these tectonic political shifts take place – the rise of an 'America First' US President, an aggressive and emboldened Russia, an ever more assertive China (not least in the South China Sea, now one of the most combustible flashpoints in the world) and a German-centric EU – the Brexit world view begins to appear painfully small-minded, obsessed as it is with doing battle with Brussels bureaucrats. No wonder that, in private at least, observers from China to Latin America scratch their heads in bemusement at the speed with which the British Conservative Party has presided over such a steep decline in British influence and power.

In the end, though, international clout depends on domestic economic strength. No country in history has been able to project sustained power around the world if the productivity, growth and ingenuity of its economy are in decline (though it can do so temporarily, as Putin's Russia attests). I have not seen anything since the Brexit referendum which alters my view that, in the long run, removing ourselves from the world's most integrated marketplace of half a billion consumers will have anything other than negative economic consequences for both the UK and the rest of the EU. The notion that what is lost through lower trade with our largest European markets – there is no Brexit scenario, even the softest, that does not involve *less* trade – could be made up through a web of bilateral agreements elsewhere will, I predict, prove to be a pipe dream. Even the much-vaunted UK–US trade deal will, soon enough, emerge as either fairly limited in scope or unacceptably controversial, especially if it involves an increase in access to the UK for US agricultural products that don't meet British animal-welfare and consumer-protection standards.

For these reasons, I do not believe that the acid test of what happens next in Britain lies in the negotiating rooms of Brussels, Whitehall or Washington. In the end, what will drive Britain's fortunes will be the degree to which current and future governments are able to radically rewire the British economy as it adapts to Brexit. If there's one thing I feel more adamant about since I first wrote this book, it is the need for far-reaching domestic economic reform, as explained in the final chapter. Put simply, a country with low productivity, persistently high deficits and accumulated debt, high levels of household borrowing, inadequate infrastructure, a woeful skills-shortage, declining household incomes and an unpredictable currency does not have great cause for complacency.

The need for far-reaching economic and social reform within the UK is underlined by the strong correlation between people in insecure employment, suffering stagnant wages, and those who voted for Brexit. For many voters the genesis of their anti-establishment sentiment was a wholly understandable reaction to the way the economy is not treating them fairly. In the

North, especially, this was allied to an accurate perception that the recovery of the British economy after the financial crash disproportionately benefited London and the South-East. I lost count of the number of good, decent people I met in my own constituency in Sheffield who told me that they were voting for Brexit because of their resentment of the way that everything was being decided down South. Ironically, then, for many voters in the North, a Brexit vote was a vote against London, more than against Brussels.

So the urgent need both to devolve power, especially to the North of England, and to revitalise the arteries of the British economy increases by the day. As I explained in the final chapter, the need for aggressive state intervention to boost house-building remains one of the most pressing tasks: the Resolution Foundation has found that rising housing costs have pretty well wiped out any income gains amongst the bottom half of households in the thirteen years up to 2015. Such a glaring social and economic injustice is crying out for radical action, including direct borrowing to cover house-building costs by government and/or local authorities. The longer governments tinker at the edges of this problem, the more likely it is that public anger will grow.

That, in turn, raises perhaps the most unsettling question of all: where will the rage go? If solutions to people's deeply felt economic, social and cultural frustrations are not forthcoming, what will voters do then? It might be hoped that as the populists fail to deliver their promised utopia – as they inevitably will – and as Brexit fails to yield the promised panacea of extra spending on the NHS and hermetically sealed borders against immigrants, then voters may turn back to mainstream politics for more workable answers. However, it is just as likely that voters will turn instead to a new generation of angry populists, with ever more extreme proposals.

So the odds are stacked heavily against the politics of moderation. But that does not mean liberalism is thwarted for good. Liberalism can survive, but only if it reinvents itself. The biggest error would be to assume that the wheel will simply turn, that the liberalism that developed at a time of sustained growth in Europe and North America in the post-war decades can be resuscitated unchanged. Liberals everywhere must heed the call for reinvention. Patriotism should be embraced, not shunned. An active state, especially when addressing market failures such as housing, should be welcomed, not rejected. Profound cultural concerns about identity, place and security should be tackled, not disregarded.

But if Liberals should be humble enough to address their weaknesses, they should also be assertive about what they have got right. Globalisation, however unsettling, is not going to be thrown into reverse. The growth of technology, population and mass transport cannot be stopped, Canute-like, by Trump and his European acolytes. Only Liberals understand that to master the modern world, we must also embrace it. Global trade, despite all the populist anger directed at it, remains one of the great sources of human development and ingenuity, as long as there are rules to protect the weak from the strong. Only Liberals understand that for governments to provide their citizens with the clean air, safe streets and secure jobs they crave, they are obliged to work hand-in-glove with other governments and with supranational organisations. The nation state cannot be isolated from its surroundings. Walls never work and always crumble, in the end.

And the populists haven't won, not yet. Donald Trump received almost three million fewer votes than his opponent. In the Brexit referendum, young voters – who, after all, will shape the future of Britain – voted overwhelmingly to stay in the EU. As much as opinion has moved sharply towards the extremes in recent years, it can shift elsewhere, too. I do not discount the possibility that within a few years opinion polls will start to show that a significant proportion of Brexit voters are disillusioned by the disruption, disappointment and disarray that may ensue, and would prefer, after all, to keep Britain within the European fold. What then? Are we, as a country, seriously going to refuse to revisit the decision to leave, even when growing evidence and public sentiment are shifting against it?

As I set out in this book, the unpredictability of politics will also demand ingenuity from politicians – especially a willingness to work beyond party divisions. The fact remains that there is no feasible way that any single party can unseat the Conservatives from power on their own – such is the combined effect of Scottish nationalism, the implosion of the Labour Party, the injustices of the electoral system and the power of the Conservative-supporting press. In fact, it is difficult to exaggerate quite how excruciatingly dysfunctional Westminster has become: an unelected Prime Minister; no meaningful pressure from the official opposition; lurid partisanship in large parts of the press; secretive decision-making; indifference towards the needs of the rest of the UK; and a refusal to countenance any meaningful political reform. Any future non-Conservative government in Westminster will need to be a combination, in some shape or form, of other parties.

So Liberals must be prepared to adapt – but must remain resolute about the merits of reason, openness and internationalism. The next few years will be crucial in determining whether Europe and the United States are able to adjust to a new world in which Asia is more dominant and 'Western' values no longer reign supreme. It is vital for the stability of the world that the nations that straddle the Atlantic grow old gracefully as new powers rise around the Pacific. Europe must not become a dysfunctional museum continent. The United Kingdom must find a way out of the hard-Brexit cul-de-sac, not least to prevent the UK from breaking up altogether. And the United States must rediscover its optimism and shun the politics of rage. Everything is in the balance right now. Liberals must work to nudge the world in a better, brighter direction.

Nick Clegg
January 2017

Acknowledgements

One of the tricky things for someone writing about their own experiences is that, for the sake of clarity, expediency or even vanity, it is easy to give the impression that you are the sole protagonist in your own story; the sole author of your actions and achievements. In politics, this is very far from the truth. Politics is, above all, a team game. Nothing I have done since I first decided to stand for elected office could have been achieved without the wisdom, hard work, creativity and loyalty of party staff, colleagues and fellow campaigners, many of whom are close friends.

Having been supported by so many people in election campaigns to be an MEP and then MP over many years – and in my offices in the East Midlands, Sheffield Hallam, the European Parliament, Westminster and Whitehall – it is inevitably impossible for me to name each and every one of the scores of people to whom I owe a debt of gratitude. Whilst I apologise to them, there are nonetheless some individuals whom it would be unforgivable of me not to thank.

Above all, this book wouldn't have seen the light of day if it wasn't for the irrepressible enthusiasm, wit and dedication of Phil Reilly, who provided meticulous research and an eye for a well-turned phrase in equal measure from beginning to end. Along with Tim Colbourne, Hollie Voyce and Vicky Booth at Open Reason, it has been a hugely enriching journey to travel together with them from an office in government to a life beyond Whitehall.

Will Hammond, my editor, has been subtle and demanding, encouraging and challenging, in exactly the right way, and I want to thank him and the whole team at Bodley Head for their willingness to publish a book about politics that departs, in many ways, from most conventional political books. My agent, Georgina Capel, has also enthusiastically nudged me along when I've felt like flagging.

It is impossible to navigate the stresses and strains, decisions and debacles of high office without leaning heavily on the friendship, moral support and guidance of close political allies. In Danny Alexander, David Laws and Paddy Ashdown, I was lucky enough to have three colleagues and friends who, unfailingly, sprang into action in the face of any crisis, offered support when there was little else to do, criticism when it was merited, and humour and loyalty through thick and thin. Danny, David and Paddy all, in their different ways, knew that the choice we had made together, to put the interests of the country first, was as unforgiving politically as it was right in principle. I couldn't have survived the numerous ups and downs without them.

I have also been lucky to have been supported throughout my time as party leader and in government by some exceptional political advisers who, with only a fraction of the resources available to their counterparts in the larger parties, achieved remarkable things: Jonny Oates, my chief of staff in government, exuded integrity in all he said and did, and is living proof that there is still space in politics for good, decent people; Lena Pietsch, my long-standing communications director, whose strong sense of principle never wavered under the daily barrage; Polly MacKenzie, who bedazzled everyone with her legendary knowledge of every nook and cranny of public policy; Matthew Hanney, whose forensic knowledge of politics is second to none, and who travelled the long distance with me from my first days as a backbench MP to my return to the backbenches ten years later; James McGrory, my Arsenal-obsessed, hard-living press spokesman, who inspired as much suspicion amongst his political foes as affection and loyalty from his friends; Chris Saunders, a walking encyclopaedia of economic policy, who single-handedly challenged Treasury orthodoxy; Ryan Coetzee, the Lib Dem's South African political strategist, whose belief in a simple message and a clear campaign helped make sense out of chaos; Tim Colbourne, whose thoughtfulness and respect for ideas put everyone else to shame; Zena Elmahrouki, a superb speechwriter, who also helped me to remember things I'd otherwise forget; Sean Kemp, whose unfailing knack to see the ridiculous in politics helped immensely in his job of working with the Conservative press team; Veena Hudson and Tim Snowball, who, in different ways, chose to join the ride long before ideas of leadership or government even arose; and many, many more. Steve Lotinga, Jo Foster, Monica Allen, James Holt, Alison Suttie, Neil Sherlock, Richard Reeves, Myrddin Edwards, Verity Harding, Alex Dziedzan, Adam Pritchard, Emily Frith, John Foster, Conan D'Arcy, Matt Sanders, Julian Astle, Ruwan Kodikara, Olly Grender, Ben Williams, Ben Rathe, Elizabeth Plummer, Bridget Harris, Christine Jardine, Shabnum Mustapha – all, in different ways, upheld liberalism and served the politics they believed in, through some exceptionally tough times.

The same is true of the special advisers who served other Lib Dem Cabinet Ministers, including Danny Alexander's Treasury team of Will De Peyer, Peter Carroll, Julia Goldsworthy, John Foster and Emma Coakley; Vince Cable's team in BIS of Katie Waring, Giles Wilkes, Ashley Lumsden, Emily Walch and Vanessa Pine; Chris Huhne and Ed Davey's team in DECC of Joel Kenrick, Chris Nicholson, Duncan Brack, Paul Hodgson and, again, Katie Waring; and Euan Roddin, who supported Scottish Secretaries Mike Moore and Alistair Carmichael.

In my Civil Service team, I was privileged to have the
support of a large number of hugely talented and dedicated
officials under the leadership, at different times, of Calum
Miller, Chris Wormald, Philip Rycroft and Lucy Smith. Civil
servants get a lot of criticism, which they are not able to
answer. My experience was that the flaws of Whitehall, such
as they are, are institutional and should never detract from
the quiet devotion to public service that thousands of hard-
working civil servants exhibit in all they do. I am also indebted
to the many dozens of astonishingly hard-working staff at Lib
Dem HQ during my time as leader, and under the leadership
of chief executives Chris Fox and later Tim Gordon. It is not
easy, to put it mildly, for a smaller party to do battle with
much larger and better-funded opponents in British politics.
One of the reasons why the Lib Dems have always punched
above their weight – and will do so again in future – is the
ferocious tenacity and ingenuity of party staff. It was painful
for them to see the party's fortunes decline, despite all their
best efforts, yet they stuck loyally to the task through triumph
and disaster.

I owe a huge debt of gratitude to the many people who helped
me in the Liberal Democrat Leader's Office in Parliament,
including Rory Belcher, Ian Sherwood, Rosie Gray, Ed Simpson
and Sian Norris-Copson, and to those in the Lib Dem House
of Commons Whips' Office – Ben Williams, Hollie Voyce, Jack
Fletcher and Joe Edwards – and the equivalent office in the
Lords – Elizabeth Plummer, Laura Gilmore, Humphrey Amos
and Giles Derrington. Maintaining discipline in Lib Dem ranks
through half a decade of consistently controversial votes in
Parliament was a remarkable achievement.

Rob Frost, Melanie Sidebottom, Barbara Masters, Alex Eagle
and Ian Turgoose have worked for me in Sheffield as one of
the best constituency teams in the country – all under the
watchful eyes of my outstanding constituency office manager,
Margaret Binks, and with the support of legions of loyal and
hard-working Lib Dem members in that great city.

As someone who received personal protection for almost six years from various teams from the Metropolitan Police, I also want to thank them for a task that is, by definition, largely invisible and unobtrusive, but is executed with great professionalism, discretion and personal warmth. And Cengiz Dervis deserves a special medal of thanks for helping me keep body and soul together in the early morning gym.

My gratitude to all my Lib Dem ministerial colleagues is unlimited: as a team, we delivered Liberal reforms within government on a scale not seen for generations. And, whatever individual misgivings some of my colleagues may have had, I could not have asked for a more steadfast and supportive group of colleagues amongst Lib Dem MPs and peers. I am very grateful to each and every one of them for the support they provided to me during my years as party leader.

My predecessors as leader of the Liberal Democrats – Paddy Ashdown, Charles Kennedy and Ming Campbell – were unstintingly loyal, discreet and helpful to me throughout my seven and a half years as leader. They understood what a challenging privilege leading a political party can be and were always available for a helpful chat, a drink and, in the case of Charles and Paddy, a cigarette when circumstances required. Charles did so with all the gentle humour and warmth for which he is so widely remembered, even though he harboured misgivings about the coalition from the beginning.

And I want to thank the millions of people who supported the Lib Dems, and still do, through the tumultuous events of recent years. British liberalism is a precious, important tradition in national public life. The ebb and flow of our fortunes is not for the faint-hearted. I am especially grateful to those who continued to believe in us when many others did not.

As I describe in this book, politics can be a pretty merciless business. It isn't easy to be a parent, a sibling, a spouse or child of a politician in the front line – particularly one in the political firing line, too – unable to defend or publicly protect the person you love. So my greatest thanks of all go to my own family - and most especially to Miriam - for showing such limitless faith in me, over the many years during which politics intruded in our lives more than I would have liked. Miriam withstood the pressures and the scrutiny with such humour, strength and grace, whilst protecting our three small children at every turn. Only she - and they - know how grateful I am to them for everything.

Notes

Introduction

p.3, 'The winner is the loser': *Winners: And How They Succeed* by Alistair Campbell (Cornerstone, 2015), p.354

1 *The Political Zoetrope*

p.15, 'Republicans have a keen eye': *The Political Brain: The Role of Emotion in Deciding the Fate of the Nation* by Drew Westen (Public Affairs, 2007), p.35

2 *Welcome to Westminster*

p.44, 'You could borrow': *The Guardian*, http://www.theguardian.com/politics/shortcuts/2013/jan/28/parliament-rifle-range

p.45, 'The essence of good': Hansard, http://hansard.millbanksystems.com/commons/1943/oct/28/house-of-commons-rebuilding

p.45, 'gesticulating about female assets': BBC, http://www.bbc.co.uk/news/uk-politics-25266177

p.45, Women make up: House of Commons Library, http://researchbriefings.parliament.uk/ResearchBriefing/Summary/SN01250

p.45, Just forty-one of 650: House of Commons Library, http://researchbriefings.parliament.uk/ResearchBriefing/Summary/SN01156

p.46, **More than a quarter of MPs**: BBC, http://www.bbc.co.uk/news/education-32692789

p.55, **'hadn't reckoned on Nick Clegg'**: *Financial Times*, http://www.ft.com/cms/s/2/3f101f44-5043-11e0-9ad1-00144feab49a.html

p.58, **'fending for themselves'**: *Sheffield Telegraph*, http://www.sheffieldtelegraph.co.uk/news/local/clegg_and_blunkett_our_hopes_and_fears_for_city_1_1526336?action=logout

p.70, **'I don't have the luxury'**: *The Guardian*, http://www.theguardian.com/politics/2010/mar/21/nick-clegg-wife-general-election-campaign

3 The Plumage of Power

p.85, **Gallingly, the decision**: *Financial Times*, https://next.ft.com/content/e42bcbc8-cc40-11e3-bd33-00144feabdco

4 The Virtue of Compromise

p.117, **'We were initially advised'**: *Efficiency Review by Sir Philip Green: Key Findings and Recommendations* (October 2010), https://www.gov.uk/government/uploads/system/uploads/attachment_data/file/61014/sir-philipgreenreview.pdf

p.118, **We still have one of the most centralised**: City Centred, http://www.citycentred.co.uk/faq/

5 Taking Power from the Powerful

p.122, **In 1951, the two major parties**: UK Political Info website, http://www.ukpolitical.info/1951.htm

p.124, **The Upper House is**: 'House of Lords: Fact vs Fiction' pamphlet by Jess Garland and Chris Terry for the Electoral Reform Society, p.5, http://electoral-reform.org.uk/sites/default/files/House-of-Lords-Fact-Vs-Fiction%20(1).pdf

p.125, **The Electoral Reform Society**: Ibid., p.13

p.125, **The average age**: ITV News, http://www.itv.com/news/2015-08-27/house-of-lords-in-numbers/

p.125, **Little more than 5 per cent**: Garland and Terry, op. cit., p.15

p.125, **David Lloyd George**: *A Short History of England* by Simon Jenkins (Profile, 2001), p.271

p.126, **The Conservatives received**: Electoral Commission, http://www. electoralcommission.org.uk/__data/assets/pdf_file/0015/190005/ Q1-2015-donations-and-loans-summary-document.pdf

p.127, **Indeed, in 2012**: *The Guardian*, http://www.theguardian.com/ politics/2012/dec/07/tory-funds-mansion-tax

6 *Burgemeester in Oorlog*

p.143, **'I'm going to be completely honest'**: *The Independent*, http://www. independent.co.uk/news/people/refugee-crisis-sweden-deputy-prime-minister- cries-as-she-announces-u-turn-on-asylum-policy-a6749531.html

p.144, **'punchbags for heavyweights'**: 'Endgames: Lessons for the Lib Dems in the final phase of coalition' by Akash Paun and Robyn Munro of the Institute for Government, http://www.instituteforgovernment.org.uk/sites/ default/files/publications/Lib%20Dem%20Conference%20Briefing%20 Paper%20final.pdf

p.153, **'I believe that ideas'**: *Purity and Danger* by Mary Douglas (Routledge Classics, 2002), p.5

p.159, **'During the election campaign'**: *Coalition* by Mark Oaten (Harriman House, 2010), p.251

7 *Was Roy Right?*

p.165, **'the only really liberal'**: 'Roy Jenkins, Europe and the Civilised Society' by Professor Vernon Bogdanor (lecture, 2013), http://www.gresham. ac.uk/lecture/transcript/print/roy-jenkins-europe-and-the-civilised- society/

p.186, **By the summer of 2015**: House of Commons Library, www.parliament. uk/briefing-papers/sn05125.pdf

p.186, **the National Trust**: BBC, http://www.bbc.co.uk/news/uk-15187147

p.186, **SNP membership quadrupled**: *The Daily Mirror*, http://www.mirror. co.uk/news/uk-news/nicola-sturgeon-turns-unelectable-labour-6640465

278 *Politics*

p.186, **The surge in Labour's membership**: *The Financial Times*, http://
www.ft.com/cms/s/0/c4ea2ac6-5d4d-11e5-a28b-50226830d644.html#
axzz4AnOlO9Jv

8 History, Grievance and Psychodrama

p.193, **'But for the fact that'**: Churchill Society, http://www.churchill-society-london.org.uk/astonish.html

p.194, **'on the whole the establishment'**: *The Rise and Fall of a National Strategy 1945–1963* by Alan S. Milward (Whitehall History Publishing, 2002)

p.195, **'England in effect is insular'**: *Britain and European Integration, 1945–1998: A Documentary History*, edited by David Gowland and Arthur Turner (Routledge, 2000), p.106

p.202, **'influence increasingly lies'**: UK Government, https://www.gov.uk/government/speeches/britain-s-foreign-policy-in-a-networked-world--2

p.206, **'would not be a responsible action'**: Hansard, http://www.publications.parliament.uk/pa/cm201011/cmhansrd/cm111024/debtext/111024-0002.htm

p.222, **'If we vote to leave'**: *Financial Times*, http://www.ft.com/cms/s/0/2e843d8e-70ed-11e5-9b9e-690fdae72044.html

9 Between the Extremes: The Return of Liberalism in an Age of Unreason

p.227, **The percentage of the US population**: *Between Debt and the Devil: Money, Credit and Fixing Global Finance* by Adair Turner (Princeton University Press, 2015), pp.2, 3

p.228, **By this measure**: *A steady job: The UK's record on labour market security and stability since the millennium* by Paul Gregg and Laura Gardiner (Resolution Foundation), p.00, http://www.resolutionfoundation.org/wp-content/uploads/2015/07/A-steady-job.pdf

p.230, **what David Brooks**: *New York Times*, http://www.nytimes.com/2015/10/20/opinion/enter-the-age-of-the-outsiders.html?smprod=nytcore-iphone&smid=nytcore-iphone-share&_r=2

p.231, **'the Age of Exhaustion'**: *The American Interest*, http://www.the-american-interest.com/2015/10/10/age-of-exhaustion/

p.234, **Wars between states:** *Slate*, http://www.slate.com/articles/ news_and_politics/foreigners/2014/12/the_world_is_not_falling_apart_ the_trend_lines_reveal_an_increasingly_peaceful.html

p.237, **'secular stagnation':** 'The Age of Secular Stagnation' by Larry Summers, http://larrysummers.com/2016/02/17/the-age-of-secular-stagnation/

p.237, **Gordon argues:** 'Is US economic growth over? Faltering innovation confronts the six headwinds' by Robert J. Gordon (National Bureau of Economic Research), http://www.nber.org/papers/w18315.pdf

p.237, **'Self-reinforcing credit':** Adair Turner, op. cit., p.6

p.238, **Just over a quarter of a century:** *The Times*, http://www.thetimes. co.uk/tto/opinion/columnists/article4662534.ece

p.238, **It is a cruel irony:** *Financial Times*, https://next.ft.com/content/ c86df908-3d07-11e6-8716-a4a71e8140b0

p.239, **Again, the outcome:** *This is Money*, http://www.thisismoney.co.uk/ money/markets/article-3661740/Banks-airlines-housebuilders-pound-hit-Brexit-slide-continues-Osborne-speaks.html

p.240, **A recent report:** Centre for Economic Performance, http://cep.lse. ac.uk/pubs/download/brexit05.pdf

p.240, **Most strikingly:** Full Fact, https://fullfact.org/immigration/ impacts-migration-local-public-services/

p.242, **'We have to constrain':** Adair Turner, op. cit., p.190

p.243, **'free market private credit creation':** Ibid., p.250

p.243, **'There is no subtler':** Ibid., p.231

p.244, **As the Bank of England:** Bank of England, http://www.bankofengland. co.uk/research/Documents/workingpapers/2015/swp571.pdf

p.245, **relative incomes have fallen:** Institute for Employment Studies, http://www.employment-studies.co.uk/resource/precarious-work-and-high-skilled-youth-europe

p.245, **the incomes of British pensioners:** Institute for Fiscal Studies, http:// www.ifs.org.uk/pr/hbai2013.pdf

p.245, **the over-sixties are:** Ibid.

p.245, **pensioner poverty:** Institute for Fiscal Studies, http://www.ifs.org.uk/ tools_and_resources/incomes_in_uk

p.245, **It doesn't help that:** Ipsos Mori, https://www.ipsos-mori.com/research-publications/researcharchive/3575/How-Britain-voted-in-2015.aspx

p.245, **nor that the proportion:** Office for Budget Responsibility, http://cdn. budgetresponsibility.org.uk/41298-OBR-accessible.pdf

p.246, **The Resolution Foundation estimates:** Resolution Foundation, http://
www.resolutionfoundation.org/wp-content/uploads/2016/02/Audit-2016.
pdf, p.16

p.246, **Today, the under-fifties:** Policy Exchange, http://www.policyexchange.
org.uk/images/publications/housing%20and%20intergenerational%20
fairness.pdf

p.247, **There are an estimated:** Intergenerational Foundation, http://www.
if.org.uk/wp-content/uploads/2011/10/IF_housingrel_defin_LE2.pdf

p.248, **'England is perhaps':** *England Your England* by George Orwell, http://
orwell.ru/library/essays/lion/english/e_eye

p.252, **Michael Gove's infamous declaration:** *The Telegraph* online,
http://www.telegraph.co.uk/news/2016/06/21/michael-gove-compares-
experts-warning-against-brexit-to-nazis-wh/

Index